William + Susanna White ~ see p 54
(+ sons Resolved + Peregrine)
? See p 130

Richard + Elizabeth + 5 daughters
(57 grandchildren)

MW01485776

WEAKER VESSELS

Also by Donna A. Watkins

• *Diverse Gashes: Governor William Bradford,*
Alice Bishop, and the Murder of Martha Clarke,
Plymouth Colony, 1648

WEAKER VESSELS

The Women and Children Of

Plymouth Colony

Donna A. Watkins

American History Press
Staunton Virginia

Staunton, Virginia

(888) 521-1789

Visit us on the Internet at:

www.Americanhistorypress.com

First Printing – December 2021

To schedule an event with the author or to inquire about bulk discount sales please contact American History Press.

Names: Watkins, Donna A., author.
Title: Weaker vessels : the women and children of Plymouth Colony / Donna A. Watkins.
Description: Staunton, Virginia : American History Press, [2020] | Includes bibliographical references and index.
Identifiers: LCCN 2020017765 | ISBN 9781939995346 (paperback)
Subjects: LCSH: Pilgrims (New Plymouth Colony) | Women--Massachusetts--History--17th century. | Children--Massachusetts--History--17th century. | Massachusetts--History--New Plymouth, 1620-1691. | Massachusetts--Social conditions--17th century.
Classification: LCC F68 .W34 2020 | DDC 974.4/02082--dc23
LC record available at https://lccn.loc.gov/2020017765

Manufactured in the United States of America on acid-free paper.

This book exceeds all ANSO standards for archival quality.

This book is dedicated to Dennis, with love and gratitude.

Author's Note

In many cases I have modernized the language of the Pilgrims for ease of understanding, unless the meaning is obvious. I have also standardized the spelling of names, using Eugene Aubrey Stratton's *Plymouth Colony: Its History & People, 1620-1691* as my main authority.

Unless otherwise noted, I have also referenced Samuel Eliot Morison's 1952 edition of William Bradford's *Of Plymouth Plantation, 1620-1647,* published by Alfred A. Knopf, New York, as my standard.

The Pilgrims used the Julian Calendar (also called Old Style, abbreviated as OS), with the new year beginning on March 25. I have chosen to cite the dates using our modern calendar, the Gregorian Calendar (known as New Style, and abbreviated as NS), with the new year beginning on January 1.

Table of Contents

Prologue – A Brief History of Plymouth Colony   1

Chapter 1 – Martyrs of the *Mayflower*   9

Chapter 2 – Laws and Standards   24

Chapter 3 – Chastity and Courtship   40

Chapter 4 – Marriage and Fidelity   54

Chapter 5 – Divorce   67

Chapter 6 – Domestic Violence   80

Chapter 7 – Children in Service   98

Chapter 8 – Notable Women of Plymouth   125

Chapter 9 – Slander, Defamation, and "Unnecessary Talking"   145

Chapter 10 – Unclean Carriages and Lascivious Acts   166

Chapter 11 – Children's Deaths   180

Chapter 12 – Danger and Desperation   194

Chapter 13 – Growing Old in Plymouth Colony   215

Chapter 14 – Plymouth Colony Becomes Plymouth County   237

Epilogue   252

Acknowledgments   255

Endnotes   258

Bibliography   289

Illustration Credits   300

Index   302

About the Author   321

"Ye husbands, dwell with [your wives] as men of knowledge,

giving honor unto the woman, as unto the weaker vessel...

that your prayers be not interrupted."

-1 Peter 3:7, Geneva Bible

"Though in the kind and extent of many duties, the same things

are required of wives which are required of children and servants,

because God hath made them all inferiors,

and exacted subjection of all."

-William Gouge, *Of Domesticall Duties, Eight Treatises*

III. Treatise. Of Wives Particular Duties

Chapter 11. "Of Wife-like Courtesie and Obeysance"

London, 1622

Prologue

A Brief History of Plymouth Colony

After sixty-six interminable days aboard the *Mayflower*, pitching about at the whims of the sea and living below deck in dank and crowded conditions, many of the ship's passengers were no doubt disappointed when the gray desolate shore of Cape Cod greeted them. In the middle of winter, the scraggly trees visible on the shoreline were bare, and the weather was bitterly cold. The Pilgrims were facing challenging conditions and they were exhausted from their Atlantic crossing. And so they prayed, did some laundry, and prayed some more. They were in a pitiful state, but they were not defeated. They were determined to wrench control out of a very frightening situation; it was in their history to do so.

One of the main reasons they had set sail was to relocate to a place where they could exert dominion over themselves and their environment. From their initial meetings back in Scrooby, England, the little group of religious dissenters saw themselves in a position of opposition. It was themselves against the government, they believed; and also against the established church and some of their more conforming neighbors. This "principle of opposition" permeated all their decision-making. Under God, this little group would bind themselves together, set their own standards, and keep watch over each other's behavior. By exerting control over themselves and the group, they would create the strength to meet any challenge.[1]

They had no way yet to know that while the New World would offer opportunities, it would also offer temptations, to which even the most fervent of them would succumb. But they never stopped trying. In their laws, rules, and social expectations, they struggled to restrain each other's behavior, resorting to harsh, and at times even cruel, corporal punishment. Those at the bottom of the social

The Old Manor House, Scrooby, with its beehives.

order—women, children, and servants—often literally felt the sting of the law.

The roots of this society dated back nearly fifteen years to a tiny village in northern Nottinghamshire, England, where a small group of religious dissenters began meeting in the manor house in Scrooby under the leadership of William Brewster. A handful of men secretly met to discuss and debate the tenets of the official English church against those of the non-conformists. In 1606, they decided to join the nascent Separatist movement, and they entered into a sacred contract among themselves: "The Lord's free people joined themselves (by a covenant of the Lord) into a church estate, in the fellowship of the gospel, to walk in all His ways made known, or to be made known unto them, according to their best endeavors, whatsoever it should cost them, the Lord assisting them."[2]

Entering such a covenant and establishing their own church, thus circumventing the established English church and the king, was illegal, and it put them in real danger.

By 1607, the crown had learned about the Scrooby group and their situation became more perilous. William Brewster became a hunted man, and several of their ministers were excommunicated from the Anglican church. The little band decided to leave England and resettle in more liberal Holland, where they hoped to enjoy tolerance for their dissenting views. At first, they settled in Amsterdam, but soon decided that the existing Separatist churches there did not give them the autonomy they sought. Next, they moved to Leiden. It was a lovely city, a "fair and beautiful city, and of a sweet situation," and it was also a manufacturing center. To support themselves, many of the Pilgrims worked in the fabric trade as weavers of cloth and ribbons, quite a change from their previous lives as yeomen and tenant farmers in England.[3]

The group lived in Leiden for twelve years, worshiping in their own way, working hard at the looms they assembled in their own homes, and trying to remain separate from the Dutch and their vibrant society. Before long it became clear that their children were growing up under a different cultural influence, one that allowed for perhaps a little too much freedom, and this troubled them greatly. To add to this, they were still under surveillance from England for having published books that criticized the Crown and the bishops. After much deliberation, they decided it would be best to move again, this time to the New World across the sea.

After securing financial support from a group of London investors, they arranged for two ships—the *Mayflower* and the *Speedwell*—to transport them. After hiring the former and buying the latter, they sold many of their personal possessions and prepared for their huge undertaking. Originally, the plan was to join the Virginia Colony. They would repay their investors with profits earned by setting up their own fishing industry. They were going to use the *Speedwell* as a fishing boat, manufacture their own salt to preserve the fish, and ship their catch back to London. However, the investors decided that the little group of Separatists could not produce enough to make the new colony profitable, and they recruited several additional passengers from London to join the adventure. The Pilgrims were not informed of these extra people who were joining their party until the last minute. They must have felt not only surprise, but also betrayal. "These strangers," Bradford called them, subscribed to a variety of religious beliefs, some conformists, some dissenting, some indifferent. The point was that they were not members of the Leiden congregation who believed theirs was a religious venture, determined for them by God himself. Now the little insular group had been burdened with the challenge of dealing with, and controlling, outsiders. As things turned out, this was only one of the problems they would face, and not the worst one.[4]

After setting sail from Southampton in the two ships, the *Speedwell* began to leak, and they had to put in to shore at Dartmouth for repairs. Another attempt to sail her failed when she again proved unseaworthy, and they had to return to shore once again, this time docking at Plymouth, England. It was decided to abandon the *Speedwell* altogether, reduce the size of their company, sort and decrease their supplies, and load the remaining passengers on the *Mayflower*, and once again set sail.

All these delays would have serious consequences for the Pilgrims. They had planned to reach America before the cold season arrived. Besides the delay in sailing, the trip across the Atlantic had taken longer than expected. By the time they arrived near Cape Cod it was November, and the weather was icy-cold. They did attempt to sail south to locate the Virginia Colony, but rough seas and riptides forced them to turn back to the safety of the Cape. They dropped anchor there on November 11, 1620. It was freezing and wet, and the Pilgrims were sick and exhausted from the trials of their long voyage.[5]

The first venture ashore gave the women a chance to feel solid land under their feet again, and to do the laundry that had accumulated for over two months. The men began to explore, looking for the most advantageous site to establish a colony. On December 15, after more than a month of searching, discussion, and indecision, they settled on a site that had first been identified as "New Plymouth" by John Smith on his 1616 map of New England. They retained the name.[6,7]

Their first priority was to construct shelters so they could move off the *Mayflower*. Besides dealing with the brutal weather, the colonists were beginning to suffer the effects of their long voyage: their lack of a proper diet, their confinement, and the poor sanitation on board the ship had taken its toll. Many of them, mostly women and children, were still living onboard in the 'tween deck that had been their home during the crossing. Plans were made for houses on shore, trees were felled, and wood was cut, but the inclement weather caused

First laundry day in the New World.

delays of several days before they could start the actual building process. Bad weather was one thing, but disease was another thing entirely. People were becoming sick, and soon many were so ill they could not work; some could not even leave their beds. Before long, many of the Pilgrims began to die.

Those who were sick remained sequestered on the *Mayflower*, cared for by the women who were already tending to all the children. Conditions onboard were crowded, dirty, and fetid. By the end of winter, more than half of the Pilgrims had died. Whole families were wiped out, children were orphaned, women widowed, men left with small children to raise. Even with all the sickness and death, William Bradford wrote that "their ends were good and honorable, their calling lawful and urgent; therefore they might expect the blessing of God in their proceeding." He added that with God's blessing, "though they should lose their lives in this action,…they have comfort in the same [because] their endeavors would be honorable." Honor aside, the group experienced a devastating fifty percent mortality rate within three months of their landing.[8]

By April 1621, the tiny colony had made enough progress that the captain of the *Mayflower*, Christopher Jones, decided that he could safely sail back to England. After all they had been through, perhaps *because* of all they had been through, not one colonist sailed back to Southampton with the ship. They had made headway towards establishing a colony—a treaty had been made with the Native people, seeds were planted, and houses were built. Loved ones were buried in the new cemetery. They were on their own, but still believed God was with them.

The struggles they had survived helped to unify the colonists, and Plymouth was established as a Separatist religious settlement, just as the Pilgrims had hoped. It was governed by a combination of English law and practicality, but mainly it was run according to the "Word of God," as represented in the Bible. The Scriptures influenced every aspect of daily life in the settlement, but it was also the Pilgrims' history, their losses and sacrifices, that informed Plymouth culture.

The history of Plymouth Colony and the Pilgrims was written by men, and did not address the experiences of women and children. Did they willingly participate in the venture? Some did, but in William Bradford's own words many of the women went along only because "they must go with their husbands." Children, of course, were in the same category. Once they boarded the *Mayflower*, whether with eagerness or anxiety, these women—and their children—became subject to the same conditions and dangers as their husbands and fathers, and many of them would die.[9]

The sacrifices these women made became a part of the history of Plymouth Colony, and eventually the history of America. Those who survived that first terrible winter went on to fulfill their designated task—the production of children. That is what they were there for— to grow families and set roots in the New World. Keeping everyone focused on this ultimate goal necessitated that many controls had to be set in place. How these women reacted to these controls is where we discover the most about their daily lives.

Looking at how the Pilgrims governed themselves reveals what was important to them. They had rules, and a system in place to enforce those rules. Anyone who broke the rules was severely punished. They also had standards, some written and some implied, that reflected their ideals, and anyone who ignored those expectations would face the community's censure. They also practiced a culture of hierarchical power, which meant that men assumed leadership roles, and women, children, and servants were under their control.

In their journals and court records, all penned by men in power, they reveal their ideals and standards and tell how they kept order at Plymouth Colony. This is the colony's history from the vantage point of those at the top.

I believe it more interesting and more revealing to look at that history from the bottom, from the lowest vantage point—the experiences of women and children. A new and fuller Pilgrim history emerges, one that reflects the contributions and sacrifices of all its residents.

৩৬৩৬৩৬

The leaders of the colony who featured prominently in its history were:

John Robinson, who was a member of the Scrooby congregation who moved to Leiden with the group. Known as the "Pastor of the Pilgrims," he died before he could come to Plymouth, but his influence through his writings helped shape the culture of the colony.

William Brewster was the leader of the Scrooby congregation, a major influence in their decisions to move twice to find a situation that would allow them to have religious and cultural freedom. While he was not ordained, he did serve as the lay elder of the Pilgrim church in Plymouth and was a mentor to its long-term governor, William Bradford. He led Sunday worship and delivered sermons but was not authorized to perform the sacraments of baptism or Eucharist.

William Bradford intermittently served as Plymouth's governor for thirty years, and his influence on the colony cannot be denied. His personal sacrifices drove his innate determination to keep the colony focused on the original goal. (Governor John Winthrop called Bradford "a very discreet and grave man," and perhaps his reserve and seriousness were a result of his experiences during Plymouth's earliest years).[10] Until his death, he struggled against the forces of the New World on succeeding generations.

There were others—all men—who made the decisions that affected their wives and children. From the very start, women were part of the plan for Plymouth. Decisions in which they had little participation decided their futures.

Chapter One

Martyrs of the *Mayflower*

The sixty-six day voyage of the *Mayflower* must have been a harrowing experience for the Pilgrims onboard. The ship that challenged the roiling Atlantic was only about one hundred feet long and twenty-five feet wide overall. The passengers, all 102 of them, were crammed into the fifty-by-twenty-foot gun deck under a claustrophobic five-foot ceiling. They likely fashioned tiny cubicles for themselves, marginally private spaces for families to sleep in and store their belongings. Fresh water was scarce, so bathing and laundry were deferred until the end of the voyage. Human waste was deposited in simple buckets, most likely secured to the deck to prevent them from spilling. At intervals the contents were dumped into the sea.

Meals were usually served cold, except when the sailors caught fish and cooked them on board. The English found some tastier than others. John Josselyn's diary of his 1638 crossing of the Atlantic noted: "The thirteenth day we took a shark, a great one, and hoisted him aboard. … The seamen divided the shark into quarters. …After they had cooked him, he proved very rough grained [and] not worthy of wholesome preferment; but in the afternoon we took a store of bonitos, or Spanish dolphins, a fish about the size of a large mackerel, beautiful with admirable varieties of glittering colors in the water and was excellent food."[1]

The *Mayflower* left extremely late in the sailing season, and once it put out to sea from Southampton it took over two months to reach Cape Cod, more than 3,000 miles later. Progress across the vast Atlantic Ocean was dependent on the winds and the currents; the little square-rigged merchant ship was constantly pitching, rolling, and heaving in the rough sea. Passengers were relentlessly tossed about, and many were seasick most of the time. Women and children

The *Mayflower* at sea.

were kept below deck, where it was deemed safer. While it may have been a more protected place for them, it was also a dark, stuffy, and humid environment. No one recorded how families kept their children safe and occupied day after day, while all the while controlling their own personal anxiety.

The ordeal took its toll on the Pilgrims. The close quarters, lack of nutritious food, persistent seasickness, and constant cold and dampness affected their physical and mental health. Some lasted longer than others, but within six months half of them would be dead.

William Butten

The first death among the *Mayflower* Pilgrims was young William Butten (Button). William Bradford simply states: "In all this voyage there died but one of the passengers, which was William Butten, a youth, servant to Samuel Fuller, when they drew near the coast." Butten died on November 6, 1620.[2,3]

Nothing is known for certain of William's origin as of this writing.

There was a Butten family in the Parish Register of Austerfield, where William Bradford was born, with a son William listed as being baptized on September 12, 1589. This William would have been 31 years old in 1620, hardly "a youth," and probably not the Pilgrim servant on the *Mayflower*. Perhaps he had a son who shared his name. There was another William Butten. He was baptized in Worksop, County Nottingham, on March 13, 1605, along with his twin, James. Worksop is less than ten miles from Scrooby, birthplace of the Pilgrims, so this may be the Pilgrim William Butten. If so, he would have been fifteen.[4,5]

Whoever he was, William Butten was in an enviable position as Samuel Fuller's servant. Fuller and his family were members of the Leiden Separatist congregation, and Samuel was a man held in high esteem. Bradford wrote that Fuller was the Pilgrim's "surgeon and physician," and his skill "had been a great help and comfort unto them," despite the fact that Fuller had no formal medical training. As a butcher's son, he probably picked up some knowledge of anatomy from watching and maybe assisting his father. In Leiden, he was a weaver. Nonetheless, he was the only medical "professional" among the Pilgrims, and as his servant, and perhaps assistant, Butten may have hoped to become a "surgeon and physician" himself. Where Butten met Fuller is unknown; there is no Butten/Button entry into the Leiden Membership List.[6,7,]

William Butten was buried at sea, since he died before the *Mayflower* reached Cape Cod.

The More Children

Most of the passengers on the *Mayflower* were making the voyage to the New World purposefully—many for religious reasons, some for economic opportunity. However, four small children were on board because their innocent existence was an inconvenience to a very influential man. Samuel More, scion of a wealthy family, made a deal with London merchant Thomas Weston. More paid Weston to take his children—Ellen, eight years old, Jasper, seven, Richard, six, and Mary, just four—on the *Mayflower* voyage.

They have been called the "More Orphans," but they were not orphans; they had at least three parents among them. Their legal father, Samuel More, had married his fifth cousin, Catherine (also known as Katherine) More, when Samuel was just sixteen, a marriage arranged by both their fathers to preserve their families' estates at Linley and Larden Halls, in Shropshire. Catherine, who was twenty-five at the time of their marriage, considered herself already promised to Jacob Blakeway, claiming they had a pre-contract, and that they had exchanged vows in secret. Since ancient times, this practice was recognized in England as a valid marriage. The man would declare, "I receive you as mine, so that you become my wife and I your husband." After the woman had responded in kind, the marriage was considered legal.[8]

After young Samuel More married Catherine, he worked as an aide to Lord Edward Zouche, and spent the majority of his time in London. His wife, in the meantime, bore four children. Shortly after the birth of the youngest, Samuel, who had just turned twenty-one and achieved legal control over both the family estates, acted on facts that he could no longer ignore. While English law made him their legal father, both the timing of their births and their resemblance to tenant Jacob Blakeway convinced Samuel that the rumors circulating in London were true—at least some of "his" children were in fact not biologically his.

With both estates now firmly and legally in his hands, Samuel More began proceedings against his wife. Furious at the assumed betrayal, Samuel removed the children from their mother's care and placed them with a tenant family on his ancestral lands. Catherine made many attempts to reclaim her family, at one point even resorting to violence. In the course of what seemed to be one particularly nasty fight, she swore, attacked the children's caregivers, and "did tear the clothes from their backs."[9]

Despite Catherine's efforts, the children remained with the tenant family for four years. Meanwhile, Samuel filed bigamy charges against Jacob Blakeway in the Court of High Commission. Jacob and Catherine appeared before a local bishop where they confessed to adultery, and that "they had together, often, and on repeated occasions lived an incontinent life and committed adultery together." After being fined, they agreed to stop seeing each other.[10]

It could have ended somewhat amicably there, but the couple did not stop seeing each other. In fact, they lived together with their children in Larden Hall, Catherine's family home, which now legally belonged to Samuel More. In 1619, More charged Blakeway with trespassing and property damage and was awarded four hundred pounds. Shortly thereafter, Blakeway "to prevent execution," fled. Samuel filed for divorce from Catherine, which was summarily awarded. But what was Samuel to do with the four children?[11]

Samuel More went to his employer, Lord Edward Zouche, and asked for assistance. Zouche has been an investor in the Virginia Company and was aware of another venture to the New World, the Separatist plan to found a religious colony. A contract was drawn up and More agreed to pay one hundred pounds to Thomas Weston. The agreement stipulated that the children would become full partners in the colony and would be "sufficiently kept and maintained with meat, drink, apparel, lodging, and other necessaries, and that at the end of seven years they should have fifty acres of land apiece in the Country of Virginia."[12]

Paul Harris, Samuel More's cousin, accompanied the children to London and turned them over to Weston, who in turn made an agreement with Separatists John Carver and Robert Cushman to include the children on the voyage and find them guardians. Rachel and Mary were put into the care of William and Mary Brewster, who already had their own sons—Love, thirteen, and Wrestling, six—with them. Jasper More was assigned to John and Katherine Carver, who had no children of their own, and Elinor was assigned to Edward and Elizabeth Winslow, who also had no children of their own.[13]

Sea travel in the seventeenth century was not for the faint-hearted. How the More children managed can only be imagined. In their short lives they had already been taken away from their mother, placed with a tenant family who were strangers to them, removed from those caregivers four years later, carried off to London, and then onto Southampton. They had probably never seen the sea or a ship before, and now they were setting sail on a voyage to the New World.

For their own safety, small children were kept below decks during the voyage. There were other children their ages on board, and while the More children were indentured to three different families, surely in the close quarters they stayed together and made friends with the other children. Their playmates were probably Bartholomew Allerton, who was seven, his sisters Remember and Mary, who were five and three, and Resolved White, who was five. Perhaps some childless wives and teenaged female passengers helped provide care and comfort to the children.

After arriving at Cape Cod in the dead of winter, women and children remained on board while the men explored the land, chose a suitable site for the colony, and began building houses. The lengthy voyage, limited diet, close quarters, and freezing weather caused many of the passengers to become ill. One of the first to die, in early December, was little Jasper More, servant to the Carvers, only seven years old. Bradford doesn't refer to Jasper by name, only calling him "Richard More's brother [who] died the first winter."[14]

Within two weeks, many of the other passengers had sickened. William Bradford wrote that "in two- or three-months' time, half of their company died, especially in January and February." In the bitter cold, they did not have adequate housing or enough food, and they were miserably sick, "being infected with the scurvy and other diseases." On some days two or three of the Pilgrims died. At the worst of it, Bradford says, there were only half a dozen persons well enough to care for the sick. The crew of the *Mayflower* did not escape the sickness; half of them had expired before she set sail to return to England on April 15, 1621.[15]

Among the dead that winter were not only Jasper More; both of his sisters, Elinor and Mary, also perished. Only Richard survived.

Richard More continued in his service to William Brewster. The 1627 Division of Cattle listed More with Brewster and his family in the fifth lot. When Richard turned twenty-one, he was entitled to his share of Plymouth property. On October 20, 1636, one year later, Richard More married Christian Hunter.[16,17]

On November 1, 1637, having bought twenty acres in Duxbury,

Richard sold them to Abraham Blush for "twenty-one pounds sterling." He and his wife relocated to Salem, where he became a mariner. In 1642 he joined the Salem church, and the couple's two sons, Samuel (perhaps named after his legal father) and Thomas, were baptized there. One author claims that Richard regularly sailed back and forth to England and on one voyage spent time with Elizabeth Woolnough, who became pregnant. Richard bigamously married her in England on October 23, 1645, and their daughter was baptized on March 2, 1646. (That claim has been challenged by genealogist Robert Charles Anderson, who believes there were two Richard Mores in Salem at the time).[18,19,20]

Richard and his Salem wife, Christian, eventually produced seven children. In 1674 he retired from sailing and opened a tavern. Christian died in 1676, and Richard married Jane Crumpton within two years. Jane died in 1686, and in 1688, Richard was called into court and charged with adultery, sentenced to be whipped, and to wear the letter *A*. As a result, Richard More was excommunicated from the Salem church.[21]

Attesting to Richard More's unsavory reputation, the record of the Salem church reads: "Old Captain More having been for many years under suspicion and [had] a common fame [reputation] of lasciviousness, and some degree at least of inconstancy and therefore was at several times spoke to, by sundry brethren and also by the Elders in a private way, [but] because for want of proof we could go no further. He was at last left to himself so far as that he was convicted before justices of peace by three witnesses of gross unchastity with another man's wife and was censured by them."[22]

In his late seventies, Richard More repented his wickedness, both verbally and in writing, and asked that his church membership be reinstated. In 1691 he was "by the vote of the Church forgiven and restored to his former state."[23] He died in the spring of 1694, at the age of eighty.

From the sumptuousness of Larden Hall, to the bleak shores of the Plymouth Colony, the only one of four siblings to survive the experience, Richard More lived a full, if not admirable life. Whether he ever thought of his sisters and brother again is impossible to know;

however, he did not name any of his seven children after any of them.

For all his faults, Richard More has one distinction to his name. He was the only surviving Pilgrim to be descended from royalty through his mother, Catherine.[24]

Mary Norris Allerton

Isaac Allerton boarded the *Mayflower* with his wife, Mary Norris, three children—Bartholomew, Remember, and Mary—and a servant boy named John Hooke. Isaac and Mary had been married in Leiden on November 4, 1611, and when Mary embarked on the *Mayflower,* she was well into her fourth pregnancy.[25,26]

As mentioned, after dropping anchor at Cape Cod, the men began exploring the bay, looking for a place to settle. By December 20, they had decided on a place on high ground, "where there is a great deal of land cleared, …and there is a very sweet brook [that] runs under the hill side, and many delicate springs of as good water as can be drunk." With that decision made, the men began to make great plans for this site. They would build a platform for the cannons on the great hill, "which will command all around about." The next day they would begin gathering the wood they needed to build the first houses, fetched from "half a quarter of an English mile" away. Excitement was high among the men, but higher among the women, because Mary Allerton had gone into labor.[27]

There was a terrible storm that night, "it blew and rained extremely; it was so tempestuous that the shallop could not go on land…." The storm continued into Friday, December 22, when Mary finally delivered a stillborn son. The child's name was not recorded, nor is it known where he was buried. Surely, the other wives and mothers on board understood Mary's grief and mourned along with her.[28]

Mary Norris Allerton died two months later, on February 25, 1621. Isaac would go on to briefly serve the colony as Governor Bradford's primary assistant. After Mary's death, Isaac married Fear Brewster, Elder Brewster's daughter. However, Allerton's financial dealings on the behalf of the colony came into question and led a disappointed

Bradford to lament Allerton's failings and betrayal with a biblical quote from Timothy, "for the love of money is the root of all evil."[29,30]

Like so many colonial women, Mary Norris Allerton's legacy is best reflected in her children. Bartholomew Allerton had the distinction of being one of the few *Mayflower* passengers who returned to England, but little is known of his subsequent life. Remember Allerton married Moses Maverick and settled near Salem. He is considered the "Father of Marblehead" for his work in the founding of that town as a separate settlement from Salem. Remember had seven children. Little Mary Allerton married Thomas Cushman, who succeeded William Brewster as Ruling Elder of the Pilgrim Church.[31] When he died in 1692, Cushman named four sons and two daughters in his will; a daughter, Fear, had predeceased him.[32,33,34,35,36]

When she died in 1699, Mary Allerton Cushman had the distinction of being the longest surviving *Mayflower* passenger.[37]

Dorothy May Bradford

Dorothy May was William Bradford's first wife, betrothed on November 3, 1613 in Amsterdam, when she was sixteen and Bradford twenty-three. Her father was Henry May, an elder of the Ancient Brethren, the first of several groups of English Separatists who had fled to Holland to escape persecution for their religious beliefs. [38,39]

William left Scrooby, England, in 1607, and settled in Amsterdam, where he likely met Dorothy. Within a year, the Scrooby group of Separatists had moved to Leiden, less than thirty miles south of Amsterdam, where they found jobs in the weaving industry. In 1612, William became a citizen of Leiden, enabling him to join a guild, thus increasing his opportunities and his earnings. When he came of full age at twenty-one, he inherited his family's lands back in Austerfield. He soon sold them and used the money to purchase a home of his own in Leiden.

William Bradford then travelled back to Amsterdam and made his proposal to Dorothy May. In the Dutch betrothal documents, it is noted that Henry May accompanied his daughter because she was

About a dozen children sailed on the *Mayflower*.

underage and needed permission to marry. They were married there on December 10, 1613. Within two years a son, John, was born to them. He would be their only child.[40,41]

Within the ideals of Separatism, a wife was expected to be completely submissive to her husband in all things. Bradford himself stated that wives "must go with their husbands," and in the language of the religion, that phrase meant more than that she should travel with him. It meant that she must submit to his leadership. The husband made all the decisions, and the wife was required to abide by them. When the decision was made that a group of the congregation would relocate to the New World, William Bradford volunteered to go, and it was understood that Dorothy would join him. However, they chose to leave John, who was then about four years old, behind in Holland. That decision has never been explained.[42]

When the exploring party returned after one of their onshore expeditions in which they scouted for the future site of Plymouth, they were full of excitement and stories. But someone had to take

William aside and break the terrible news that his wife had died in his absence. In the passenger list that Bradford drew up for *Of Plymouth Plantation*, he simply wrote that, "William Bradford, his wife died soon after their arrival."[43]

It wasn't until 1702, over eighty years later, that Cotton Mather revealed in his biography of Bradford the cause of Dorothy's death, that "his dearest consort accidentally falling overboard, was drowned in the harbor." That and Bradford's notation are the only primary sources that record Dorothy's passing. If anyone believed her demise was anything more than a tragic accident, no one wrote a word. This void in the historic record, this lack of an explanation by Bradford himself, certainly invited speculation into the reason for Dorothy's death. The first conjecture appeared in 1869.[44]

Just in time for the 250th anniversary of the *Mayflower* landing, a fictional account of Dorothy's death appropriated factual history. In a short story sensationally entitled "William Bradford's Love Life," author Jane Goodwin Austin, a friend of Louisa May Alcott, first raised the notion that Dorothy May Bradford took her own life. That romantic fictional story, published in *Harper's New Monthly Magazine* in June 1869, quotes an imaginary journal that Dorothy kept, claiming that while on the *Mayflower* in Cape Cod harbor she wrote: "Last night I dreamed that my mother came to me with my baby dead in her arms—my baby, my one child. Ah, child! You never loved another better than me, and yet I left you—for him. When I woke startled from my dream, he [William Bradford] stirred in his sleep, and murmured: 'Alice! Sweetest, dearest!'"[45]

In the fabricated story, William Bradford longs for his first love, Alice Carpenter Southworth, and speaks her name in his dreams. He neglects his lonely wife while participating in on-shore excursions, causing the fictional Dorothy to complain, "he speaks but little to me in any fashion. ...I wonder if he will be sorry when I am dead." In despair, she jumps into the icy Atlantic and her body is never recovered.[46]

Once the story was published, and republished in 1893, it was mistakenly accepted as factual by Bradford and Southworth heirs, and became the stuff of family legends handed down through generations. Over time, those legends became regarded as authentic history, and were published as if they were true.

There was at least one attempt to quash the fictional claim of Bradford pining over lost love. In 1931, noted historian and genealogical scholar, Gene Ernest Bowman, wrote an article for *The Mayflower Descendant*, entitled "Governor William Bradford's First Wife Dorothy (May) Bradford Did Not Commit Suicide," whose title speaks for itself. In a stinging rebuke of Jane Austin's story, Bowman cites all its misinformation item by item. Referring to the fictional journal, Bowman attacks Austin for claiming to have original historical documents, "priceless relics" that never actually existed.[47]

The problem, Bowman wrote, was that Austin's false assertion that her facts were "well-authenticated" in Dorothy's non-existent journal, led her readers to believe that she had proven that Dorothy May Bradford took her own life. "This story," he wrote, "has many times been quoted as the authority, and the only authority, for saying that Dorothy Bradford died a suicide." As a final jab, Bowman added that, considering all the factual errors in her short story, "no assertion by her can have the slightest weight."[48]

And yet the speculations continued. In 1950, Ernest Gebler published *The Plymouth Adventure: A Chronical Novel of the Voyage of the Mayflower*, which was a huge best-seller, so popular that in 1952 it was made into a movie. Gebler's book added a new twist to the story. He created a romantic involvement between the captain of the *Mayflower* and Dorothy Bradford. "In a vein of romantic speculation," wrote one movie reviewer, the film is "thoroughly respectful" and "should do nothing to shake the concepts learned at school." However, nowhere in the historical account does the *Mayflower's* Captain Jones attempt to "steal William Bradford's wife." The "crudely predatory Captain Jones," was played by Spencer Tracy; Gene Tierney portrayed Mrs. Bradford, "a firm pillar of well-starched ladyhood." Dorothy, already depressed and in despair, is confused over the captain's attention and contemplates death as she stares into the cold dark sea. She climbs on an icy barrel to get a better look and accidentally slips, falling to her death. Audiences were spell-bound. The poor historical Dorothy must have been spinning in her very real watery grave.[49,50]

Then, in 1994, Delores Carpenter published a collection of W. Sears Nickerson's papers under the title of *Early Encounters*, that revived the legends of Dorothy's death. In an essay, Nickerson (1880-1966), an historian and genealogist, related the story of Dorothy's despair that he had heard as "an old family tale." Nickerson's version parallels the Austin fictional account, right down to the claim that Bradford was haunted by his love for Alice Carpenter. As Austin before him did, Nickerson mixed genuine historical facts with a fanciful and romantic narration, such as, "although his wedded wife and the mother of his son, [Dorothy] could never hope to enter within that barrier which his first love had built around his heart."[51]

Nickerson wrote that while listening to the rhythm of the waves splashing against the side of the *Mayflower*, Dorothy thought "How blessed it would be to slip away from it all into that soothing harmony and be at peace forever." It is easy to imagine that someone in Nickerson's ancestry had read the Austin article and related it at the dinner table while passing the mashed potatoes, leaving future generations to recall the claim and consider it as fact, to be passed on and on until it has been burnished into an assumed truth.[52,53]

And yet, for all the fictional stories that have tried to explain Dorothy's death, it is not hard to imagine that a real young woman, separated from her only child, away from home and family, and facing the desolate wilderness, could have despaired, and slipped quietly overboard. The believability of the tale continues to fuel debate not only among Bradford descendants, but among otherwise respected historians as well.

In his book about Plymouth Colony, *Saints and Strangers*, 1945, George F. Willison offered that William Bradford "never mentioned her name again. There undoubtedly was some reason for this as Bradford was not a hardhearted or callous man. If Dorothy had jumped overboard, that was reason enough, for at the time nothing was regarded as so heinous an offense against the laws of God and man as taking one's life. Nor would Dorothy have been the first or last to crack in terror of the 'hideous & desolate wilderness.' ...To picture the forlorn lot or share the soul-searing experience of the pioneer women who first came to our shores is impossible for even the liveliest imagination today."[54]

In his biography of his ancestor William Bradford, written in 1951, Bradford Smith wondered: "How was it no one had been able to save her, the ship lying at anchor in a quiet harbor? John Howland had fallen overboard in mid-passage, yet they had managed to save him. Could she have drowned without a cry being heard, close to the crowded ship? ...The mystery of Dorothy Bradford's drowning has never been solved. ...Does [Bradford's brief record] hide a suicide as some have guessed? ...It is equally possible that Bradford's silence covered a feeling on his part that those aboard ship had been grossly negligent in failing to save her. Most of the crew and all the women and children were aboard. Even if Dorothy had wanted to commit suicide it is hard to see how she could have accomplished it if any determined efforts had been made to save her. ...Why could a rope not have been thrown to her?"[55]

Historian Samuel Eliot Morison offered his somewhat sexist opinion in 1956 in his book, *The Story of the 'Old Colony' of New Plymouth*: "One may suspect that [Dorothy May Bradford] did it on purpose, disheartened by gazing on the barren sand dunes of Cape Cod. How many tender hearts of pioneer women must have grown faint when they first beheld the wilderness shores of New England, so different from those of the green and placid Old England they knew!"[56]

In 2001 psychologist R. G. Kainer agreed that Dorothy definitely "ha[d] reason for despair as a young soul in an unknown wilderness," but Kainer also adds that the side effects of malnutrition and scurvy may have contributed to her depression. First recognized as a disease among sailors in the fifteenth century when longer sea voyages became possible, scurvy results from a diet lacking nutrients, especially Vitamin C. Along with joint pain, bleeding gums, loose teeth, and slow wound healing, scurvy also causes fatigue, weariness, and depression. Was Dorothy Bradford, already discouraged by her situation in the desolate wilderness, also fighting the crushing effects of depression? In such a fragile frame of mind, it is quite possible she despaired, lost all hope, and quietly slipped overboard into the frigid Atlantic.[57]

And yet, it is very possible that Dorothy's death was simply a tragic accident. The wooden railings on the bulwarks of the *Mayflower* were probably about waist-height, and the deck might have been icy. Dorothy, exhausted from the voyage, could have lost her balance while walking the deck, fallen against the railing, and tumbled over into the sea. Once her clothing became wet, it would have been nearly impossible to save her. As were all the women, she was wearing several layers of woolen skirts which would have become saturated very quickly, the weight pulling her below the surface before she could cry out.

Though he never wrote about it, William Bradford must have been deeply affected by the loss of his partner. Plymouth was a colony of families and Bradford now had none. He also may have felt some guilt over her death. It was his idea to come on this adventure, and "women must go with their husbands," as he wrote. Furthermore, his son was now motherless.

Within three years, Bradford married again, this time to a more mature woman, a widow with children of her own, and yet young enough to bear more. Alice Carpenter Southworth was more like Mary Brewster, steady and settled, committed to their religion, and strong enough to be able to withstand the rigors of colonization. She became the governor's wife and together they had three children.

William and Dorothy May's son, John, eventually did sail to Plymouth Colony. He married, but had no children.

Chapter Two

Laws and Standards

Plymouth Colony began keeping court records in 1633. Most of what we know about the women and children of Plymouth comes from those records, written evidence of some actions that may have been committed outside acceptable community standards. Descriptions and details of daily life are otherwise nearly non-existent; few women in that period could write, and even if they were literate, there was little time or inclination to record the mundane details of everyday activities. Wills and probate inventories provide much information about the material culture of the colony, but it is the court records that best describe what was deemed appropriate behavior and what was not. Also, in many of these records the secretary wrote down the actual dialogue of those charged with crimes or that of litigants bringing lawsuits against one another. We hear their feelings, their passion and anger and remorse, as they explain their complaints and offer their excuses, as real today as they were four hundred years ago.

Undoubtedly, most women in Plymouth quietly spent their days without ever having to explain their behavior to the governor or his assistants. As James and Patricia Deetz wrote, "The majority of women would have been married, living out their lives in the context of the recognized authority of their husbands, and working extremely hard to feed and clothe families that could include foster children as well as indentured servants. ... The average woman is largely invisible." Their marriage and death entries, the records of the births of their children, the wills and inventories of their husbands' estates—these are often the only written confirmations that many women even existed.[1]

Admittedly, court records document aberrant behavior for the most part; however, by knowing what was not acceptable, we can ferret out what was expected of women and children by the community.

These records are the best evidence of how women functioned within this society at large, and sometimes even in the privacy of their own homes.

In the early days of the colony, order was kept at a very personal and practical level. After that first terrible sickness, when the *Mayflower* left Plymouth to return to England, there were only about fifty Pilgrims still alive. When problems or disputes arose, the colony's leaders would gather, assess the situation, and then decide on a course of action. As the colony grew, it became necessary to create a code of laws and to write them down systematically. The first set of laws was written in 1636, and appended to as changing situations required. All laws were reviewed and updated in 1658, 1672, and 1685. Whether informal or formal, laws were respected at Plymouth, and no one was above them.[2]

First and foremost, laws were based on the Bible, which was accepted as the "Revealed Truth." John Robinson wrote, "The holy Scriptures are that Divine instrument, and means, by which we are taught to believe what we ought, touching God, and ourselves, and all creatures; and how to please God in all things, unto eternal life." To make it clearer he added, "Nothing is to be practiced, but that which is to be believed, nothing to be believed, but that which is to be taught; nothing to be taught, but according to the Scriptures." In the Scriptures, God "gives his holy law, saying, 'Do this and live,'" wrote Robinson.[3]

So central were the Scriptures to Plymouth culture that a law was passed in 1655 stating that any who "shall deny the Scriptures to be a rule of life shall receive corporal punishment according to the discretion of the magistrate so as it shall not extend to life or limb."[4]

Robinson, however, extended the intent of the Scriptures. He wrote that God's law not only prohibits evil, but also carries with it an intended opposite virtue. "He that saith expressly 'Thou shalt not kill,' means also, as well, 'Thou shalt preserve thy neighbor's life.'" These "oppositions" in the Scriptures "are diligently to be observed," warned Robinson. This principle formed the basis of the Pilgrims' belief that each had a responsibility to take care of the other.[5]

Next in line after the authority of the Scriptures were English laws. They were used as a guideline, and not adopted whole cloth. In

New England's Salamander Discovered, published in 1647, Edward Winslow explains: "I honor it [English law] and ever did, and yet know well that it was never intended for New England." There are some things in English law, he added, that we came here to avoid, "[such] as the hierarchy, the holy days, and book of Common Prayer, etc."[6]

Plymouth jurisprudence, then, was a combination of biblical law and English law, and was based on an awareness and recognition of the unique situation the Pilgrims were in. The individual codes were surprisingly practical and meant to be applied equally to all, regardless of wealth, station, or gender, and for the most part they were. And yet, the court gave themselves the option to decide whom to punish and the method of doing so. In the case law cited above, for example, the offender was to be punished "according to the discretion of the magistrate." No doubt someone accused of a crime could expect the court not only to consider the crime itself, but also that person's reputation in Plymouth.

But, it is in the manner in which the laws were enforced that reveals subtle details about the Pilgrim culture.

Pilgrim Watchfulness

Laws and standards were enforced not only by the courts, but also from within the community itself through the practice of *watchfulness*. According to Robinson's teachings, each Pilgrim was responsible for the other, not only physically, but also spiritually. Encouraged by both the government and the church, community watchfulness meant that each member kept an eye on the other for their own good. John Robinson and William Brewster proudly wrote that the Separatist congregation in Leiden was as "knit together as a body in a most strict and sacred bond and covenant of the Lord, of the violation whereof we make great conscience; and by virtue whereof we do hold ourselves straightly tied to all care of each other's good, and of the whole by everyone, and so mutually."[7]

Snooping and tattling were integral to the colony's governing system, encouraged by both the courts and the church. Their purpose was to prevent violations of Plymouth's laws and standards. William Bradford wrote that evil acts might not have been any more prevalent in Plymouth than any other place, but "they are here more discovered and seen and made public by due search, inquisition and due punishment; for the churches look narrowly [to limit or restrict] to their members, and the magistrates over all, more strictly than in other places."[8] Robinson wrote that "God has established fellowships and communities of men to procure their mutual good, and to fence them the better, on every side, against evil. ...Christians are most bound by virtue of their association, to help, and assist...their brethren and associates against [evil]." He went so far as to offer that "He that bears with the vices of his friend makes them his own."[9]

Necessary to the effectiveness of Pilgrim watchfulness was a vastly different concept of privacy than that which we assume today. Basically, there was little, if any, opportunity for solitude and seclusion in Plymouth. While this was true in England as well, the Pilgrims intensified this social reality. Early homes were small, fifteen to twenty feet in width and depth, consisting of one room dominated by a large fireplace at one end. While a dwelling may have been divided by a simple wall, with the inner chamber serving as a bedroom, there was no guarantee of privacy, as it was common practice for anyone to enter another's home at any time, uninvited.[10]

Houses were small, families were large, and the most basic of daily activities took place inside in crowded circumstances. Pilgrims living in such packed environments may never have acquired a sense of privacy. They had little expectation of enjoying any solitude or experiencing concealment of their personal activities. Beds were shared by several family members and children and servants slept on the floor nearby. As a result, the scant four hundred or so square feet of floor space may have been covered with adults and children sleeping shoulder to shoulder during the night. Dressing, washing, the necessities of bodily functions, all took place in the common room.

During the day, with so many people coming and going to and from the house and performing chores inside and out, keeping any actions private would have been nearly impossible. By necessity and for convenience, doors were probably left open during the daytime

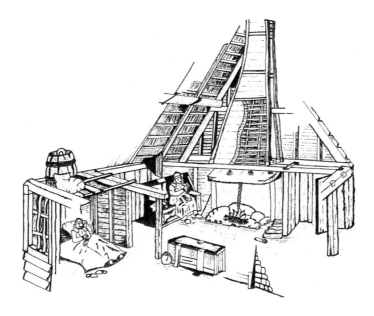

The Billington family house.

except in the most inclement weather. Besides the physical environment of the home limiting any expectation of privacy, cultural practices regarded anyone who sought time alone as secretive and suspicious. "God hath made man a sociable creature," wrote Robinson.[11]

There were locks at Plymouth. In a deed dated 1645, Richard Chadwell sold his property in Sandwich to Edmond Freeman, including his dwelling house, "with all the doors, locks, dressers, benches, glass, and glass windows...together with all lands to the said house belonging."[12] However, it is unclear how often doors were locked. In the Pilgrim mind, a closed door, never mind a locked one, meant that most likely something forbidden was going on behind it.

When any colonist observed or assumed that some illicit act had taken place, such as discord in a neighbor's household that was egregious enough to disturb the peace, the incident was reported to the town's representative on the Grand Inquest, or grand jury. This was a panel of men, seventeen of them in 1637, who swore to "enquire of all abuses within the body of this government."[13] That representative would investigate the complaint, and if warranted, bring it to the attention of the entire panel, who would then review the evidence. If they agreed that further action was necessary, they would bring the issue to the court's attention as an item of "Presentments by the Grand Inquest."

At this time, there were two types of courts held in Plymouth. The Courts of Assistants met the first Tuesday of every month, according to law.[14] These courts included the governor and his assistants, whose numbers varied from meeting to meeting. The second type of court was the General Court, which in the early years included the governor, his assistants, and all freemen. By 1671, as the colony grew and spread, a third type of court was instituted, the Selectmen's Court, which included deputies from each township to represent its freemen.[15] The General Courts were usually held in June, when elections were held, and in October.

Two types of cases were tried by the courts, criminal and civil. In civil cases, evidence was reviewed, and decisions were subsequently handed down by the magistrates. One example was the repayment of a debt. On October 31, 1666, John Rickard sued Elizabeth Moore for a debt of fifteen shillings. Elizabeth paid the debt and court costs with— surprisingly—one of her petticoats.[16,17]

Civil and criminal cases could come before either court, but by law the Courts of Assistants "shall not try any matters of weight without the major part of the assistants be present," and no cases would be tried unless there were at least four assistants present.[18] It was the responsibility of the jury of inquiry to present their cases to the court, "so they may be prosecuted by the governor by all due means."[19]

If the court found that the accusation was a genuine breach of the colony's laws or standards, and if the offender was then found guilty, the courts would decide the punishment. For example, a man who tried to court a woman without her parents' or master's consent, would, by law, "be punished either by fine or corporal punishment or both at the discretions of the bench and according to the nature of the offense."[20] Punishments for specific crimes were not always defined by Plymouth law.

Punishments

Following Pastor John Robinson's advice that behavior "can be restrained in the most, and worst, only by the fear of punishment," any violations of Plymouth law or colonial standards carried a penalty. Some offenders might receive a verbal warning, some were fined, others were severely beaten, but all penalties were administered in public, purposefully designed to cause maximum humiliation and shame. This was one way in which the Pilgrims confirmed community standards. Punishments should be public, wrote John Robinson, so that the "fear and warning [extend] to many." While reprimands must be administered with "sorrow and commiseration," they also must be severe enough—"temporary torments" he calls them, "grievous to conceive of, how much more to undergo,"—to be effective, not only for the good of the community, but also for the salvation of one's soul.[21]

Punishments were meant to cause pain severe enough to make an impression not only on the criminal's body, but also on his or her spirit. A public whipping was humiliating, drew blood and left scars to remind the offender of the "state's Godly authority."[22] However, several punishments common in other American colonies were not among the approved punishments in Plymouth. For example, the Pilgrims did not use the ducking stool, a chair into which an offender was tied and then dunked into water, nor did they employ the brank, an iron cage worn over the head designed to impair speaking and prevent gossiping.

Public Censure

The most basic form of punishment was the official admonition, also known as a warning. For example, on October 7, 1651, Rachel Ramsden, a married woman, was on trial in the court "for lascivious going in the company of young men." She was admonished, released, and ordered to watch her step, or in court parlance "to labor to walk inoffensively." The young men were not named nor charged. Yet, in this small community, public censure was no small penalty. Everyone would know what you had done; your reputation was damaged, and your behavior would be under even more scrutiny in the future.[23]

Still, the courts had compassion. In 1635, Elizabeth Warren's servant, Thomas Williams, was brought into court for "speaking profane and blasphemous speeches against the majesty of God." When she reprimanded him "to hear God and do his duty," the boy remarked that "he neither feared God, nor the devil." After the shock wore off, the court deemed that the boy's words were "judged to be spoken in passion and distemper," and let him go with an admonishment. Governor Bradford, however, dissented and "would have had him punished with bodily punishment, as the case seemed [at least to him] to require."[24]

Fines

Fines would be imposed in cases of more serious offenses. They ranged from just a few shillings to many pounds. Since currency and coin were scarce in the colony, commodities were often used as a medium of exchange. One common method of payment was a specified amount of corn. In 1633, it was rated at six shillings per bushel,[25] but the exchange rate could fluctuate. For example, in later years the value of a bushel of "Indian corn" would be about three shillings.[26] The point is that you had to pay your fines or your taxes with your own labor with corn which you grew and harvested yourself.

It took a lot of labor to produce corn; an acre would yield about eighteen bushels.[27] So it was no small punishment when on April 1, 1633, John and Alice Thorpe were sentenced to sit in the stock and were fined forty shillings (two pounds) because "his wife conceived with child before marriage." Due to their "present poverty," they were given one year to pay the fine. That would be long enough to plant, grow, harvest, and shuck enough corn to fill six bushels, or the production of about one-third of an acre, almost enough to pay the fine.[28]

To put the value of a two-pound fine into some perspective, on October 7, 1651, Giles Rickard, Sr., of Plymouth, paid to George Russell, of Scituate, five pounds, ten shillings for a house and land at Wellingsly, near Plymouth. The deal included not only the house, "with all the rooms, ...boards, shelves, doors, [and] locks," but also the two acres of land which the house was standing on, and also seven acres of upland nearby.[29] A fine of five pounds could be the equivalent of what a colonist might spend to buy an entire farm.

The Stocks

Not only did the aforementioned Thorpes owe the court a fine; they were also sentenced to sit in the stocks. The stocks were heavy wooden frames with holes for ankles and wrists, holding the convicted firmly seated in place and on public display. The offender would be made to "sit in stocks" for a specified period of time on Meeting Day outside the meeting house, when everyone in the colony was required to attend church services, exposing him or her to public ridicule and shame. Every community had to have its own stocks. In 1637, Duxbury and Scituate had neglected to build theirs and were ordered by the court to erect their stocks within a year or "to be fined by the court for their default."[30]

Another example of combined punishments was addressed on May 7, 1661, when Ann Savory was brought into court with several charges against her. She was at home "on the Lord's day," instead of being at "public exercise," and was discovered to be in the company of Thomas Lucas, "at unseasonable time." Furthermore, she was found "drunk at the same time under a hedge, in uncivil and beastly manner." For being with Lucas, she was sentenced to sit in the stocks; for being found drunk, she was fined five shillings; and for "profaning the Lord's day," she was fined an additional ten shillings.[31]

Whipping

Those convicted of more serious crimes were sentenced to corporal punishment in the form of whipping. There were several forms of whipping: a common whipping, a severe whipping, and being whipped

The stocks and whipping post.

twice, once in Plymouth town and a second time in the lawbreakers' hometown. Using a switch to administer discipline was a normal practice in Plymouth; parents commonly used a bundle of twigs to punish their children. But administering "stripes" was another matter. The lawbreaker would be tied to a sturdy post, stripped to the waist—male and female alike—and thrashed on the bare back with a leather or rope whip. A common whipping was often seven stripes; a severe whipping could be as many as thirty stripes. Sometimes a "tormenting whip" was used, made with three cords with knots tied in the end of each.[32] The beating would be administered in public, near the meeting house, again on meeting day when nearly all Pilgrims would be present, both adults and children.

Whipping was brutal and left raw wounds, but the courts were not cruel. In 1639, Dorothy Temple had a child out of wedlock and was "censured to be whipt twice." Dorothy fainted after her first whipping, and the courts decided to spare her the second round.[33] Perhaps some kind soul treated Dorothy's painful lacerations with seal oil, which was what the Native Americans used for cuts and sores.[34]

Often miscreants were offered a choice—pay a fine or get a

whipping. While this practice favored the wealthier residents, it was also believed that those who were more successful were those who worked harder. It was only the most desperate who had to chose the whip over the fine.

Sometimes a crime was found to be so offensive that the courts ordered multiple punishments, including banishment from the colony. For example, in July 1683, Jonathan Dunham was arrested for breaking into John Irish's home. Dunham had abandoned his family and had been "wandering about from place to place as a vagabond in this colony." He met a young woman named Mary Ross along the way, who, according to his testimony, somehow enchanted him. Mary Ross, he claimed, "said he must do what she bade him."[35]

It was her idea, Dunham claimed, to go to the house of John Irish, in Little Compton, and in the course of their "antics, tricks, and foolish powers," start a fire in the house. The couple threw John Irish's dog into the flames. Irish testified that they fired a gun several times, burnt some of his belongings, almost burned down his house, and terrorized his young children. John had to summon his neighbors to help him fight off Dunham and Ross and rescue his family.[36]

The court ordered Dunham to be whipped at the post and "to depart forthwith out of the colony." Should he delay, he would be whipped again. As for Mary Ross, for her crimes and "for her uncivil and outrageous railing words and carriages to the Deputy Governor, and afterwards before the whole court," she was sentenced to be whipped. Afterward, she would be "conveyed from constable to constable out of this government towards Boston, where her mother dwells." How her mother managed her wild, unruly daughter is not known.[37]

Whipped at the Cart's Tail

The court occasionally ordered that the wrongdoer be whipped at the cart's tail. This punishment was usually reserved for women involved in sexual offenses, and was particularly humiliating.[38] The woman would have been stripped to the waist, tied with a rope to the back end of the cart, walked through the main street of town, all the while being continuously whipped. For instance, on September 3, 1639, two women, Mary Mendame and Jane Winter, were sentenced to be "whipt at a cart's tail," both for "acts of uncleanness," the colony's euphemism for sexual misdeeds.[39]

Branding and the Scarlet Letter

Branding was reserved for especially heinous crimes and used only for male criminals. The permanent mark labeled the offender for life, and wherever he went he could be immediately identified as a criminal. However, there was a temporary type of label used in Plymouth. Convicted women—and sometimes men—could be ordered to wear an appliquéd fabric letter on their clothing; most often it was the letter A for adultery.

The penalty exacted in a case in 1656 required the woman involved to wear the letter *B*. Katherine Aines, "for her unclean and lascivious behavior with…William Paule, and for the blasphemous words that she hath spoken," was sentenced to be whipped at Plymouth and afterwards at Taunton, "on a public training day." (A "public training day" was a compulsory military event to train Plymouth's self-armed militia.) She was also ordered to wear the letter *B*, signifying her crime of blasphemy, "cut out of red cloth and sewed to her upper garment on her right arm. Should she ever be seen without it, "while she is in the government," she was to be "forthwith publicly whipped." However, Katherine was determined not fully responsible for her crime. As head of the household and responsible for the behavior of all under his roof, Katherine's husband, Alexander was punished as well, "for his leaving his family, and exposing his wife to such temptations." He was sentenced to sit in the stocks while his wife and William Paule were being whipped and was also ordered to pay the charges incurred during his wife's imprisonment.[40]

By punishing Alexander as well as the transgressing couple, the courts were reminding the community of the husband's responsibility to control his wife's behavior. The courts did demonstrate some consideration for him, however; because "the said Aines is very poor," he was permitted to pay twelve pence a week until the charges were paid in full.[41]

Hanging

Capital crimes were punishable by death by hanging, the only category of crime with a specific punishment, according to Plymouth law, first cited in 1636. Capital offenses included treason, willful murder, witchcraft, arson, sodomy, rape, buggery, and adultery. Between 1630 and 1690, ten felons were hanged in Plymouth Colony, nine for the crime of murder. In 1630, John Billington, a *Mayflower* passenger, was convicted and hanged for murdering John Newcomen, the first time the colony dealt with a capital crime. Four men—Arthur Peach, Thomas Jackson, Richard Stinnings, and Daniel Cross—were convicted of murdering a Native American and sentenced to death. Daniel Cross escaped, but the three others were hanged in 1638.[42] Thomas Granger, a teenager who was hanged in 1642, convicted of "buggery with a mare, a cow, two goats, diverse sheep, two calves, and a turkey." [43,44,45] (This unusual case will be discussed later.)

Three Native Americans were charged, convicted, and found guilty of murdering another Indigenous person, John Sassamon. Tobias, Wampapaquan, and Mattashunnamo were all tried by jury on June 1, 1675. The jury members, "this English jury," was joined by "some of the most indifferentist, gravest, and sage Indians," who "fully concurred" with the decision.[46] (The murder of Sassamon, a friend of the colonists who tried to remain loyal to them as well as to the natives, brought tensions between the groups to a breaking point and led directly to King Philip's War.) In 1690, John Armand de la Forrest was condemned to hang for murder. "Immediately before his execution," the court record states, he "confessed himself guilty of the murder."[47]

Even though hanging was the prescribed punishment for murder, not all murder cases resulted in a hanging. For example, on March 5, 1685, an Indigenous woman named Betty was indicted for killing her husband, known as Great Harry, by throwing a stone at him. When she was first interviewed, "she denied it, but afterwards owned the fact, but said she did not intend to kill, but by throwing of a stone at a bottle of liquor and missing the bottle, she hit the said Indian, her husband, on the side of the head, whereof he died." The grand jury indicted her for murder. However, the petty jury found her to be "guilty of homicide by misadventure," or what we would call manslaughter. There was no hanging.[48]

As will be discussed later, another case of murder also went unpunished. A servant boy, John Walker, died after mistreatment by his master and mistress, Robert and Susanna Latham.

Alice Bishop was not so fortunate to escape the noose. The only woman who was hanged at Plymouth, Alice Bishop murdered her four-year-old daughter, Martha Clarke, on July 22, 1648.

The day started out as most did. A visiting neighbor, Rachel Ramsden, testified that she found Alice to be "as well as she had known her at any time." Little Martha was asleep in her bed. At Alice's request, Rachel went to fetch a kettle of buttermilk from "Goodwife Winslow," (Mary Chilton Winslow, John Winslow's wife) who lived nearby.[49] Upon Rachel's return, things were very different, as she testified to Governor Bradford:

> Rachel, the wife of Joseph Ramsden, aged about 23 years, being examined, [said that] when she came [back] she found [Alice Bishop] sad and dumpish; she asked her what blood was that she saw at the ladder's foot; [Alice Bishop] pointed into the chamber, and bid her look, but [Rachel] perceived [Alice] had killed her child, and being afraid, she refused, and ran and told her father and mother. Moreover, she said the reason that moved her to think she had killed her child was that when she saw the blood, she looked on the bed, and the child was not there.[50]

The testimony of the jury of inquiry was especially gruesome:

> We declare, that coming into the house of the said Richard Bishop, we saw at the foot of a ladder which

leads into an upper chamber, much blood; and going
up, all of us, into the chamber, we found a woman
child of about four years of age lying in her shift upon
her left cheek with her throat cut with diverse gashes
cross ways, the wind pipe cut and stuck into the throat
downward, and a bloody knife lying by the side of
the child, with which knife all of us judged, and the
said Alice confessed to five of us at one time, that she
murdered the child with the said knife.[51]

No motive for the murder was offered, and Alice freely confessed
to the jury of inquiry on the day of the crime and was arrested. On
August 1, 1648, she appeared before the Court of Assistants:

At a Court of Assistants held at New Plymouth, the
first of August 1648, before Mr. Bradford, Governor,
Mr. Collier, Capt. Myles Standish, and Mr. William
Thomas, Gentlemen, Assistants, the said Alice, being
examined, confessed she did commit the aforesaid
murder, and is sorry for it.[52]

Alice was kept in jail until the General Court convened two months
later, on October 4, 1648. This length of time would determine whether
Alice was pregnant, which was important because it was not the custom
to hang a pregnant woman. At that October court, held during the
heavily-attended Duxbury annual fair, the grand inquest jury found
the case against Alice Bishop to be a "true bill." Immediately following
the acceptance of the indictment, the petty jury assembled, reviewed
the case, and found Alice, "guilty of the said felonious murdering of
Martha Clarke aforesaid."[53,54]

It was up to the governor and his assistants to decide how Alice
would be punished. They followed Plymouth law in this capital case:

And so, she had the sentence of death pronounced
against her, that is, to be taken from the place where
she was to the place from whence she came, and thence

to the place of execution, and there to be hanged by the neck until her body is dead, which accordingly was executed.[55]

Why Alice Bishop murdered her daughter is not known for certain. No motive was recorded. Her execution at the Duxbury fair meant that Alice Bishop was hanged before a large crowd, which most likely included her husband and surviving daughters.[56]

Chapter Three

Chastity and Courtship

Marriages were not arranged by parents in Plymouth Colony. Young people were free to choose their own mates; courtship was, however, conducted under the watchful eye of the entire community. There were no known or recorded dating rituals, no dances, nor any hangouts where those of marriageable age might congregate. Men and women met through their usual daily activities, perhaps at church meetings, weekly markets, or while performing chores or errands. Many had known each other since childhood.

Once a couple began eyeing one another, everyone would notice there was an attraction. This was a community that was very watchful, nowhere more so than in matters of sexual temptation. The fitness of the match was no doubt discussed, perhaps even before the couple themselves were ready to admit they were interested in each other. Once they were close to making a commitment, the parents would meet and, if they approved, the young man was then permitted to begin formal courting. This stemmed from a law passed by the courts in 1636 that stated that "none shall be allowed to marry that are under the covert of parents but by their consent and approbation." Young men and women were free to choose their own prospective partners, but before marriage could occur, both sets of parents had to give their approval of the union, or the courts would step in.[1] Such was the case on March 2, 1652, when Jonathan Coventry was called into court for courting Katherine Bradbury, who was a servant to "Mr. Bourne" of Marshfield. Young Jonathan had not obtained the consent of her master. Probably fearing the worst, Jonathan "departed the government," according to a marginal notation in the court record, abandoning his pursuit of Katherine before the case could be tried.[2]

If the relationship progressed to the engagement stage, an

announcement of the upcoming marriage would be made at church meetings and a notice posted on the door for three succeeding weeks, giving anyone who protested the proposed union plenty of time to object. Once this notice was made, the couple was considered to be under contract, which changed everything for them; they immediately became subject to the laws and rules and customs that governed marriage in Plymouth.

Courtship

With or without a contract, if a promise of marriage had been made, the courts saw that as a formal and binding agreement. If broken, the offended party could sue for damages, as did one John Sutton. On October 1, 1661, Sutton brought a civil lawsuit against Mary Russell, suing her for two hundred pounds. Mary, John complained, had promised to marry him, and then engaged herself to another man. The jury agreed he had been wronged, and ordered Mary to pay fifteen pounds damage, a very weighty fine, thus signifying the seriousness of the offense. She was also ordered to pay the cost of the suit, which came to one pound, ten shillings, six pence.[3]

While it was the custom in Plymouth for parents to help their children with gifts of land at the time of marriage, sometimes the gift was in cash or commodities, as was the case with James Willet and his intended, Elizabeth Hunt. On November 1, 1679, Willet, of Swansea, sued Peter Hunt, Elizabeth's father, for two hundred pounds, "for non-payment of the sum of one hundred pounds in money, or the value thereof, due unto him." Hunt had promised to give Willet the money, "grounded upon and in consideration of his marriage with Elizabeth." Hunt, Willet complained, had paid only a portion of the agreed amount.[4]

James and Elizabeth had already been married for six years— since April 17, 1673—when Willet brought the lawsuit. After hearing the case and considering the evidence, "the jury found for the defendant," Elizabeth's father. He was awarded the costs he incurred in defending himself against the Willet's lawsuit. No mention was

Pilgrim courtship.

made of the originally promised two hundred pounds. Perhaps the court felt that James Willet had received the dowry in other ways over the ensuing years.[5,6]

Clearly, the Pilgrims were concerned about keeping control over the colony's young people, especially in their marriage choices. By 1638, the courts had added serious punishments for those who engaged in relationships without parents' or masters' approval: "If any shall make any motion of marriage to any man's daughter or maid servant not having first obtained leave and consent of the parents or master so to do, [he] shall be punished either by fine or corporal punishment or both at the discretions of the bench and according to the nature of the offense."[7]

There was hope, however, for those who could not obtain parental consent. They could be allowed to marry, the law said, "with the consent of the governor or some assistant to whom the persons are known, whose care it shall be to see the marriage be fit before it be allowed by him."[8]

Parents had other issues to consider aside from their disapproval of their child's choice of a mate. One concern was that either party might not be fit for marriage and procreation. On March 2, 1647, Francis

Crooker appeared before the court asking for permission to marry Mary Gaunt. The problem was that Francis had an ailment which might render him unfit for marriage. He was required to produce a "certificate under the hands of Mr. Chauncy and some other approved physician, that the disease with which he is sometimes troubled be not the falling sickness." Only after Francis proved that he did not have epilepsy would he be approved to marry. Apparently, Charles Chauncy, preacher at Scituate, a physician, and later president of Harvard, cleared Francis. He and Mary were married that same year and settled in Marshfield.[9,10]

One young man, Richard Taylor, appeared before the courts to ask for the governor's help in obtaining permission to marry Ruth Whelding, whose father would not provide consent. The case came to the courts on October 27, 1646 when, after hearing all the evidence, Ruth's father was persuaded that the match was a good one. The record states: "In the case between Gabriel Whelding and Richard Taylor, about his daughter Ruth, the said Gabriel promised his free assent and consent to their marriage." It was a successful union. The couple went on to have seven children, two sons and five daughters. After twenty-seven years of marriage, Ruth died in an unfortunate boating accident in December 1673.[11,12,13]

Arthur Howland, Jr. faced fines for pursuing Elizabeth Prence. On March 5, 1667, Howland was called into court for "inveigling of Mistress Elizabeth Prence and making motion of marriage to her, and prosecuting [persuing] the same contrary to her parents' liking, and without their consent, and directly contrary to their mind and will." Elizabeth's parents clearly did not approve of Arthur.[14]

Arthur and Elizabeth were both members of prominent Pilgrim families. Arthur was the nephew of *Mayflower* passenger John Howland, and Elizabeth was the current governor's daughter. Besides the humiliation of being brought into court, Arthur was fined five pounds, and asked to post sureties to insure his good behavior. He was ordered to "desist from the use of any means to obtain or retain her affections as foresaid." On July 2, 1667, an apologetic Arthur Howland, Jr., appeared before the court, promising he would "wholly desist and never apply himself for the future, as formerly he hath done, to

Mistress Elizabeth Prence in reference unto marriage."[15,16]

The problem Governor Prence had with young Arthur was probably that he was a Quaker, and Prence had a very strong position on Quakers: "They were such a people as deserved to be destroyed, they, their wives, their children, their houses and lands, without pity or mercy."[17]

But Arthur and Elizabeth were determined to be together, and their love would not be denied. On December 9, 1667 the couple was married.[18] Their subsequent life together was a difficult one. Arthur was constantly beleaguered by the Marshfield Church for his Quaker faith. In 1684, he was jailed for refusing to contribute to minister Samuel Arnold's salary. During his incarceration, Arthur was, in his own words, "allowed neither bread nor water, or anything to lie on but the floor, nor anything to cover me, ... nor so much as [a] fire by their order."[19] Two years before, Arnold had ordered that the couple be shunned, and forbade all church members from eating and drinking with them. He even urged Elizabeth not to associate with her own husband.[20]

Elizabeth, still a woman of strong mind, "withdrew from them and told them if they would not or could not produce some clear scripture rule for what they had done to her husband she could not partake with them in that which she thought was such an unchristian act without sinning against her conscience...."[21]

Elizabeth stood steadfastly with her husband, and they produced at least five recorded children. It is not known how Governor Prence dealt with having Quaker grandchildren, given his earlier opinions.

Sex Before Marriage

Fornication, or sexual relations between a man and a woman outside of marriage, was against Plymouth law. Not only was the act considered immoral as an offense against the seventh commandment, but there was also the more practical concern that the community would have financial responsibility for an illegitimate child. For both reasons, charges were vigorously prosecuted.

In the 1636 written code of law, fornication was considered a criminal act. Along with "other unclean carriages," fornicators would be punished "at the discretion of the Magistrates according to the nature thereof." In 1645, the law was amended and strengthened to standardize the punishment. The offending couple would be punished either by whipping or by paying ten pounds each and would be imprisoned for not more than three days. That law also officially recognized a difference between couples who had entered into a formal contract to be married, who had obtained the consent of their parents or guardians, and who had made "a solemn promise of marriage in due time to each other before two competent witnesses," and those couples who had not done so.[22]

For example, on the same court date in 1633, two couples were charged with fornication. John and Joan Hews were charged that "Joan conceived with child by him [John] before they were publicly married, though in the time of contract." They were sentenced to sit in the stocks. John and Alice Thorpe were likewise charged and likewise sentenced to the stocks; however, they had the added fine of forty shillings. Unlike the Hews, the Thorpes had not been under contract.[23]

Fornication was the most common sexual offense to come into court; it has been estimated that up to twenty percent of Plymouth's married couples engaged in premarital sex, as evidenced by subsequent pregnancy.[24] The number may have been much larger; there is no way to count those couples who had sex and did not become pregnant. (In comparison, a Public Health Report published in 2007 stated that between 1954 and 2003, "Almost all Americans have sex before marrying."[25] With the availability of birth control now, unwanted pregnancy can be avoided.)

Couples who had entered into contract were less likely to have relations before marriage, indicating perhaps that those who officially stated their intentions were more likely to be law-abiding and dutiful. Of sixty-nine cases of fornication recorded between 1633 and 1691, only four had occurred during the period of contract. Of those sixty-nine cases, forty-six percent eventually married, and forty-eight percent never married.[26]

Through the imposition of fines and corporal punishment, the couple was pressured into marriage after having "carnal copulation." Once they were married to each other, the fine would be reduced to five pounds each and they would be imprisoned, but they would not be whipped. If they could not pay the fine, then both parties would be whipped. Consequently, poorer couples faced the possibility of dreadful corporal punishment. Apparently, the threat of a whipping was the courts way of discouraging unfettered sexuality among the poor, which would not only maintain community standards, but also lessen the possibility of the colony having to support large needy families.[27]

The most obvious evidence of the crime of fornication was the birth of a full term child less than nine months after marriage; and in this watchful community, someone was counting. In March 1652, Thomas Launder was charged with "having a child born within thirty weeks after marriage." At that same court, Nicholas Davis was charged with "having a child five weeks and four days before the ordinary time of women after marriage."[28]

The courts would not be fooled. On March 1, 1670, when Bethiah Tubbs accused John Prince, Jr., "that he had begotten her with child," she cited the date the child was conceived. Prince denied the charge. While the court was in session, Bethiah went into labor and delivered a child "come to full perfection," that is, a full term baby. The court decided that "the time being computed that she accused him to have done the act, ...was found not to answer to the time of the child's birth." Prince was cleared of all charges. Four years later, on June 24, 1674, Bethiah married Joseph Hanmore in Marshfield.[29]

Two cases came before the court on March 14, 1688. Jeremy Hatch and his wife were bound over "for his wife's having a child at nine and twenty weeks after marriage; [making it] a possibility that the said child might have been born before the time of nature." The child died soon after birth and the couple were charged only court costs. On the same day, John Merritt and his wife Elizabeth were fined fifty shillings and court costs for fornication. Their child was "born twelve weeks too soon, that is to say, at twenty-seven weeks after marriage or thereabouts."[30]

In 1671, the laws were updated and became somewhat more

lenient to those who fornicated while under contract. Fines were lowered, and imprisonment was at the discretion of the court. If the fines were not paid, however, the offending couple would be whipped. For those who engaged in sexual activity without promise of marriage, the punishment was a fine of ten pounds each, three days in jail, and a whipping. Should anyone think that the courts were condoning sex outside of marriage, they further decided that all transgressors "shall be convict[ed] in public court; and their fines to be paid in money."[31] Public humiliation was added to the punishment, and they were not allowed to pay fines with a commodity.

As serious as the crime was, the courts were not without compassion. Pressure to marry was strong in Plymouth, and some women were desperate enough to trade their chastity for a chance of becoming a wife. Such was the case of Jane Powell, servant to William Swift of Sandwich. One fateful evening she met David OKillia (also known as Ogillior), "an Irish man, servant to Edward Sturgis."[32]

On June 8, 1655, Jane was presented in court by the grand jury "for an act of fornication by her own confession upon examination." On October 4, 1655, the court addressed the case again and Jane was again charged with fornication. She testified that "she was allured thereunto by him [OKillia] going for water one evening." She hoped that he would marry her, "being she was in a sad and miserable condition by hard service, wanting clothes, and living discontentedly." She "express[ed] great sorrow for her evil," and the court cleared her, "for the present," and ordered her to go home again.[33]

But this story had a happy ending. In 1657, "David Okillia, Irishman," of Yarmouth, took the oath of fidelity and became a freeman.[34] He and Jane were married, and their first child, Sarah, was born in 1660. They would eventually have seven children. David's will was proved on July 27, 1697, listing "my loving wife, Jane" as his sole executrix. Jane never remarried and lived on in Yarmouth. She died there on October 17, 1711, leaving scores of OKillia (Kelly) descendants. David is remembered as "a person of considerable prominence in the community."[35,36]

In the fall of 1663, another case was heard in which the woman had hoped to marry her lover. On October 5, Elizabeth Soule, daughter of

George and Mary, made a complaint against Nathaniel Church, suing him for two hundred pounds. Church, she claimed, had "committed the act of fornication with her, the said Elizabeth, and [afterward]… denying to marry her."[37]

Six months earlier, on March 3, 1663, the court had charged the couple with fornication and fined them. Elizabeth, perhaps in an effort to repair her reputation, returned to court and claimed that Nathaniel had intended to marry her. The jury agreed, and awarded Elizabeth ten pounds damage, plus court costs. But four years later, on July 2, 1667, when she again stood before the court accused of fornication with a different and unnamed man, the courts were not so understanding. Since this was her second offense, she was sentenced to be whipped. The unnamed man may have been Francis Walker. They were married shortly thereafter.[38,39,40,41,42]

The governor and his assistants considered the circumstances of each fornication case individually, and even though they failed to record the full details, their decisions indicate that there was more to the story than had been entered into the record. For example, three cases of fornication came before the courts on the same day, October 29, 1670, each with a different outcome. William Rogers was the first to appear, "for committing fornication before marriage." He was sentenced to pay a fine of five pounds, "in money." If he could not, or refused to pay the fine, he would be whipped.[43] His choice was not recorded.

The next case was a charge of fornication between Mary Adkinson and her then husband, Marmaduke Adkinson. The court had ordered Mary's father, Edward Jenkens, to pay three pounds fine, "for and in the behalf of his daughter, Mary Adkinson, who is fined for having carnal copulation with her husband, Marmaduke Adkinson, before marriage and before contract." Apparently, the couple could not afford the fine. When her father later paid, she was freed from jail.[44]

The third case incurred the largest fine, without explanation. "At this court, Jabez Snow and his wife were fined the sum of ten pounds for having carnal copulation with each other before marriage."[45]

As shown in the above cases, even if the couple married after committing fornication and conceiving a child, they were still liable to be punished. In another example, November 8, 1638, the court considered the case of John Smyth and Bennett Moorecock. Bennett became pregnant by John before marriage. He was ordered to appear in court after the child's birth and to remain in the colony. John and Bennett were married and yet he was still "censured" for fornication and ordered to be whipped, "which accordingly was done."[46]

Any conviction of a crime could mar someone's reputation for life. It was, therefore, important that the court look at all the circumstances. Take the case of Robert Whitcomb (Whetcombe) and Mary Cudworth, who appeared in court on March 5, 1661. The couple was charged for "disorderly coming together without consent of parents and lawful marriage." They were fined ten pounds and imprisoned. The couple testified that they were "desirous to be orderly married," and were married on March 9, 1661, three days later.[47]

It may be that they, in fact, believed themselves already married. The clue is in the word "orderly." Henry Hobson apparently had illegally conducted a ceremony for the couple, perhaps a Quaker ceremony. On that same date, March 5, 1661, Hobson had been ordered to appear in court, "to answer for his derision of authority in counterfeiting the solemnizing of the marriage of Robert Whitcomb and Mary Cudworth." The case was heard on June 10 and held over until the October court so that witnesses could attend. The witnesses were Robert Whitcomb and his wife, Robert Ale and his wife, and Ezekiel Mayne. The case was never heard, and no further record has been found.[48,49]

However, a full year later, on March 4, 1662, after two years of marriage, the couple was once again back in court. Robert and Mary, "having since been orderly married, and living orderly together, and following their callings industriously, and attending the worship of God diligently, as is testified by some of their neighbors, of good report," the court decided to reduce the fine from ten pounds to five. Furthermore, since they were considered a poor family, the court asked the colony treasurer "to be slow in demanding the remainder" of what they owed to the colony.[50]

A curious case of fornication came before the court on July 4, 1679, when Jonathan Higgins was charged with "committing fornication with his wife's sister [probably Hannah] after his wife's death." He was fined twenty pounds, an unusually large amount for fornication. It may be that the court also considered the crime to be an incestuous act, since Higgins was her brother-in-law, although related only through marriage. Several of his friends appealed to the court, "earnestly," and the fine was reduced to ten pounds.[51] Jonathan may have married his sister-in-law, Hannah, although no record has been found. He did father five more children after his first wife's death.

When an act of fornication produced a child and the couple did not marry, the courts made great efforts to seek out the father and order him to pay child support. Otherwise, the colony would need to support the abandoned mother and child in what was already a very poor community. For example, in a 1672 civil case, Mary Churchill was not only pregnant; she had been abandoned by her lover. The court made certain that she received support for herself and the child. On October 30, 1671, she named Thomas Doty (Doten) as the father, who "having begotten her with child, is departed the government and it is doubtful whether he will return again, and having left her in a poor deplored condition." She sued to attach "such goods and chattels, and all dues and rights appertaining to the said Doty to be for her support."[52]

Mary produced a list of Thomas Doty's assets, with the help of the Plymouth constable. These included "Thomas Doty's third of a boat, in partnership with Lt. Morton and Thomas Howes, his third likewise of a parcel of nets in the same partnership, with his third of the roads, anchors, and sails appertaining to the said boat; and also a gun in the custody of Ephraim Morton, a rapier at George Morton's, forty shillings for the hire of the boat due from Richard Willis, and a parcel of boards in the custody of diverse persona." The court ordered that the responsibility for Mary and the child be on the father, who had assets, instead of supporting her with public assistance.[53]

However, after running off, Thomas apparently had a change of heart, returned to Plymouth, took up his fishing business again, and married Mary Churchill.[54]

The case of Thomas Boardman (of Sandwich, not Thomas Boreman of Barnstable, a different family) was especially complex. On August 7, 1638, Thomas was charged with fornication with Lucy, "his now wife, and did beget her with child before they were married

together, which, upon examination, was confessed by them both."
Apparently, the crime was committed across the sea, and Thomas, "left
the child (so unlawfully begotten) living in England." No matter that
the crime was committed in a distant country under a different set of
laws, in Plymouth Colony Thomas was still considered guilty of the
act. He was sentenced to be "severely whipped, which was performed
accordingly, and to find sureties for his good behavior." Lucy, it seems,
was pregnant again, and would be "censured when she is delivered, as
the bench shall think fit."[55]

Boardman had been known to the court for his actions a year
earlier. The list of volunteer soldiers for June 7, 1637, did not include
Thomas. He was listed under another category, "Such as will go if they
are pressed." Thomas, perhaps a Quaker, would serve only if forced to
do so. His reluctance to serve his community may have influenced the
court to further address this case.[56]

On August 11, three days after the charge of fornication, the court
gave Boardman a fuller explanation of the "good behavior" the court
expected from him. He shall "appear at the General Court to be held
for this government in January next, [and] not depart the same without
license." He was also expected to "bring testimony under the hand of
the alderman of the ward and published in London, or else some other
sufficient testimony, that a man child, begotten upon the body of Lucy
his now wife, before marriage, was living when he put for the same to
nurse." He was then released.[57]

Boardman apparently reformed and went on to serve as surveyor
of highways in Sandwich in 1644, and on the Grand Inquest in 1648.
Lucy died in 1676, and Thomas married Elizabeth Rider Cole. He
left three children when he died in 1689. The fate of the child born in
England is unknown.[58,59,60]

Loose Women

Hannah Bonney stood before the governor and his assistants on
October 27, 1685, charged with two counts of fornication. The first
was with John Mitchell, who was convicted and sentenced to be

Pregnancy was the most obvious
evidence of fornication.

severely whipped." He also had to post a bond ensuring his good behavior until the next court convened in March. Furthermore, he was held in jail "'till the sentence be performed." The second man charged was "Nimrod, negro," with whom Hannah had a child. He received the same sentence as John Mitchell and was ordered to pay child support of eighteen pence per week for a year, "if [the child] live so long." If he or his master could not pay, the deputy governor would "put [him] out to service" to earn the money. Hannah was "sentenced to be well whipped."[61]

When the acts of loose women were especially egregious, they were charged with the crime of "whoredom." In 1665, Sarah Ensign was charged with whoredom, "aggravated with divers circumstances, found guilty and whipped at the cart's tail." It was left to the magistrate's discretion to decide how many stripes Sarah would receive, but the court ordered that the whipping "not to exceed twenty."[62]

John and Elizabeth Loe were well known to the courts before the charge of whoredom against her in 1678. John Loe was fined five shillings for being drunk on March 2, 1669, one year later for being drunk a second time, and on March 5, 1672, fined forty shillings, "or to be whipped," for "profaning the Lord's day by servile labor and contemptible words." On June 3, 1673, Joseph Roes of Marshfield, after being charged with "much familiarity" with the wife of John Loe, paid a bond of twenty pounds for good behavior, and promised not to keep company with Elizabeth, and to not leave the colony.[63]

On June 5, 1678, Elizabeth Loe swore "by the name of the everlasting God, that Phillip Leonard, of Marshfield, is the real father of the child last borne of [her] body, begotten in whoredom." Elizabeth was charged with whoredom, and not adultery, because she was now a widow; sometime between 1673 and 1678, John Loe had died. Elizabeth was convicted and sentenced to be whipped. Phillip, who "hath not cleared himself to the satisfaction of the court," was determined by the court to be the father, and ordered to pay two shillings and six pence each week for child support until the child turned seven, "if it live." He was also ordered to post a bond of thirty pounds to ensure that he complied. The child support would cease when the child "do attain the age of seven years," the age at which many children were put out as servants and presumably no longer the responsibility of their parents.[64]

Chapter Four

Marriage and Fidelity

It is in the colony's laws governing marriage that Pilgrim ideals and morals are most clear. The Pilgrims intended to establish a permanent colony at Plymouth. To do so they needed stable families who would produce children. Marriage, therefore, was considered the customary state for all. By law, those marriages needed to be harmonious and monogamous.

It wasn't just for procreation that marriage was so revered. Families were the basis of government—and control—at Plymouth. The head of the household, the father in most cases, oversaw what went on in that house and he answered to the grand jury both for his behavior and that of all who lived within. From the grand jury it was only one step to the governor and his court of assistants.

It is no surprise, therefore, that the first marriage among the Pilgrims took place within six months of the landing of the *Mayflower*.

The First Marriage

Of the eighteen adult women who sailed on the *Mayflower*, all of whom were married, only five survived the first winter: Eleanor Billington, Mary Brewster, Katherine Carver, Elizabeth Hopkins, and Susanna White. (The high mortality rate among women can be partly explained by the fact that they stayed on board the *Mayflower* in "damp, filthy and crowded quarters," caring for the sick, while the men were on shore in the open air.) Katherine Carver and Susanna White were soon widowed; and then Katherine died shortly after her husband. While there were several teenage girls on board the *Mayflower*, they were too young to wed. That left Susanna as the first woman available for marriage, and there can be little doubt that she was actively courted.[1]

Edward Winslow, twenty-five years old, was the successful suitor, and on May 12, 1621, the first marriage in Plymouth Colony was celebrated. Winslow's first wife had been Elizabeth Barker, who accompanied him on the *Mayflower*. They had no children of their own, however, Edward and Elizabeth had taken one of the More "orphans," eight-year old Ellen, into their care. During the terrible "first sickness," both Elizabeth and Ellen died, leaving Edward alone.[2,3]

Susanna White was the wife of William White. She boarded the *Mayflower* with her husband and son, Resolved, who was probably around five years old. She was also pregnant. Her second son, Peregrine, was born on November 11, 1620, while the ship was at anchor in what is now called Provincetown Harbor. Susanna's husband, William, died during the "first sickness," on February 21, 1621, leaving her a widow with a five-year-old and an infant.[4,5,6]

Edward and Susanna's wedding was performed by the magistrate in a civil ceremony, "according to the laudable custom of the Low Countries, in which they had lived." The Pilgrims were fashioning their lives according to Scripture and "nowhere found in the Gospel" was an example of the marriage rite "to be laid on the ministers as a part of their office," Bradford explained. All subsequent marriages in the colony would be simple civil ceremonies, usually held in the home of the bride's parents.[7]

It was a good match. Along with Susanna's two sons, the couple would have five more children of their own. The marriage lasted thirty-four years until Winslow's death in 1655.[8]

Marriage Laws

Once officially married, expectations for the newlyweds were simple: the couple must live together under the same roof, they must live harmoniously, and they must engage in a sexual relationship that is both "normal" and exclusive. Husbands and fathers were in charge, and were expected not only to provide for the family, but also to control all behavior within the household. It was believed that a happy and

Pilgrim wedding.

exclusive marriage bond was vital to the success of Plymouth Colony.[9]

In 1646 marriage laws were tightened. Not only did marriages need to be publicly conducted by a magistrate; they also needed to be formally recorded by the town clerk in the official records. This amendment addressed the occasional cases of colonists marrying themselves privately and secretly.[10]

On March 8, 1679, Thomas Burman, Jr., was cited by the courts "for being married in a clandestine way, contrary to the law of this government, [and] is fined five pounds." The "clandestine way" may be a reference to the old English custom of a couple privately marrying themselves, as we have already discussed above in the section on the More children. Referred to also as "de verba de praesenti" marriages, this form of marriage was basically a verbal contract between a man and a woman.[11,12]

In another action by the courts, William Gifford was charged with taking a wife "without orderly marriage on March 5, 1684." Gifford was a Quaker, and the court may have objected to his being married in the Quaker manner by merely speaking promises to each other during meetings, rather than by an official Pilgrim magistrate who would have duly entered the marriage into the colony records. However, there must have been more to the story, for the record added, "as there were many circumstances in the action that did alleviate the fault, [Gifford] is only fined fifty shillings."[13]

Any violations of the colony's laws and standards would have been reported by concerned neighbors to the grand jury, who would have investigated. Those unions that were unhappy, non-functional, or a disturbance to the peace of the neighborhood were referred to the courts. The violations cited above incurred fines, but punishments varied and were usually imposed on both the husband and the wife. Besides fines, a couple could be ordered to sit in the stocks or be referred for corporal punishment.

Contentious Living

A couple who could not get along were called before the courts for their behavior. One example is the Ransom couple. On October 29, 1669, Robert Ransom and his wife were in court to answer for "their contentious and unworthy carriages each to other in their walking [conducting themselves] in marriage condition." Robert and Hannah (sometimes called Susanna) were admonished "to live better in that behalf." They promised to do so and "were for the present cleared."[14]

Robert had been before the courts before, and was known to be hot-tempered and confrontational. He had been a "servant sometimes" in Sandwich to Thomas Dexter, Jr., and complained against his master in court on August 1, 1654, saying that he had been "hardly used and unreasonably dealt with." The court investigated, and decided to allow Robert to transfer his indenture to Thomas Clarke, who bought out the remaining portion of his servitude.[15]

Before he was released, however, the court, "admonished [Robert Ransom] to carry himself better than he had formerly." Apparently during the court's investigation, it was learned that he had been "stubborn against his master," and they ruled that "in case he should behave himself as formerly, he should not escape corporal punishment." Along with Nathaniel Fish, who was complicit in the case when he gave Ransom a place to stay when he left the home of Thomas Dexter, Ransom was "committed to the custody of the marshal a night and part of a day."[16]

For all his problems, Robert Ransom was made a freeman in 1657. However, he was back in court in 1663, charged with "breach of the Sabbath," and was fined ten shillings. Unable to control his temper and resorting to "turbulent and clamorous carriage in the court," Ransom was sentenced to be jailed, "during the pleasure of the court." Two years later, in 1665, he was yet again in front of the magistrates for calling William Hawkins a "rogue," and insulting him.[17,18,19]

In 1670 Robert was once again charged, this time "for speaking wicked and reproachful words against the governor and magistrates." While he was cleared of the charges because there was only one witness against him, the court added that the accusation certainly sounded like something Ransom would say, (it "spake like unto the said Ransom's language,") citing Robert Ransom's reputation as an angry, quarrelsome man as evidence in court against him. In 1673, he was admonished for "[using] abusive words, tending to the breach of peace to John Andrews." Ransom was charged with selling rum without a license and fined five pounds in 1680, and the following year fined again, ten shillings, "for reviling the ministry."[20,21,22]

For all his nastiness, Ransom and his no doubt long-suffering wife, Hannah, managed to stay together and had a large family of seven children.[23]

Abandonment and Separation

One of the issues that most concerned the courts were those occasions when a husband and wife lived apart from one another. The main concern was that the woman and her children were not under the supervision of the head of the house. But there was also a very practical concern that the abandoned family would become a financial burden on the community. These types of cases were vigorously investigated.

It is not known why, but on April 4, 1650, Katherine Warner and Mary Mills ran away from their husbands in Maine. When they appeared in Barnstable, "in the jurisdiction of New Plymouth," they were considered lawbreakers. They were summarily apprehended, along with Thomas Wallen, George Way, and Richard Carle, all of whom had helped them escape. After they were questioned by the court, the men confessed to aiding the women and Carle admitted that he stole his father's boat, "which they came away in."[24]

It was ordered that Katherine Warner, Mary Mills, and George Way "be sent from constable to constable to the place from whence they came, a place called Winter Harbor." Thomas Wallen and Richard Carle were jailed, pending further charges.[25] Were the women escaping abusive marriages? Was it a spur-of-the-moment lark? Sadly, no further Plymouth record exists to prove it one way or another.

In 1659, in another case, John Spring's wife, Lydia, was not living with him in Watertown, but had lived three or four years in Scituate. The court ordered her to "repair to her husband with all convenient speed." But they gave her another option, just in case there may have been more to the story than John Spring was telling. She could instead meet with Mr. Alden in Duxbury "to give reason why she did not [return to her husband]." If she did not take either choice, the court promised to "take a speedy course to send her to her said husband."[26]

Lydia had previously been married to Thomas Hatch, and had lived in Scituate until her remarriage after his death. Why she chose to remain in Scituate and not live with John Spring in Watertown is not known. Perhaps she was comfortable among friends, or maybe the marriage was not a happy one. Apparently, she did not abide by the court order to rejoin her husband; she was still living in Scituate in 1655, around the time of John's death. The court did not pursue the matter, and John left all his property to his son when he died, excluding her from his will, and denying her the customary "widow's third." In this case, the court permitted a couple to live separately, most likely to preserve the peace.[27]

Isaac Harris' case was one of abandonment. On October 29, 1668, he was charged with leaving his wife, Mercy, and their child, and neglecting to provide for their care. Harris was warned to "provide for his wife that which is necessary for her comfortable subsistence," and if he continued to neglect her, "a further course shall be taken by the court to constrain him to do it."[28]

Isaac did not comply. Mercy's father, Robert Latham, took up the case eight months later. On July 5, 1669, Latham testified of the "great neglect of the said Harris in not taking care for his wife's comfortable subsistence, being departed the government." It wasn't just his daughter's "comfortable subsistence" that he was worried about. Harris, Latham testified, had left Mercy and her child "to be burdensome to the said Robert Latham, her father."[29]

Isaac was the son of Arthur Harris, one of the original settlers of Bridgewater. Isaac's wife, Mercy, was the daughter of Robert Latham and Susanna Chilton Winslow. Susanna was the daughter of Mary Chilton (who was long-supposed to have been the first female to set foot at Plymouth in 1620).[30]

The court ordered and authorized Bridgewater's selectmen to "take notice of what sizable estate appertains unto the said Isaac Harris, and to take it into their custody, and to improve it for the relief and subsistence of his wife aforesaid, and that they be careful to keep a due account of their receipt and disbursements on that behalf." Did losing his "sizeable estate" move Isaac Harris to reconsider his situation? Perhaps, because the couple reconciled and eventually had eight children.[31,32]

Rowland Wills was charged for living apart from his wife a few years later, on October 29, 1670. Wills had been invited to Scituate by John Williams, perhaps as a tenant farmer. Wills had not been formally approved as a resident of Plymouth, but after promising to bring his wife to Scituate, Wills was allowed to stay on, "until his next crop is reaped." Having his wife living with him demonstrated to the courts his stability and commitment to the community. If his wife failed to come and live with him, however, he would be ordered "to depart the government."[33]

Having an unofficial citizen—especially a single man—living in Plymouth troubled the court. After all, anything could happen. The court reminded John Williams that he had financial responsibility for any damages that Rowland Wills might cause, "to save the town of Scituate from any damage that may accrue unto them by the said Rowland Wills as long as he lives on the farm, or until his term is out."[34] No further record of Mr. Wills has been found.

Problems in Sexual Relations

One of the requirements of a Plymouth marriage was that the couple have monogamous and "normal" sexual relations, the assumption being that the pair would have children who would contribute to the growth of the colony. Cases involving complaints of neglecting this marriage duty did come before the courts, brought by both husbands and wives, but the case of John Williams, Jr., and his wife, Elizabeth, was especially exasperating for the courts. What started as a complaint from his wife, led to all kinds of revelations for the courts to untangle.[35]

Williams was the son of John Williams, Sr., an industrious and successful resident of Scituate since before 1640. John, Jr., was made a freeman in 1653, and served as an ensign in the Scituate military company. He was, nonetheless, impulsive, and an inveterate law breaker who appeared before the courts on numerous occasions. His wife, Elizabeth, was the daughter of Rev. John Lothrop of the Scituate church.[36,37]

(Williams' estate at the time of his death in Scituate in 1694 was valued at over 350 pounds, considered a large fortune for the time and place. Jeremy Dupertuis Bangs correctly notes that "his immense wealth must be considered a factor in the circumstance that a large amount of antisocial behavior on Williams' part met with little effective opposition.")[38]

Trouble in the marriage first came to the attention of the courts in 1663. On October 5, John Bayley, Williams' servant, sued his master for one hundred pounds. Bayley accused Williams of slander and defamation, complaining that Williams had said that his wife "was Bayley's whore," and that he could prove it. The jury found for Bayley, awarded him ten pounds plus court costs. The two men continued to work together, but it was an uneasy relationship. On March 1, 1664, Williams and Bayley were fined three shillings, four pence, by the court "for breaking the peace by striking one another."[39,40]

On June 7, 1665, after there were several complaints from the community, John Williams, Jr., and his wife, Elizabeth, were charged with "disorderly living." He was faulted for "abusive and harsh carriages towards her both in words and actions, in special his sequestration of himself from the marriage bed." John countered with an accusation of his own. Elizabeth, he claimed, was "a whore, and…a child lately borne of his said wife [is] by him denied to be legitimate."[41]

This sparked the court's attention, and it immediately sent for his wife. "After the hearing of several things to and fro betwixt them," the court was not convinced of Elizabeth's alleged adultery. The couple was admonished "to apply themselves to such ways as might make for the recovering of peace and love…." The court assigned a monitor, Isaac Buck, who was the town clerk for many years, "to be officious therein," that is, to keep an eye on their behavior.[42,43]

Three months later, on October 3, 1665, the court again addressed the charges against John Williams, reminding everyone once more that he was not sleeping with his wife and accusing him of "not attending that reformation expected from him." Elizabeth Williams' brother, Barnabas Lothrop, spoke for his sister, testifying that he had witnessed continued abuse, which served to add more charges against John Williams.[44]

The court was still hopeful the couple could reconcile, that a separation could be avoided, and that John's behavior might improve. They exhorted him "to amend his ways," and gave him another chance; he was released.[45]

That was when Elizabeth Williams spoke up. It was a rare occurrence in colony courts for a woman to confront the governor and his assistants. Her request was a simple one, that her honor and her reputation be restored to her in an official public statement. With her reputation under attack and considering all the "diverse scandalous reports cast abroad concerning her, [she] desired that open proclamation might be made in the court tending to the clearing of her name." The court complied by issuing a remarkable statement, one that exonerated her from blame, and declaring that she "hath behaved herself as one that hath faithfully observed the bond of wedlock." Furthermore, it was added that "she and her friends hath been much wronged by such reports."[46]

Having her name cleared of adultery provided Elizabeth's husband an opportunity to pursue a civil suit against Thomas Summers, who had been spreading rumors that Elizabeth had been unchaste. Even though Williams had been doing the same thing, he nonetheless sued Summers for "abusing of her [Elizabeth Williams] in reference unto unchastity." Williams was suing for the grand sum of five hundred pounds. The jury decided for Williams but fined Summers only twenty pounds in damages, plus court costs. Summers was ordered to make a public acknowledgement that he wronged the couple and apologize for his "scandalous and reproachful speeches."[47]

John Williams was relentless in his abuse of his wife. On May 1, 1666, eight months after he successfully sued Thomas Summers for his slander, John was back in court, "to make answer for his continued abusing of his wife, by unnatural carriages towards her both in words and actions, by rendering her to be a whore, and for persisting on in his refusing to perform marriage duty towards her according to the law of God and man." A jury trial was set for the following June and in the meantime, the court finally agreed that the couple could live apart; Elizabeth would stay with friends and John would pay her expenses.[48]

The following month, on June 5, 1666, it was Elizabeth's turn to bring charges. In writing, she complained against her husband for his continued abuse, "both in word and deed," defaming her reputation, and "by persisting in his refusing to perform marriage duty unto her according to what both the law of God and man requireth." He should have been "a shelter and protection unto her," Elizabeth explained, instead he "hath endeavored to reproach, ensnare, and betray her."[49]

The jury found for Elizabeth, but one outcome of a public jury trial that John may not have anticipated was that he was obliged to admit that he was unable to carry out his marital responsibilities, "himself also declaring his insufficiency for converse with women." John Williams was impotent, and by his own actions everyone knew about it.[50]

On that same date, after almost three years of complaints and "contentious living," the court finally decided that the couple could officially and lawfully be separated. The court gave Elizabeth "her liberty at present, to depart from him unto her friends," at least temporarily, since "it is not safe nor convenient for her to live with her husband." John was ordered to continue to support her, "to allow her ten pounds yearly to maintain her while she shall be thus absent from him." It was the court's hope that John was still redeemable, that he might "apply himself unto her in such a way as she may be better satisfied to return to him again."[51]

For defaming and abusing his wife, John was also ordered to "stand in the street or marketplace by the post with an inscription over him that may declare to the world his unworthy carriages towards his wife." Apparently, Elizabeth still had some affection for her husband, asking that he be spared this humiliation, which was allowed. However, the court let stand the order that since John's "wicked carriages" were "very disturbing and expensive to this government," and he was fined twenty pounds.[52]

One year later, on June 5, 1667, Elizabeth was back before the court demanding back spousal support. John was ordered to post yearly bonds to assure his payment, which must have fueled his anger against his wife. In October that same year, John sued Thomas Summers again, this time for "dalliance" with Elizabeth, resulting in pregnancy.[53]

By this point, the court must have been weary of dealing with John Williams. They ordered that Williams and Summers come to a written agreement that would settle their differences hopefully once and for all. The agreement, guided by Nathaniel Morton and Constant Southworth, declared that John Williams would withdraw the charges against Summers (which must have been determined to be false), and that they would not "trouble or vex each other in or about these matters aforesaid." Should either party break this agreement, the guilty one would pay the other five hundred pounds, a huge sum.[54]

Elizabeth Williams was also a party to the agreement, promising that she and John would "release and discharge each other aforesaid from all matters expressed in this paper," including any legal actions obtained in the Boston court, where Elizabeth was living with her brother. It was further agreed that Summers would pay Williams thirty shillings, and that Williams would pay Summers "forty and three pounds twelve shillings and six pence" to settle any pending differences between them.[55]

If John Williams thought that was the end of his legal problems, he had a surprise coming. Constant Southworth, Plymouth's Treasurer, stood up and complained that John had forfeited on a bond for

Elizabeth's support and owed the colony twenty pounds. The jury found for Southworth for "the forfeiture of the bond and the cost of the suit." And then, James Cudworth, Joseph Tilden, and Robert Studson (Stetson), representing the town of Scituate, stepped up and sued Williams for seventeen pounds because he "doth neglect or refuse to satisfy the penalty or forfeiture." In this case John was more fortunate; the jury found the defendant innocent of the charge.[56]

The following year, once again, the court had to deal with John Williams and Thomas Summers. On March 5, 1668, Thomas Summers sued John Williams for five hundred pounds, pursuant to their agreement prohibiting either of them from "vexing" one other. Summers accused Williams of violating the agreement, and, therefore, wanted full damages. The jury agreed and awarded Summers "the forfeiture of the bond of five hundred pounds." Williams had lost, and he was not a gracious loser. Williams turned around and sued Summers for five hundred pounds, claiming that Summers' suit was in violation of their agreement. The jury found for Summers, giving Williams two defeats in one day.[57]

Finally, the court had had enough. Once again, an agreement was written, "signed and sealed" by Williams, and "witnessed by several gentlemen" who were attorneys for both parties. The agreement stated that John Williams would "discharge" Thomas Summers "from all differences, whether concerning Elizabeth, my reputed wife, or whatsoever else." John also released Thomas from any "actions and causes of actions that are or might have been," including "bonds, bills, debts, awards, or arbitrations, judgments, [and] executions, together with all controversies whatsoever."[58]

John Williams, Jr., died in Scituate in 1694; his will was proved on July 10 of that year. He left his residence farm to his nephew, William Barker, "to be possessed by him when 21 years of age," and another property to his "ancient servant," his one-time adversary, John Bayley. Williams mentions three "Indian Servants" in his will—Will, George, and Thom—two of whom "I obtained with my sword and with my bow," apparently captured as children during King Philip's War. Williams requested that George and Thomas be freed and known by the surname Williams.[59]

John and Elizabeth Williams were still married at his death, but he did not mention her in his will, vengeful to the very end. However, the courts instructed the executor, John Barker, to "always reserve to Elizabeth the widow of said deceased, all such rights in said estate as per law belong[s] to her."[60] She would get her widow's third.

Chapter Five

Divorce

There were no laws in Plymouth concerning divorce. However, the courts had the power and discretion to grant them on a case-by-case basis. Grounds for such action could include adultery, bigamy, desertion, and impotence.[1]

Separatists in Plymouth recognized that divorces were sometimes necessary, especially in the case of adultery. Divorce, wrote Pilgrim Pastor John Robinson, was really a civil matter. It "was never approved by the Lord in the court of heaven,...but permitted only in civil courts, without bodily punishment." He believed that "as marriage is a medicine against uncleanness, so adultery is the disease of marriage, and divorce the medicine of adultery." Divorce does not cure the guilty, Robinson added, but is necessary "for the easing of the innocent."[2]

Twelve cases were considered by the Plymouth courts that included a request for a divorce. The couples were Burges, Hacke, Tubbs, Hewett (addressed in the next chapter), Halloway, Skiffe, Williams (John and Sarah of Barnstable), Atkinson, Stevens, Glover, Clarke, Williams (John and Elizabeth of Scituate, already discussed). The first was in 1661, and the last in 1686. Of the twelve, five were adultery cases, four were abandonment, one was brought for bigamy, and two for impotence. Seven of the requests were granted, three were allowed to separate but not divorce, and two couples reconciled.

Six of the divorce requests were filed by women, although one of those six was filed by the litigant's father (Atkinson). While wives were under their husbands' complete authority, when the peace and order within the community was threatened, a woman's request for divorce was taken seriously. Nonetheless, there had to be a very good reason behind the request, and proof was required. Only two of the requests filed by women were granted, one for adultery and one for bigamy. In the two cases where the wives asked for divorces because their husbands were impotent, neither was granted a divorce, but they were permitted to legally separate.

Take the case of Nathaniel and Dorothy (Lettice Gray) Clarke. Dorothy was so eager for a divorce that she lied to the court and put her husband through a humiliating ordeal.

On June 4, 1686, Dorothy made a petition to the court; "I am sorely afflicted that I have this sad occasion to petition to God and you, for in that Mr. Nathaniel Clarke hath not performed the duty of a husband to me, for he is miss-formed, and is always unable to perform the act of generation." Dorothy was thirty-eight at the time, and had previously been married to Edward Gray, who died in 1681, and with whom she had six children.[3,4]

Nathaniel, born in 1643, the son of Thomas Clarke and Susanna Ring, strongly disagreed with the charge of impotency, "affirming the contrary." To settle the matter, the court ordered that "his body be viewed by some persons skillful and judicious." Three physicians were named for the task and Nathaniel ordered to "show himself to them." At the next court, on July 6, 1686, Dorothy again presented her request and complaint, but the court, presumably after getting the physician's report, "did not see cause to grant a divorce as she desired."[5]

While the charge of impotency was not proved, on July 10, 1686, the court allowed the couple to separate. There was "such an uncomfortable difference between the said Clarke and his wife," that the court feared "they should ruin each other in their estates." The court's solution was to have Dorothy and Nathaniel enter into a contract, a property settlement of sorts, that stipulated what each was to retain. Each would keep the assets they brought into the marriage with them, and hold each other harmless for any "obligation, bond, or debt" each had incurred before or during the marriage. Each also had to post a bond of five hundred pounds guaranteeing their compliance with the agreement.[6]

In less than a year's time, Nathaniel had made a bad decision. He aligned himself with the government of Sir Edmund Andros, who in December 1686 had arrived in Boston with a commission from King James which made him the governor of all of the "Dominion In of New England," which encompassed the Massachusetts Bay Colony (including present-day Maine), Plymouth Colony, Rhode Island, Connecticut, and New Hampshire. Each independent colony was now subject to his rule. Andros was widely hated and considered "excessively odious" for "his meanness and rapacity" in the colonies. Eight men were chosen from Plymouth to serve on his council; seven resigned, and only Nathaniel Clarke supported the new governor and served on his commission.[7,8]

In April of 1689, King James was overthrown, and Governor Andros was apprehended in New York. Andros was permitted to return to England, but Nathaniel Clarke had some explaining to do back in Plymouth. The colonists wasted no time to once again govern themselves; after nearly three years of Andros, the courts began to meet without delay. On June 7, 1689, Nathaniel Clarke was brought before the court, and declared to be "a public enemy to (and disturber of the peace of) this colony." He was required to post a bond of two hundred pounds to appear at the next court. There is no further follow up to this charge, but Nathaniel was also in trouble with the Plymouth Church.[9]

On July 7, 1689, one month after he was declared by the Plymouth Court to be a public enemy, the Plymouth Church challenged him to answer for missing public worship. Not only that, it was claimed that "Nathaniel Clarke had like Esau despised his birthright, by many words and carriages condemned the church," and so was "cut off…as an unprofitable branch" and expelled from the church. His estranged wife Dorothy also had her own problems with the congregation for some small offenses she had committed, but she repented, apologized, and was forgiven.[10]

Nathaniel Clarke lived on for nearly thirty years; he died on January 31, 1717, at the age of seventy-four, leaving no descendants. Dorothy outlived him, dying in Plymouth in 1726 at the age of seventy-three.[11,12]

Bigamy

A rare case of bigamy came before the court on July 7, 1680, when Nicolas Wade brought his daughter, Elizabeth Stevens, into court to complain against her husband, Thomas Stevens, who was described as "a man of a debauched life, expressed by his pluralities of wives." Thomas, it seems, had a wife in Boston, another wife (and children) in England, and yet another in Barbados. The court was quick and furious in its response.[13]

After considering the facts, the court decided to release Elizabeth from her marriage bond, "Elizabeth is clearly and absolutely released from her conjugal relation and engagement with the said Thomas Stevens and the said covenant of man and wife between Thomas Stevens and Elizabeth Stevens is dissolved and at an end forever." She was declared free to remarry. Thomas, "for his abominable wickedness," was sentenced "to be severely whipped at the post."[14]

Desertion

Communication was difficult and achingly slow within the colonies, and even more so with England. It could take years to locate a man who had deserted his family, leaving his wife and children dependent on family, friends, neighbors, or community support in his absence. In the case of Mary Hacke, she wanted to remarry.

Mary Hacke appeared in court in June 1667, accusing her husband of desertion. She "solicited the court to have liberty to bestow herself in marriage." She had "diverse testimonies" to prove that "William Hacke, her husband, is dead, he having left her about three years since, and went for England." Mary and William had a son, William, Jr., born November 15, 1663.[15,16]

The case must have taken up a full day; Mary was in and out of the court room as she gathered her evidence, and various actions were taken. He must be dead, she testified. "She never received any letter from him since, nor any other intelligence from or concerning him." She produced further testimony as evidence "that he is deceased." Notwithstanding, the court was not satisfied with the evidence she produced, at least not satisfied enough to "grant her liberty of marriage at the present." Yet, curiously, they were sufficiently satisfied to begin proceedings to process his estate.[17]

Mary was granted letters of administration, and she quickly produced an inventory of "the estate and goods of William Hacke that was left in the hand of me, Mary Hacke, at the departure of my husband." He owned some property, a house and land, and three acres of meadow that was "not paid for." Debts due to him were eight pounds, and he owed a Mr. Gibbins sixteen pounds, who "paid for [Mary] and her child's maintenance since her husband departed from her." The court also asked that anyone who had any debts from William Hacke's estate should come forward within a year, "a twelvemonth and a day of this date," to record their claims.[18] As of this writing, it remains a mystery who "Mr. Gibbins" was and why he had paid to support Mary Hacke and her child. It is also not known if Mary Hacke remarried.[19,20]

James Skiff's case was simple, in comparison. Skiff had been resident of Sandwich, but moved to "the Vineyard," (Martha's Vineyard, as it is now known). On May 10, 1671, he petitioned the court for a divorce from his wife, based on desertion. He charged that she "hath unlawfully forsaken her lawful husband, James Skiff, and is gone to Roanoke, in or at Virginia." There, Elizabeth, "hath taken another man for to be her husband, and we have received several testimonies of it."[21]

The court agreed that James had been abandoned, and granted his request, "a lawful bill of divorce from the former woman, namely, Elizabeth, the daughter of Mr. Naighbor Cooper, inhabitant of Boston; that James Skiff is free from the aforesaid woman, which was his lawful wife; and that the aforesaid covenant of marriage is now dissolved and of non-effect."[22]

Six years later, in March 1677, James Skiff remarried. His second wife was Sarah Barnard, daughter of Robert Barnard of Nantucket. They had five daughters and a son. James became a deacon of the church and died sometime after 1719. Sarah lived until 1732.[23]

Adultery

On the subject of divorce, John Robinson stated that adultery was the primary reason to grant a dissolution of marriage. To him it was a terrible crime. Adultery, by definition the act of a husband or wife having sexual relations outside the marriage, threatened not only individual families, but because the very foundation of Plymouth's stability was the family unit, the community as well. It was vital to Plymouth's success that families live in harmony and respect the colony's laws and standards.

Plymouth's first written laws, set down in 1636, listed adultery as a capital crime. Plymouth law was based on the Bible, and Leviticus 20:10 reads, "The man that committeth adultery with another man's wife,…the adulterer and the adulteress shall die the death." However, it seems the Pilgrims were uneasy with such a severe punishment. While the crime was technically listed as a capital one by letter of the law, the punishment of death was not specifically prescribed, and no one was hanged in the colony for adultery. The courts decided each case individually and imposed whatever punishment was appropriate considering the circumstances.

By 1658 the growth of the colony was making life more complicated, so the law regarding adultery was rewritten. While it was no longer deemed to be considered a capital crime, it could still result in severe punishment. The new law read: "That whosoever shall commit adultery shall be severely punished by whipping two…times; namely once while [in] the court." The second whipping would presumably take place in the criminal's home community. Should there be a second infraction, the lawbreaker would "wear two capital letters, namely AD, cut out in cloth and sewed on their uppermost garments on their arm or back; and if at any time they shall be [seen] without the said letters while they are in the government…to be forthwith taken and publicly whipped."[24]

Adultery was the complaint in the first case of divorce in Plymouth in 1661. On June 10 of that year Thomas Burges, Jr. was charged with "an act of uncleanness committed by him with Lydia Gaunt." So disgraceful was his crime that he was sentenced to be "severely whipped," twice—once in Plymouth Town and again at Sandwich. The couple was ordered to wear "the capital letters to be worn according to the law," that is, the letters "AD" for adultery, but "it is for the present respited until the court shall discern better of his future walking."[25]

Almost immediately, Elizabeth Bassett, Burges' wife of thirteen years, "urgently solicited the court for a divorce." Thomas, "manifesting little dislike thereof, and some of their relations concurring therein," the court considered "the particulars mentioned" and granted the first divorce in Plymouth Colony. Given the evidence of the betrayal, the settlement was quick: Elizabeth was awarded one-third of his estate, "viz., lands, goods, chattels, as her proper right forever." Thomas was also to give her a bed and bedding, "with some other small things." As a result, Elizabeth had no need to rely on public assistance from the colony for her support.[26,27]

Thomas went on to marry Lydia Gaunt, his partner in adultery, and they moved to Newport, Rhode Island. There they had a son, named after his father, in 1668.[28] It is not known what became of Elizabeth Bassett Burge.

Samuel Halloway's wife, Jane, was evidently a handful. On December 8, 1669, the Taunton townsmen stepped up and sent her to Plymouth's court because "her carriage towards her husband was so turbulent and wild, both in words and action, as he could not live with her but in danger of his life or limbs." During her trial, "her carriage before the court was so audacious as was intolerable," and earned her a jail sentence.[29]

After one night in jail, "in close durance [confinement]," Jane "manifested great pensiveness and sorrow for her said miscarriages and engaged to carry better for the future." Her husband earnestly entreated on her behalf, and Jane was "set at liberty that she might go home with her husband, and so to pass upon trial in hopes of better practices for the future."[30]

Those hopes were dashed when three months later, on March 1, 1670, the case was readdressed; it was obvious that Jane was pregnant, and the child's father was in doubt. Jane Halloway was reported to the court for "horrible and abusive speeches and actions by her spoken and done against her husband and others, not only in other places, but in the presence of the Court." Jane was sentenced to be whipped, but because she was with child, "the execution of the said sentence is referred until she shall be delivered."[31]

Jane had a complaint of her own, charging that Jonathan Briggs

"Her carriage before the court was
so audacious as was intolerable."

"had committed adultery with her two several times." The court
investigated, could not confirm her charge, and "the said Jonathan
Briggs was cleared before the court." But Jane's claim was enough for
Samuel, her husband. He wanted a divorce, citing that she "not only
more horribly abused him, as is manifested by the testimonies to the
above said presentment, and at other times, as is above hinted, but
also confessed that she hath committed adultery with diverse persons."
The court postponed granting the divorce until the next court, "being
willing to take mature advice and deliberation about it, as is behooveful
so weighty a matter."[32]

On June 7, 1670 Halloway again "importuned the court for
a divorce from his wife, Jane Halloway, expressing himself much
aggrieved with her continued opprobrious and audacious asserting
and affirming that she had committed adultery with Jonathan Briggs."
The court requested that the authorities in Taunton interview Jane,
"as soon as she can conveniently after her being up out of child bed,"
to determine if indeed she and JonathanBriggs had been intimate. If,
after investigation, she persisted in her claim, the court would grant
the divorce.[33]

Jane had a history of being high spirited. On June 3, 1668, she was
called into court along with Mary Phillips, and each were fined three

shillings, four pence, "for breaking the King's peace by striking each other." Even with Jane's troublesome reputation, she and Samuel still reconciled. There is no record of them pursuing the request for a divorce, or the charges of adultery, and in fact they remained married. Two more children were born to them, joining Samuel, born in 1668, Nathaniel in 1670. Easter was born in 1673, and John in 1674, after they had reconciled.[34,35]

The case of Mary Jenkens Atkinson had many complications, one of which was the question of whether her husband, Marmaduke, was dead or alive.

Mary, daughter of Edward Jenkens, was found guilty on October 29, 1670, of "having carnal copulation with her husband Marmaduke Atkinson before marriage and before contract." Mary and Marmaduke must have been very poor, because her father was ordered to pay her fine of three pounds. One year later Mary was back in court answering to an accusation of adultery with John Backe. He denied the charge and asked for a jury trial, during which he was found guilty. Mary swore before the court that the child that "was now living with her" was John's and not her husband's. They were given their choice of punishment— to be whipped or to pay ten pounds; they chose the latter.[36,37]

But there were more questions to settle, and eventually a request for a divorce. Mary's legal husband, Marmaduke Atkinson, had died, and the exact date of his death was uncertain. If it was determined that he died before Mary and John Backe were intimate, then Mary's crime would be one of fornication and not adultery. The fathers of both Mary and John had to post a surety to guarantee they would return to court and face charges once Marmaduke's date of death was determined. In the meantime, John's father, Isaac, would "pay or cause to be paid" three pounds a year for eight years for child support.[38]

It was later sworn in court that Marmaduke Atkinson had not indeed died, but instead had abandoned his wife. On March 1, 1675, Edward Jenkens "petitioned the court that his daughter, Mary Atkinson, may be divorced from her husband named Marmaduke Atkinson, declaring that he, the said Marmaduke Atkinson, had left the said Mary, his wife, and absented himself from her the full term of seven years and more, neither coming at her nor providing for her."[39]

Arguing his case before the court.

Curiously, the court declared that while there was no legal basis to grant a divorce, they did declare her to be "no longer bound, but do leave her to her liberty to marry if she please." And she did. Mary Jenkens Atkinson soon married Robert Cooke.[40] Nothing further has been found in the records.

Other cases were even more involved, such as the nasty litigation between John and Mary Glover of Barnstable in 1686. On June 4, John, "a cooper" who owned his house, land and shop, petitioned the court for a divorce from his wife. He accused her of having committed adultery "by entertaining some other man or men into bed fellowship." What was worse, John continued, "by her filthiness and baseness [Mary] infect[ed] him, her said husband, with that filthy, annoying disease called the pox, to his great sorrow and pain, ruin of his estate, and hazard [to] his life."[41,42]

The court heard both sides of the case and at first decided to postpone its ruling, but then John, clearly exasperated, appeared— "in his own person"—before the court, "praying" them to grant his freedom. The court, "on their further and due consideration" relented and "declared a separation and divorce" for the couple. The ruling was that "John Glover hath herewith a total freedom."[43]

After his divorce, John moved back to Dorchester, where he had been born, and remarried. In 1689, he had a son, but in 1690, he died, only thirty-five years old, possibly from the effects of his disease.[44]

The divorce case of William and Mercy Tubbs had it all: desertion, adultery, and a rebellious and stubborn wife with a reputation for being generous with her affections.

On June 3, 1668, William Tubbs requested a divorce from his wife, Mercy Sprague Tubbs, on the grounds of desertion. The couple had been married for thirty-one years, having joined together November 9, 1637. They had three surviving children: Samuel, born about 1638, Bethiah, about 1641, and William, 1654, all born in Duxbury.[45,46,47]

Things apparently were fine for about fifteen years, but on March 2, 1652, Mercy Tubbs, thirty-five at the time, was ordered to appear at the June court "to answer for mixed dancing, whereof she is accused." She was cleared of the charge but given a warning. Ten years later a much more serious charge was levied against her.[48]

On June 1, 1663, Joseph Rogers was brought into court charged with spending an unseemly amount of time in the company of Mercy, "the wife of William Tubbs." Their relationship had given the court cause to "suspect that there hath been lascivious acts committed by them," and that they had been going on for some time. Rogers denied the charges and had in fact sued Rebecca and Alice Pierce for twenty pounds three months earlier, "for sundry defamations, and particularly for reporting that they saw the said Joseph and Mercy, the wife of William Tubbs, lying under a blanket." Before the case could be heard, Rogers stormed out of court, a "contentious departing," and was fined five pounds for the tantrum.[49,50]

Rogers was ordered to leave town by June 20, "and stay away from Mercy and her house on pain of whipping." The court held Mercy's husband, William Tubbs, accountable as well; he was "strictly charged not to tolerate [Rogers] to come to his house…as he will answer the same at his peril."[51] As head of the household, William Tubbs was responsible for all that occurred under his roof.

The court took further action in October 1663. Mercy was fined twenty pounds for "lascivious behavior," and Joseph Rogers was also fined twenty pounds. William Tubbs, the wronged husband, was fined ten pounds, as was William Randall, who apparently was somehow involved in the infidelity.[52,53]

On June 8, 1664, the contentious marriage of William and Mercy Tubbs again attracted the court's attention. William Paybodie, who had been Duxbury's deputy to the General Court between 1654 and 1663, apparently took it upon himself to write an order of separation for the couple, which was witnessed by Lieutenant Nash and John Sprague. However, this order was not officially recognized by the courts. Paybodie was fined five pounds for assuming more authority than he had been allowed. Nash and Sprague were each fined three pounds. However, the courts did allow Tubbs to publish a notice that he was "disowning all [his wife's] debts that she make to any from this time forward as not intended to pay any of them to any person whatsoever."[54,55]

In 1665, Mercy was in trouble again. John Arthur (perhaps Archer?) was summoned into court "to answer for abusive speeches and for entertaining the wife of [Peter] Talmon and the wife of William Tubbs." Arthur denied the charges, claiming he had evidence to clear him, and the case was not pursued. [56]

Four years later, on June 3, 1668, William Tubbs petitioned the court for a divorce. Mercy, he claimed, had "for a long time sequestered herself from him, and will not be persuaded to return to him." Mercy had fled to Rhode Island. On William's behalf, the Plymouth court wrote to the Rhode Island court and asked them to find and inform Mercy of William's request, giving her one month to reply.[57]

After receiving a response from authorities in Rhode Island, the court decided that Mercy, "being a woman of ill fame and light behavior," had abandoned her husband, moved to another colony, and there "pretended she is at liberty." She could not be persuaded to return to him, "as she ought to do." Before witnesses, Mercy vowed that "she will never return again unto him while her eyes are open."[58]

After considering Mercy's adamant response, the court finally granted William Tubbs a divorce on July 7, 1668. He was free to remarry, which he did. Four years later he married Dorothy Jones, the widow of William Jones. Interestingly, the couple signed an agreement, a kind of pre-nuptial agreement, in which William Tubbs granted to Dorothy his house and land during her lifetime. After her death, the land would "return to my heirs." William and Dorothy had two children, Benjamin, born 1673, and Joseph, born 1675.[59,60]

On March 4, 1674, two cases of defamation and slander were filed against William Tubbs and his second wife, Dorothy. Isaac Barker complained that the couple were telling others that Barker had "said and threatened that he would ruinate them,…root and branch." The complaint was withdrawn. At that same court, John Perry sued William Tubbs for one hundred pounds because Tubbs had been spreading the false story that Perry had made derogatory comments about the governor and the magistrates. The court found in Tubbs' favor.[61]

After her declaration of independence in 1668 from Rhode Island, Mercy Tubbs disappeared from the historical record. One of her lovers, Joseph Rogers, stayed in Duxbury and married Abigail Barker, Isaac's sister, in 1667.[62]

William Tubbs died on May 2, 1688, and named his second wife, his "loving wife Dorothy," as sole executrix of his will, and all five children as heirs.[63]

Chapter Six

Domestic Violence

As already stated, three things were required in a Pilgrim marriage: the couple must live together, the marriage must be a peaceful one, and their sexual relations must be exclusive and "normal." These were not only religious standards; they were reflected in the laws, and situations that fell outside these standards were addressed in court. Yet, the courts were reluctant to challenge the authority of the husband or to become involved in the affairs of an individual household.[1]

It was a careful balancing act. As a result, abuse within the home was addressed in Plymouth statutes in a rather circumspect and broad way. The 1636 law stated, "That all such misdemeanors of any person or persons as tend to the hurt and detriment of society, civility, peace, and neighborhood to be enquired into by the Grand Inquest and the persons presented to the court that so the disturbers thereof may be punished and the peace and welfare of the subject comfortably preserved."[2] This law covered any type of discord within a household that disturbed the peace of the neighborhood.

In contrast, the Massachusetts Bay Colony addressed spousal abuse directly. In 1641, Massachusetts adopted a Body of Liberties. Under the heading "Liberties of Women," the government stated that: "Every married woman shall be free from bodily correction or stripes [whipping] by her husband, unless it be in his own defense upon her assault. If there be any just cause of correction [of the wife], complaint shall be made to Authority assembled in some court, from which only she shall receive it." Plymouth law was not that specific.[3]

Whether by design or accident, Plymouth's broad law served as an umbrella decree covering all types of violence among family members. However, it was accepted that husbands were dominant in a marriage; wives were expected to be compliant. It was his duty to correct his wife when he alone identified a need. Was it "correction" or abuse when, in 1663, Ralph Earle was called into court to answer for "drawing [dragging] his wife in an uncivil manner on the snow." He was fined twenty shillings (one pound), an amount sufficiently painful to demonstrate the court's disapproval, yet he was not sentenced to physical punishment.[4]

While the Pilgrims gave the male head of a family full control over his household, which included physical discipline of both wife and children, they did not tolerate brutality, and punishments for this type of violence could be severe.

Husbands as Abusers

On August 1, 1665, John Dunham, Jr., appeared in court to answer for "his abusive carriage towards his wife in continual tyrannizing over her, and in particular for his late abusive and uncivil carriage in endeavoring to beat her in a [debauched] manner, and for affrighting of her by drawing a sword and pretending therewith to offer violence to her life." Dunham was sentenced to be "severely" whipped; however, his wife intervened, and he was released with only a warning and a fine. We will never know whether it was her terror of an abusive husband or her affection for him that motivated her to speak up. He was ordered to stop beating his wife, to post a bond of twenty pounds, and to appear at the October meeting of the court for a review of his behavior.[5]

Wives often spoke in defense of abusive husbands. For example, on March 2, 1669, Thomas Lucas was brought into court "for abusing of his wife and children." He promised "reformation" and his wife testified that since her complaint, "he hath not abused them as aforesaid," and so "Lucas was cleared of this presentment."[6]

This was the second time Lucas, a blacksmith, had been charged with beating his wife. The first was in March 1664, when he was in court charged with "being drunk the third time," and for "abusing of his wife to her danger and hazard." Thomas Lucas appeared in court several times for drunkenness and was sentenced to be whipped on many of those occasions.[7]

A chronic alcoholic, Lucas died on January 6, 1679. The record reads: "Being very ancient and decrepit, in his limbs, and it being very cold, and having drunk some drink, got a violent fall into a ditch, in a very dangerous place, could not recover himself, but bruised his body, and lying all night in the cold, so he came by his end."[8]

The first name of the wife of Thomas Lucas is not found in the court records. She could not have had an easy life, living with Thomas and his drinking, while mothering his seven children. Most likely, there was chronic physical abuse in the Lucas household that was never reported to the authorities.

Spousal abuse could be vicious and dangerous. On June 5, 1671, Richard Marshall was called into court for "abusing his wife by kicking her off from a stool into the fire." Marshall was sentenced to "sit in the stocks during the pleasure of the court."[9]

In the case of Joseph and Rachel Ramsden, it is not clear what the risk was to Rachel, but the court stepped in to protect her. The couple was married in March 1645, when she was about twenty years old. She was the daughter of Francis Eaton, *Mayflower* passenger, and the stepdaughter of the infamous Francis Billington. Ramsden ran a pine-tar kiln, heating pine wood and collecting the sap. This sap, or "tar," was used both as a waterproofing agent and as a seal for open wounds. The Ramsdens lived "remotely in the woods," deep in the pine forest. They had a son, Daniel, born in September 1649.[10,11]

Three years after the child's birth, on May 4, 1652, the court ordered Joseph to move his wife and child to "some neighborhood [where] she may be in a way of help as necessity shall require." Rachel has been "exposed to great hardship and peril of losing her life," the court complained. Apparently, Joseph did not comply because four years later the court again ordered him to move his family, adding that if he did not, the "his house would be pulled down."[12]

The issue in these two cases may have been that Rachel, living so far away from other women, could not obtain help during childbirth. She may have experienced labor alone and had a very difficult time. Apparently, any other infants that the couple may have had did not survive; Daniel is her only recorded child. Rachel died before October 1661, and the cause of her death is unknown.[13]

Wives as Abusers

Household violence was not limited to brutal husbands. In Plymouth, wives were also brought before the courts and charged with abuse. Joan Miller was ordered to appear in court on March 6, 1655, charged with "beating and reviling her husband [Obadiah], and egging her children to help her, biding them knock him in the head, and wishing his victuals might choke him." Cryptically, Joan was sentenced to be "punished at home."[14]

Children as Abusers

The case of the Bessey girls and their attack on their stepfather, George Barlow, is one brimming with violence and irony. On October 1, 1661, three young sisters, Anna, Mary, and Dorcas Bessey, were brought into court charged with "unnatural and cruel carriages" towards their stepfather, George Barlow. The girls, twenty-two, twenty, and sixteen, respectively, were the daughters of Anthony and Jane Bessey; their father had died in May 1657. Jane remarried, to George Barlow. Dorcas was fined ten pounds and Mary twenty, and all three were ordered to appear at the next court in March.[15,16]

Anna Bessey's culpability was addressed at the next court. On March 4, 1662, she was found guilty of "unnatural practice towards her father-in-law [stepfather], George Barlow, in chopping of him in the back." Anna was fined ten pounds and ordered to be publicly whipped. The whipping was delayed because of "her present condition." Anna was pregnant and would marry Andrew Hallett, presumably the child's father, that same year.[17,18]

Dorcas and Mary were found guilty of the same charges, "though not so high degree, were both sentenced to sit in the stocks." Mary was "sharply reproved by the court, as being by her disobedience the occasions of the evil above mentioned." Apparently, it was Mary's behavior that started the melee, but all was not well in the Barlow household. At the end of the court record it is stated that "George Barlow and his wife were both severely reproved for their most ungodly living in contention one with the other and admonished to live otherwise."[19]

George Barlow was not an entirely sympathetic victim. He was known to be a mean drunk, "to be drunk, and then to be mad, and to beat his wife and children like a madman, and to throw the things of the house from one place to another." Historians have judged him "a bad man," and even worse, "a hard-hearted, intolerant, tyrannical man, abusing the power entrusted to him, and seemingly taking delight in confiscating the property of innocent men and women, or in dragging them to prison, to the stocks, or the whipping post." Where did he derive such authority? In 1658 Barlow was appointed marshal of Sandwich, Barnstable, and Yarmouth, and he went after Quakers with a vicious enthusiasm, responsible for "a system of terrorism in the old colony." His habit, wrote another historian, "was to take not what was to be most valuable to the authorities, but what would be most poignantly missed by the Quaker families."[20,21,22]

With a checkered past as a failed preacher behind him, Barlow first appeared in Sandwich in 1657. As marshal, he was appointed to "act as a constable, by apprehending felons or other suspicious persons, keeping of the peace, serving of warrants, or any other public service that of the said constable may be required." The region was a hotbed of Quakerism, and the Pilgrims took a harsh view of Quakers. On June 7, 1659, by order of the court under Governor Prence's leadership, the Quakers, "are judged by the court grossly scandalous as liars, drunkards, swearers, etc.," empowering Barlow to take a hard line against them. He fulfilled his duties with an offensive combination of violence, intimidation, and terror.[23]

On June 23, 1658, Barlow arrested two Quaker preachers, Christopher Holder and John Copeland, who were on their way to Sandwich. Barlow brought them before the selectmen of Sandwich, who refused to charge the two men. Barlow took the prisoners to his own house, kept them there for six days, and then brought them to Thomas Hinckley in Barnstable, an assistant of Governor Prence. Hinckley was in agreement with Barlow's view of Quakers, and he sentenced them to be punished. The two men were whipped, "thirty-three cruel stripes laid upon them with a new tormenting whip, with three cords, and knots at the ends, made by the marshal, and brought with him." The residents of Barnstable, who had not seen such proceedings before, were shocked. Their response was that "however erroneous Quakerism right be, such conduct on the part of their rulers did not consist with the religion of Jesus." One of the witnesses was said to have remarked, "Who would have thought…that I should have come to New England to witness such scenes?"[24,25]

Barlow was known to attack at night. For example, in March 1659, William Newland "did say in court, that George Barlow [did] break up his house in the night, whereby he suffered much damage." Barlow's authority was hard to escape. Thomas Butler was fined ten shillings at the same meeting, "for refusing to assist the marshal Barlow in the execution of his office."[26]

The courts did respond when Barlow blatantly overstepped his authority. On March 5, 1661, he was called before the courts, "for charging Benjamin Allen to sit in the stocks at Sandwich the greatest part of a night without cause." Furthermore, Barlow was ordered to return to Allen a shirt "and some other small linen, which he took from him."[27]

In May of 1665, Barlow was back in court charged with "attempting the chastity of Abigail, the wife of Jonathan Pratt, by alluring words and acts of force, being to the affrighting and much wronging of the said Abigail in the house she dwells in, being then alone." Barlow denied the charge, but the court "saw cause to require bonds of him for his good behavior" until the June court, and charged him twenty pounds.[28]

Not surprisingly, Barlow also had a drinking problem. On March 6, 1666, he was fined ten shillings "for being drunk the second time." In attempting to make an arrest, he was so drunk, "that he could hardly forbear vomiting in the bosom of him whom he pretended to press [take into custody.]"[29,30]

Quaker historians have written Barlow a sad end: "Barlow died as his lived, a poor miserable drunkard. No loving hand smoothed his brow in death, and no stone tells where he lies." Actually, George Barlow owned many assets at his death: a home and eight acres, pigs, horses, cows, oxen, tools, household furnishings, and clothes. He named four sons in his will, which was proved October 31, 1684. To Aaron and Moses Bessey, his stepsons, he left five shillings each, with the cryptic notation, "that is all I give them." To Jane and the two sons he had with her, John and Nathan, he gave what amounted to about eight acres, his house, his farm stock and equipment, and his "household stuff."[31,32,33]

Jane died in August 1693, outliving George Barlow by nine perhaps more peaceful years, and left an estate of thirty-eight pounds. After the court case in 1662, Dorcas and Mary Bessey disappear from the historical record. Anna Bessey married Andrew Hallet shortly thereafter, presumably the father of the child she was carrying at that time.[34]

Problems Between Parents and Children

Mary Foster Morey and her son, Benjamin Foster, appeared in court on March 2, 1689, answering a complaint that "her cruel, unnatural and extreme passionate carriages so exasperated her said son as that he oftentimes carried himself very much unbeseeming him and unworthily toward his said mother…." So turbulent was the relationship between mother and son that "several of the neighbors feared murder would be the issue of it." Benjamin was not a child; he was in his late twenties but apparently he could not get along with his mother.[35]

Mary Bartlet married Richard Foster on September 10, 1651. They had two children, Mary, born March 8, 1652, and Benjamin, born about 1654-5.[36] After Foster died, Mary married Jonathan Morey on July 8, 1659. They had three children: Jonathan, 1661, John, 1666, and Hannah, born sometime between 1673 and 1675. Her son, Benjamin had been before the courts on March 5, 1685, charged with "striking and abusing Joseph Buck." He was found guilty and sentenced to pay "three and four pence [each] month, and five shillings to the country."[37] Yet, he must have had some redeeming qualities, because in October 1686 he was called to sit on the colony's petty jury.[38,39,40,41,42,43]

Mary Foster Morey "owned her fault [in the relationship] and seemed to be very sorry for it and promised reformation." Benjamin "owned with tears his evil behavior towards his mother." The magistrates were satisfied with the testimonies; Benjamin received an admonition and Mary was warned to engage in "better walking," that is, to watch her step. Her son was permitted to remain with her until the June court, and in the intervening time they would be watched for improved behavior.[44]

It is believed that Benjamin Foster had an illegitimate daughter, Maria, born in 1685. The child's mother was known only as Mercy; she later married Samuel Lawrence. The child would have been four years old in 1689, when Benjamin and his mother were called into court for their behavior. Perhaps the child and Benjamin's involvement with Mercy was the subject of the arguments between mother and son.[45,46]

Benjamin Foster died intestate in 1690, probably unmarried. His mother, Mary, died two years later, on September 26, 1692. The illegitimate child Maria married John Trowbridge in 1711 and had two daughters.[47,48]

Parent/Relative Abusive to Children

Discipline of children in Plymouth would be considered unnecessarily harsh by today's standards. Parents were expected to punish their children as part of their religious and social acculturalization. This was not considered child abuse, so only a handful of cases appear in the court records. Those cases usually resulted in little or no punishment for the accused adult. Again, as head of the family, the father had full responsibility for what occurred in his home. This was a religious standard in the colony, so his authority was rarely questioned.

Rape and incest were a different matter entirely. Plymouth law included rape as a capital crime, but there is no mention of incest. Yet, at least three times in the colony's history they were forced to deal with this transgression. It was a difficult offense to prove because it was the custom that there be at least two witnesses to a crime to secure a guilty verdict. While there were punishments inflicted on the offenders, often the child was sent right back to the home where the assault took place.

On August 7, 1660, Thomas Atkins was brought into court "having been apprehended and committed to jail for committing incest with his own daughter, named Mary." Mary was about twelve years old at the time and it was she who made the complaint to the court. Her words were that her father "had committed the said act sundry times with her." Atkins, about forty years old, lived near the Kennebec River at the Plymouth trading post. Upon hearing his daughter's complaint, Atkins denied that "he ever had to do with her in that kind." Still, he was held over in jail until the matter was taken up again in October that same year.[49]

On October 2, the grand jury heard the evidence, and indicted Atkins. The petty jury, however, found him not guilty. When the jury questioned Atkins, he admitted "that on a time he being in drink in the night season in his own house, he offered some unclean, incestuous attempts to his own daughter, Mary Atkins, aforesaid, in his chimney corner, as he himself, in part, confessed." There were no witnesses to the incident and the jury believed him that no actual incestuous rape had taken place. It may not have been rape, but it certainly was at least attempted rape because he was sentenced to be whipped, and then "set at liberty to return to his own home," and his daughter.[50]

The courts addressed another case of rape within the family on July 13, 1677. Lydia Fish accused Ambrose Fish, who was possibly her brother or perhaps her half-brother, "of having not the fear of God before his eyes, did wickedly, and contrary to the order of nature, on the twentieth day of July last past before the date hereof, in his own house in Sandwich, in this colony of New Plymouth, by force carnally know and ravish Lydia Fish, the daughter of Mr. Nathaniel Fish, of Sandwich aforesaid, and against her will, she being then in the peace of God and of the King." As in the case above, Lydia was the only witness, and the courts settled on whipping Ambrose instead of hanging him. Ambrose was sentenced "to suffer corporal punishment by being publicly whipped at the post, which accordingly was inflicted, and the prisoner released."[51,52]

Two challenging cases of sexual abuse came before the courts, one case of incest in 1669, one of child murder in 1679, both of which involved the daughters of Christopher Winter.

The charge of incest between Christopher Winter and his married daughter Martha Winter Hewitt resulted in a pregnancy. On March 2, 1669, father and daughter appeared before the court "on suspicion of committing incest with each other…a very heinous and capital crime…." Both father and daughter were charged equally, "committing incest with each other."[53]

The relationship between Christopher and Martha, in her twenties at the time, actually came to light through her husband, John Hewitt. When Martha became pregnant, presumably by her father, Christopher immediately tried to find her a husband, inviting John Hewitt to court his daughter. Winter "hasten[ed] the marriage" to Hewitt even though he complained "he [Winter] had no comfort in the match." Apparently neither did Martha. The record notes her reluctance as it was revealed in her "carriage [behavior] that day that they were married."[54]

John Hewitt became aware of his wife's pregnancy soon after their marriage. He realized that he could not possibly be the father, so he confronted Martha, who "will not discover the father of her child." The court later cryptically noted that in her stubborn refusal, "she has more than ordinary grounds to be unwilling to disclose." Martha, however, did confess to her father-in-law that her husband was not the child's father.[55]

There is some evidence that the relationship between father and daughter was not consensual. Martha showed signs of having been the victim of an attack. Winter himself had warned Hewitt that Martha was nervous and "that his daughter was apt to be frightened." One time, he explained, he came home unexpectedly and surprised her, and she was so alarmed "that she fell into a swoon."[56]

The case returned to the court again on June 1, three months later. This time Christopher Winter was indicted "on suspicion of committing incest with his daughter, Martha Hewitt." The grand jury found "not the bill, and so he was released." Martha, however, "having a bastard borne of her body, which was groundedly suspected to be begotten by her said father, though not legally proved, as above said," continued to refuse to name her child's father. She was therefore convicted of "whoredom" and sentenced "to suffer corporal punishment by whipping at the post." Winter went free and his daughter, whom he most likely raped, suffered the pain and humiliation of a public whipping.[57]

At the same court, John Hewitt requested and petitioned to be divorced from her. Undecided on how to proceed, the court referred the case forward to the next meeting in July. However, on July 5, the court still could not decide because "the case appeared very difficult in reference to some particulars," and it was put over until the October court. There is no mention in the October court records of Hewitt's request, however, it is apparent that John and Martha found a way to reconcile. The couple's first child, named Solomon, was born in 1670, and they went on to have two more sons and four daughters.[58,59]

Christopher Winter's will, dated 1680, sworn in 1684, reveals a favoritism towards his daughter. He named Martha as his executrix. Although he had other daughters, he left Martha "all my housing and lands…also my horses, cattle, sheep, swine and all my servants and my household stuff, corn, provisions, beds, bedding, clothes, linen, woolen and all that part and whole of my estate in[side] house and out[side] of it during her natural life." (Among Christopher Winter's asset was listed "ye neger a man servant" worth eleven pounds. It seems that Winter was one of the first slave owners in Plymouth.) In the event of Martha's death, Christopher directed that all his assets be left to a "my grandchild, Winter Hewitt."[60,61]

Winter Hewitt was one of Martha's children, presumably fathered by her husband, John. As to the fate of the illegitimate child Martha was carrying during the trials, who would have been born in 1669 or 1670, the record is silent. It is possible that Solomon was that child. To give the child the name of Solomon, recalling the biblical story of the king who had to decide which of two women were really an infant's mother, is a curious and perhaps telling choice.

Another of Christopher Winter's daughters, Anne, married Robert Batson on July 13, 1676. Two years later, on June 5, 1678, Robert charged Charles Wills, "that he had lain with his [Batson's] wife." Baston further claimed that Wills was the father of the child born to his wife. The court investigated and determined that Wills was not guilty and they "cleared him thereof and from keeping the child," meaning that Wills did not have to pay child support. However,

Anne was charged with "uncleanness," and her father posted a bond of fifty pounds assuring that she would appear in court to answer the charge.[62,63,64]

During their inquiry, the court learned that Robert Batson "hath frequently companied with his said wife by bedding with her, both before and after the child was born." Clearly the court had no way to prove with certainty who the child's father was, since both men were sleeping with Batson's wife. However, they made the decision that it was the husband who was the child's legal father. Family stability was everything in Plymouth and with this decision the Batson family unit was preserved.[65]

It was presumably this unnamed child, about two years old, who was found dead in their home. On March 25, 1679, a jury was authorized to "search out the cause of the death of the child of Anne Batson." The jury reported that it found "nothing that might be the cause of its death." However, the child, of unnamed gender, had injuries in the lower abdomen, "the private members there being a settling of red and black, and the members being swelled." Lacking supporting forensic evidence, the court could not determine cause of death, but evidently they were suspicious and ordered that "Anne Batson and several of the family…touch the dead child."[66]

Requiring the suspects to lay their hands on the corpse was known as "trial by touch" or "trial by ordeal." Dating back to medieval times, this practice was an ancient supernatural method of proving guilt or innocence. It was believed that if the body began to bleed freshly from its wounds when touched by a suspect, it was God's verdict that he or she was guilty of the murder. "Anne Batson and several of the family" touched the corpse as directed, however, "nothing thereby did appear respecting [the child's] death." Anne did not reappear at court, as ordered, on the charge of uncleanness. She had fled the colony, and as a result her father had to forfeit at least part of his bond. There is no further mention of the name Batson in the court records.[67]

Clearly the child's death was caused by physical abuse, probably of a sexual nature. The primary suspect, Anne, had run away and could not be found, the results of the "trial by touch" was inconclusive, there were no witnesses, and so no one was held responsible. But there is something else curious about this case. Among the twelve jurors were five women, an extremely rare occurrence in the colonies. They were Abigail Snow, Faith Winslow, Martha Powell, Mary Williamson, and Mary Branch.[68] English law allowed for "matron's juries" in cases when a suspect had claimed to be pregnant and needed to be examined to confirm the claim. In the Batson case it may be that the court wanted the opinion of those most familiar with childcare and hygiene, and so they included women who were mothers on the jury.

Home Invasions

Then as now, not all violence in the home originated from family members. A woman at home alone was unprotected and vulnerable to attack. In 1668, Samuel Worden was away when two men broke into his house, "in the dead time of the night," and terrorized his family. According to Worden's complaint, Edward Crowell and James Maker approached his house and threatened to break the door down or enter through the window if not admitted. Once inside, the two men boldly went to Worden's bed and "attempt[ed] the chastity of his wife and sister by many lascivious carriages," terrifying the women and their children.[69]

The court addressed the case on October 29 and found the two men guilty. Crowell and Maker were each fined ten pounds and had to post bonds of forty pounds. They also had to pay Samuel Worden all the costs he incurred "in the vindication of his wife's innocence." Apparently, Samuel's wife had been unfairly accused of willing complicity in the crime.[70]

Threats from Native Americans were especially fearsome to the colonists, and attack by the "savages" was never far from the colonists' minds. They always kept their firearms close at hand, just in case. There were a handful of court actions involving Native Americans who had broken into private homes and terrorized the households.

As more immigrants settled in New England, tension between the native people and the new colonists increased. The Native Americans'

Weapons carried from fear of attack.

land was being encroached upon, and as Plymouth grew so did the strain and friction between the two groups. A case of Indian home invasion came before the court on March 1, 1664. In Barnstable, five Natives forced their way into the house of Robert Shelly, "affrighting his family, and other abuses." All of those charged were sentenced to sit in the stocks and ordered to pay Shelly five shillings, "in work or otherwise."[71]

Another case was heard years later. "Sampson, alias Bump," was charged with "most insolent and intolerable carriages towards" Elizabeth Vaughan and Samuel Eaton's wife, Martha. Sampson came into George Vaughan's house when he was not at home, "and held up his knife at the said Elizabeth Vaughan several times in a threatening way and manner as if he would have wounded her, with other insolent carriages that much affrighted her." He "wickedly" twisted the neck of Martha Eaton, "to the endangering of her life." The women sent for Francis Billington, Martha Eaton's father, to come to their aid, and he was met with "insolent carriages." For terrorizing the women, Sampson was sentenced by the court "to be severely whipped at this present court and to be branded in the shoulder with a Roman P, which accordingly was inflicted." Sampson was whipped and branded for the offense of perversion.[72]

The courts likewise protected the American Indian families from invasions by colonists. John Woodcocke and Adonijah Morris, for example, entered a Native American's home in 1655 to settle debts owed them. Woodcocke "[took] away an Indian child and some goods." Morris also stole a variety of things. For his outrageous act of kidnapping, Woodcocke was sentenced to sit in Rehoboth's stocks for an hour on training day and pay a fine of forty shillings (two pounds). Morris was fined the same amount. Presumably the child was returned to his or her parents, no doubt traumatized by the ordeal.[73]

After King Philip's War, the colonists took the opportunity to try the Native Americans for war crimes. "King Philip" was Metacom, the second son of Massasoit, who sat down with the Pilgrims in March 1621 and signed a treaty of peace and mutual defense. At that time, the colonists numbered about fifty people. Things had changed a lot since then. As the population grew, the Indigenous People felt threatened, and relations became strained.

Metacom lead the effort among the Native people to drive out the English. During the war, which lasted just under two years (1675-1677), twelve colonial towns were destroyed, and hundreds of colonists were killed. In August 1676, Metacom was captured, brutally beheaded, and quartered. His head was jammed on a spike and displayed at Plymouth for twenty-five years.

In March 1676, at the height of the war, an incident occurred that was emblematic of the entire conflict. Eleven Natives broke into William Clarke's home near the Eel River and murdered his wife, Sarah. According to Increase Mather's journal:

> March 12, 1676. This Sabbath eleven Indians assaulted <u>Mr. William Clark's house in Plymouth</u>, killed his wife, who was the daughter of a godly father and mother that came to New England on the account of religion, and she herself also a pious and prudent woman: They

Attack on a home.

also killed her suckling child, and knocked another
child (who was about eight years old) in the head,
supposing they had killed them… And whereas there
was another family besides his own entertained in Mr.
Clark's house, the Indians destroyed them all, root and
branch, the father and the mother and all the children.
So that eleven persons were murdered that day, and
under one roof; after which they set the house on fire.[74]

While Mather's account was vivid, it was greatly exaggerated.
When the case was considered by the courts, on July 7, 1676, only
the murder of Sarah Clarke was cited. William Clarke was a merchant
and had been trading with the Indians. He stored his inventory in
his warehouse, which also doubled as his home. Among his goods
were firearms, powder, and shot, items extremely attractive to Native
Americans at war.[75]

The case was taken up by the courts just before Metacom's capture
and execution. An Indigenous woman was the court's informant and
she named two men, Woodcocke (apparently no relation to the John
Woodcocke mentioned above) and Quanapawhan, stating that "they
were present and actors in that bloody murder of Mistress Sarah

Clarke." Those two accused named a third, John Num, and "upon examination," all three "confessed they were present at the committing of that horrid murder and outrage, and so had a hand as co-partners therein."[76]

John Num also confessed that "he was of that company that [had earlier] murdered Jacob Michell and his wife and John Pope." All three were sentenced to die, "which accordingly immediately was executed. But, before they died, they named the instigators of the crime, Tatoson and Keeweenam.[77]

Keeweenam admitted that that he had "lately been at the house of William Clarke, at the Eel River." The house was "slightly fortified," he reported to his confederates, "and that it was well furnished with necessaries." Only three people lived there, he said, and that most of them would be at meeting on the Lord's Day. Even if they left a man at home, "they might soon dispatch him, and then they would meet with no opposition, but might do as they pleased." On his information the plan was executed and "on which the night following, (this being on the last day of the week), the said Tatoson went towards Plymouth, and on the morrow following, in the morning about nine or ten of the clock, he with his company did this cruel villainy."[78]

Keeweenam was called before the court, and while he denied committing the murder, he did admit he gave all the necessary information to Tatoson. The court noted that had Keeweenam reported the plan to the government, "it might have prevented the following mischief." Keeweenam was given the opportunity to speak for himself, "but said little or nothing to any purpose."[79]

The court considered all the evidence, the "three positive testimonies who witnessed as abovesaid, and with all divers concurring circumstances, which have a tendency to the clearing up of the case, do judge, that the said Keeweenam is worthy to die." He received the sentence of death, but the manner of execution was somewhat unusual. The court ordered "that his head…shall be severed from his body, which was immediately accordingly executed."[80]

Besides the three already mentioned—Woodcocke, Quanapawhan, and John Num—the court recorded the names of the other eight "who were copartners in the outrage committed at William Clarke's house, at the Eel River, in the township of New Plymouth, on the 12th of March 1676." They were, Thomas Tatoson and his nephew, Thomas Piant, Musquash, Sanballett, Wapanpowett, Uttsooweest, and Woonashenah. Their subsequent fate is unknown.[81]

A bounty was put on Thomas Tatoson's head on July 22, 1676, along with Penachason. Should any Native American bring in either one of them, "their reward for each of them [would be] four coats." The reward for "every other Indian that shall prove merchantable," that is, suitable for sale as a slave, would be one coat each.[82]

Following this case, the court established a new policy regarding Indigenous People who might surrender to the colony during and after the war, stating that "They should find favor in so doing." But, there were conditions. If they had committed a murder "in the field in a soldier-like way," they were forgiven. But, had they any role in a murder like that at the Clarke home, they would be fully punished by the courts. Furthermore, any Native Americans who entered the colony, "in a clandestine way, not applying themselves to the authority of this jurisdiction for liberty, shall not expect the benefit of the indemnity formerly showed to other Indians that did come in in an orderly way, but shall be forthwith taken up and disposed of, as other captive Indians, to the colony's use."[83,84]

"Disposed of" usually meant being put into forced labor in the colony or sold into slavery and shipped to the Caribbean. There they would most likely die from disease or the harsh labor conditions on the sugar plantations there.

Chapter Seven

Children in Service

Hard physical labor was vital for the success of Plymouth Colony. Living in a subsistence economy based on farming, individual families often could not supply enough labor to support themselves. One solution was to take in children as indentured servants. These children, for the most part, were treated as members of the family, living in the same house, eating the same food, and being provided with clothing. According to the conditions of their indenture agreement, they might even look forward to a lump payment at the end of their service period. This interval usually lasted seven years, or until the child reached twenty-one years of age.

The system was carefully monitored. Indenture agreements were formal written documents that were entered into the court record. (There probably were informal agreements between parents for hiring out children for short-term work, like helping during a harvest, but those were not supervised by the courts.) Along with the necessities, servants received indoctrination into Plymouth culture, religious training, and a rudimentary education. Masters had full responsibility for the well-being of their indentured servants and were also held responsible for their behavior.

For example, on July 7, 1646, when Charles Thurston, servant to William Hanbury, got into trouble for "reveling and disguised dancing," he was sentenced to pay a fine or to be whipped. It was his master who paid the fine, although Thurston had to promise the court to pay Hanbury back, even if it meant he would have to extend his indenture beyond the completion date. The court also stipulated that he would have to make up the time he missed while away on his revels, as he had "absent[ed] himself from [Hanbury's] service without his said master's consent." His merry behavior came at a high price—two more years of service.[1]

Children gathering kindling.

Charles Thurston had been in the courts before. On June 5, 1644, he was charged with "abusing his mistress," and ordered to be whipped at the post. However, "the young men of Plymouth" petitioned the court to stay the sentence, "upon trial of his good carriage until the next court." His friends must have believed Thurston was redeemable, and, with only a warning, he was given a second chance to control his aggression. At the next court, held March 3, 1645, Thurston was discharged, apparently having mended his violent ways against his master.[2,3]

In another case, the master of a servant girl was asked to pay her medical bills. On May 3, 1659, a complaint was made against John Williams, of Scituate, referred to earlier, for the "hard usage of a daughter of John Barker, deceased." The child, Deborah Barker, who was Williams' niece (his sister, Anna Barker's daughter), was living with him under his guardianship. She was removed from his care and sent to live with Thomas Bird until the next court. Deborah, "being weak and infirm," presumably from the rough handling by Williams, needed care to restore her health. Bird was asking the court for "means for her cure," that is, funds for her medical treatment. The court agreed to consider the request and asked that all parties appear at the next court, "to clear up the case betwixt the said John Williams and his kinswoman, the said girl."[4]

On October 6, 1659, the case was readdressed. Williams denied the charge of abusing the child, "producing many evidences to clear his innocence." While the proof did not support the charge of abuse, perhaps the court was not entirely convinced of his innocence. Deborah was allowed to choose a new guardian, and she decided to stay with Thomas Bird.[5]

Bird was a curious and unexplained choice. As of this writing, no relationship has been found between Thomas Bird and Deborah Barker. In 1662, he was charged with "adulterous practices and attempts, so far as strength of nature would permit," with Hannah Bumpass. Thomas was sentenced to be whipped twice. Hannah was also charged "for yielding to him, and not making such resistance [not calling for help] against him as she ought." Bird also had to pay Hannah ten pounds, "for the wrong he hath done her."[6]

Nonetheless, in his will, presented to the court on October 4, 1664, Thomas Bird left Deborah Barker Buden five pounds.[7]

Masters were expected to carefully monitor their servants' conduct while mentoring them to be responsible citizens of Plymouth. Anyone who interfered in that relationship was called into court. For instance, on January 14, 1637, Edith Pitts complained in court against her master, John Emerson, accusing him of abuse. John was ordered to appear at the next General Court to answer the charge; Edith was also ordered to appear, and not "depart [the colony] without license." Emerson posted a bond of forty pounds for good behavior and appearance at the court, as directed.[8]

There is no further record of a resolution of that particular charge. However, John Emerson was brought into court on March 5, 1639, for "entertaining of other men's servants at unlawful times, diverse and sundry times." On September 3, 1639, Emerson was fined for "suffering disorders in his house by drinking."[9] It was the charge of drinking with other men's servants that drew the court's attention. He was a bad influence.

Reasons for Putting Children into Service

There were many reasons a child might be placed into the care of another family. Poverty was the most common justification. Sometimes there was dissention within a family, or a child was out of parental control and needed a firmer hand. One rationale that is not mentioned in the court record, but may have been practiced, if unconsciously, is that the child was overindulged at home. The Pilgrims' pastor in Leiden, John Robinson, wrote that it is dangerous for parents to favor one child over the others in a family, "either for its beauty or wit or likeness to themselves, or some other fancied good in it." There is grave danger in that partiality, he warned: "Sometimes the Lord takes away such before the rest, to punish the father's fondness." Even if the child survives, there may be serious problems. The favored child, "if surviving, prove the worst of all the rest, as growing hereby proud, and arrogant in themselves, presumptuous upon their father's love, and contemptuous of the rest of their brethren, and sisters…." It would be better for everyone, he advised, if such a child were placed with another family.[10]

Poverty

By far the most common reason children were put into service was poverty. There was no reliable form of birth control in the seventeenth century, and the usual interval between pregnancies was two years. While infants did not always survive, families could still be quite large, and the father might be unable to provide properly for his children. The courts could step in, and they did so when it was obvious that children were at risk in the family home. Boys might be enrolled into an apprenticeship with a craftsman, a form of indenture that included training in a specific trade for a prescribed amount of time. Most often, the child's role was as a servant in the home, helping care for younger children and performing daily chores.

Poverty was clearly the reason Samuel and Elizabeth Eddy put their children into service. Samuel was a freeman who owned land but was too poor to support his family. The couple explained to the court that "having many children, and by reason of many wants lying upon them,...they are not able to bring them up as they desire." In 1645, Samuel put his seven-year-old son John into the care of Francis and Katherine Goulder. The agreement was that John would stay with the Goulders until he reached the age of twenty-one. Two years later, seven-year-old Zachery (Zachariah) Eddy was placed with John Brown under similar agreement. In 1652, Caleb Eddy, nine years old, was also sent to live with John Brown.[11,12,13]

The Eddy boys did very well. John grew up to be a large landowner in Taunton and Zachariah settled in Swansea, where his brother Caleb served as a deacon of the church. A fourth son, Obadiah, settled in Middleborough. All had large families.[14]

Then there was the case of the Billingtons. John Billington, his wife Eleanor, and their two sons, John and Francis, *Mayflower* passengers, were referred to by Bradford as "one of the profanest families amongst them." They were trouble from the start, he wrote, for "he and some of his had been often punished for miscarriages." "I know not by what friends," Bradford complained, "[that the Billingtons were] shuffled into their company."[15]

John Billington, Sr., holds the distinction of being the first man hanged in Plymouth Colony. In September 1630 he was executed for the murder of John Newcomen. John, Jr., died shortly before his father was hanged, but Francis grew to manhood. He married Christian Penn, the widow of Francis Eaton, in July 1634. She brought her four children into the marriage: Samuel, Rachel, Benjamin, and an unnamed child whom William Bradford uncharitably and bluntly described as "an idiot." Francis and Christian's first child, Elizabeth, was born in July of 1635. They would have eight more children together.[16,17,18,19]

The Billingtons, who lived in Playne Dealing or North Plymouth as it is called today, were regarded by the community as an unproductive bunch, seemingly content to live in extreme poverty. As their family grew, the situation became critical and they began to put their children into service. Soon after Elizabeth's birth, on February 11, 1636, Christian's son Benjamin Eaton, aged seven, was put into service with Bridget Fuller, the widow of Samuel Fuller. Six months later, on July 5, 1636, Samuel Eaton, who was about sixteen years old, was bound to John Cooke, Jr., for a term of seven years, "to get at the end of term three suits of apparel, 12 bushels of corn, and a heifer." (Cooke was a neighbor of the Billingtons.) On April 5, 1642, Elizabeth Billington, seven years old, was placed with John Barnes and his wife Mary. (Daughter Rachel Eaton was not bound out but was kept at home, most likely to help tend younger children.)[20,21,22]

More children continued to be born to the couple. By 1643, the Billingtons were living in life-threatening poverty, and were receiving public assistance from the town. Worried about the children's well-being and probably fearful that the town could not afford to support the family for much longer, the townsmen stepped in on January 14, 1643. They forcibly removed some of the children from the home. "Concerning the placing and disposing of Francis Billington's children according to the act and order of the court," four Billington children were taken from the family and placed with others who agreed, under certain conditions, to take them into their families.[23]

The eldest of the brood, Benjamin Eaton, almost fifteen years old, who had originally been placed with Bridget Fuller in 1636, was subsequently re-placed with John Winslow, with whom he was supposed to stay until he turned twenty-one. No reason was given for the switch. Winslow agreed "to find him meat, drink, and apparel during the said term and pay ten pounds for his service...."[24]

Joseph, who was six or seven years old, went to John Cooke (who already had taken in his brother Samuel), "until he be twenty and one years" and agreed to "find him meat, drink, and apparel during the said term." Giles Rickard took the five-year-old Martha and agreed to "keep her and find her meat, drink, and apparel until she shall accomplish the age of twenty years or be married with consent...." Within a month of her marriage, the agreement provided that Martha's husband would receive thirty shillings, "towards the appareling of her." The other little girl, Mary, was assigned to Gabriel Fallowell, under much the same circumstances, except Fallowell needed financial help taking on the extra responsibility. John Winslow would pay him "thirty-three shillings, four pence for the first three yars next after the taking of her."[25,26]

Six months after taking Joseph Billington, John Cooke, Jr., was having problems with the child. He constantly ran away, going back to the Billington family and home. On July 4, 1643, the court ordered that Joseph "shall be returned to his said master again immediately and shall so remain with him during his term." If he runs away again, and his parents take him in, the court ordered that "Francis and Christian, his wife, shall be set in the stocks every lecture day during the time thereof, as often as he or she shall so receive him, until the court shall take a further course with them." "And also," the court ordered, "if Benjamin Eaton, now living with the said Francis Billington shall counsel, entice, or inveigle the said Joseph [his brother] from his said master, that then he shall have the same punishment with his father and mother." (How Benjamin, who had been placed first with Bridget Fuller, then with John Winslow, came to move back to his parents' home is not recorded).[27]

After their children were taken from them, and without reliable birth control, the Billingtons went on to have five more children. They were Isaac, born in 1644, an unnamed child who died young, Rebecca, born in 1648, who evidently also died young, Dorcas, born in 1650, and Mercy, born in 1652.[28]

Through the second generation the Billingtons continued to rely on the public assistance to survive. Dorcas became pregnant at twenty-two, unmarried, and was "sentenced to pay a fine of five pounds by the next July court...for committing fornication with [name missing] or to appear at the said court and to receive corporal punishment by whipping." She stubbornly and persistently refused to name the child's father. Apparently, she was unable to pay the fine; she was whipped after all.[29,30]

The unlucky Billingtons received another blow in 1666. On February 5 of that year the town court appointed three men—Edward Gray, William Clarke, and William Crow—to take up a collection from the town's inhabitants as soon as possible, "for the relief of Francis Billington he having lately suffered great loss by the burning of his house."[31,32]

In 1669, Francis and Christian moved to Middleborough and settled on their "great lot," as part of the land grant issued to all first comers. Francis told his son, Isaac, that after the devastation from the Indian Wars, he could no longer make a living on his land in Playne Dealing.

At a meeting in Middleboro on July 20, 1683 the town addressed the situation of Dorcas and her illegitimate child, who were living with her parents. It was decided that her father, Francis Billington, could not adequately care for Dorcas and the child, "being in present want." It was left to "the wisdom and discretion of the selectmen…to the disposing of his daughter Dorcas her lad." Dorcas never named the father of her child, so there was no one to turn to for financial support. She was ordered to put the child into service with another family. The record is silent on the outcome, but in 1686, Dorcas married Edward May. Her son would have been fourteen years old. It may be that Dorcas and Edward had three more children, but their parentage has not been proven for certain.[33,34]

Francis Billington died in Middleborough on December 3, 1684, shortly after Christian's death. With all their troubles, they both lived to be nearly eighty years old. But even after death Francis and Christian continued to be a controversial family. There was some unfinished business over property rights and it was Isaac's eldest daughter, Desire, who tackled the problem.[35]

When Francis Billington died, there was no probate record filed. Isaac Billington, who had been caring for his parents in their dotage, assumed he was his father's only heir. On May 11, 1665, Francis had deeded to Isaac "the quantity of fifty or threescore acres" in an area that later became Middleborough, to be awarded after his death, "for natural affection."[36]

Once more a Billington appealed for public assistance. On March 1, 1704, Isaac and his wife Hannah (Glass) Billington petitioned the court for reimbursement for the seven years they cared for his parents.

"Though I lived comfortably at Marshfield," Isaac argued, his father Francis "urged [him] with the greatest importunity to go with him, alleging that he should perish if I did not." Isaac relocated his family to Middleborough, "to take care of and provide for my aged parents, according to their request." For seven years Isaac provided "both house, food, and apparel for them and kept them both in sickness and health. At their deaths, Isaac also paid for their funerals.[37]

Isaac wanted to be reimbursed from the town's treasury on the grounds that if he had not cared for his parents, the colony would have had to. Isaac claimed that Lieut. Tompson, the selectman of Middleborough, promised him that his father's entire estate, "whatever divisions and allotments of lands," should be his, "if I would take care of them and not suffer them to want." Otherwise, if Isaac did not intercede, "all must be sold by the selectmen for their relief." Isaac even figured out his expenses, estimated at six shillings a week, "would amount to above ten times the value of all the lands. He added that "none of the rest of the relations...never did anything towards relieving [their parents] in their wants."[38]

Isaac's claim was a dubious one. It was outside the authority of the selectmen to decide how an estate should be divided; likewise, the Plymouth court declined to consider the claim. One problem facing Isaac was that it was unclear exactly what Francis Billington had owned. Some of his holdings were sold off during his lifetime, and others were in his children's names. Isaac's daughter, Desire, thirty-one and unmarried, took up the challenge of sorting out who owned what. In 1706, she received the rights to her father's property and set out to clear the titles and claim ownership once and for all. She was able to get documents from her aunts relinquishing any rights to Billington property, but she still needed her uncles' involvement.[39]

In 1718, Desire married James Bonney, who was able to purchase land her uncles, Francis and Samuel, had received from their father. One more entanglement over Billington's original holdings was settled in 1724, too late for James Bonney, who had died earlier, to see the issue resolved. Through her own persistence Desire Billington Bonney had finally settled her grandfather's estate. She then conveyed all ownership to her stepson, James Bonney, Jr., "all right and title in the share of land which did formerly belong to my grandfather Francis Billington." The issue was finally closed, but all the original Billington properties passed out of the family name.[40]

Friction Within a Family

There were instances when discord within a family was drawn to the court's attention. Children were sometimes "put out" to get away from the problems at home, and in at least one case a son was put into service because his family could not control his behavior.

On October 2, 1660, Thomas Lombard, Sr., of Barnstable (also known as Lumbart or Lumbert), stood before the court requesting that his son, "as be by him freed." The boy, Thomas complained, "hath carried stubbornly against his said father," and should be placed with another family, an "honest, godly family." Jedediah, who was twenty years old at the time, was offered the chance to choose his own foster family, or the court would find one for him.[41]

The problem with Jedediah may have been that he was associating with Quakers, since he would marry Hannah Wing in 1668, daughter of Daniel Wing, a well-known Quaker in Sandwich. It appears, however, that father and son reconciled before Thomas' will was written in 1663. He left Jedediah land, a mare, and full access to his mother's home.[42,43]

Unsuitable Parents

The courts also stepped in when parents were considered unable to fulfill the responsibilities of raising their children. The Everson family is a good example.

John Everson was a man who could not settle down and make a go of things in Boston. Considered a transient of "ill behavior," he was asked to leave Boston in 1663. By 1668 he and his three young children appeared in the Plymouth Colony records. There is no trace of his wife in Plymouth, so she may have died before 1668. He apparently found a family willing to take him and his children into their household, at least on an unofficial basis.[44]

This situation made the courts very uneasy. They preferred that all prospective residents of the colony be reviewed and approved before settling. Everson, already evicted from Boston, would certainly not have been approved. Just to make things clear for everyone, Plymouth Town records for October, 1668, state that, "the Selectmen shall henceforth have full power to require any that shall receive any stranger so as to entertain them into their house, to give security unto them to save the town harmless from any damage that may accrue unto them by their entertainment of such as aforesaid." In other words, if you bring any outsider into your home, you assume full responsibility for that person's care and behavior. Clearly, the Everson family was on the court's mind when they wrote this because immediately following this order, the record states that, "It was likewise agreed that John Everson be forthwith warned to depart the town with all convenient speed."[45]

Looking more closely at the situation, it became obvious to the court that Everson was not a suitable parent and that his children were at risk. In 1668, the Town of Plymouth, with the consent of John Everson, placed his two-year-old son, Richard, with William Nelson, Sr., "to be and remain with him until he hath attained the age of one and twenty years...." The next year, on July 29, John Everson allowed his daughter, Martha, to be adopted by Robert Barrows, "to be...with him as his own child from this time forward." The youngest child, John, was apparently placed with Stephen Bryant, Jr., who raised him as his own son and gave him eight acres of land in his 1690 will, "in consideration of love and good will."[46,47]

John Everson then disappears from the historical records. Whatever his shortcomings as a father, Everson apparently made good choices about where to place his children, seeing that all three grew up to be successful adults. Richard married in 1698, and even though he and wife Elizabeth "were fined four pounds for committing fornication together when single persons," he became a prosperous landowner who had five children with Elizabeth, and two more with his second wife, Penelope. Martha married Hugh Briggs of Taunton and had three children. Likewise John was a success, if judged by the numerous land transactions in his name in the area. He married an Elizabeth as well, last name unknown, and they had five children.[48]

The three Everson children eventually reunited and settled in Plympton. In 1717, the Everson boys petitioned the Massachusetts General Court to recognize the "the northeast part of Plympton, near (Jones) river" as the township of Kingston. At their request, the town was incorporated in 1726. It measures about twenty square miles today and as of 2010 had a population of over 5,500 inhabitants.[49,50]

There was at least one case addressed by the court of the placement of an orphan. On October 27, 1680, the situation of six-year-old Sarah Nesfield was discussed. Her father was killed, "slain by the Indians in Capt. Pierce's fight," and his daughter was "left at Manomet…in a destitute condition." Tristram and Anne Hedges took in the child but requested "some satisfaction" from the town to cover their expenses. However, since Manomet "is in its infancy," and still establishing itself, it was agreed that the community could not offer public funds for relief. A compromise was reached, and it was agreed that the town would pay three pounds to the Hedges instead of the five pounds granted by the court.[51]

But Sarah was not well-placed with Tristram and Anne. The following March the court ordered that Sarah Nesfield be removed from the Hedges' household and that "the town of Manomet do prepare and provide a fit place for the said child." The town was also relieved of any payment to the Hedges. Sadly, there is no further record of Sarah Nesfield's fate. She was most likely put into service with another family who would provide better care for her.[52]

Another orphan was rescued by the courts the following year. On July 7, 1681, Robert Marshall, Jr., "a poor orphan left at Plymouth, his friends many of them being deceased," was put into the care of Samuel Seabury of Duxbury.[53]

Apprenticeships

In many cases, male children were put into indenture for a specific period so they could learn a specialized trade or craft. The parents of the placed child often covered the cost of that training. In 1653, Benjamin Savory, nine years old, was placed with John and Alice Shaw, to remain with them until the age of twenty-one. The Shaws promised to teach Benjamin to read and write and to teach him "whatsoever trade the said Jonathan Shaw can do." At the end of his service, Benjamin would receive five pounds or a cow, and two suits of clothes. Benjamin's father paid John Shaw thirty shillings in the transaction. Included in the terms was the condition that if either Thomas Savory or his wife died before the end of the period, then Benjamin's service contract would transfer to Jonathan Shaw, John Shaw's son.[54]

Two years into the agreement, a note in the record states that "Jonathan Shaw is cleared of any engagement unto Benjamin Savory." The thirteen-year-old was placed into the care of Shaw's brother-in-law, Stephen Bryant, with the agreement that Benjamin be "instructed in husbandry," and receive five pounds at the end of his term. There is no further mention of Benjamin Savory in the Plymouth records.[55,56]

Occasionally, a master did not provide the special training he promised, and those cases came before the courts. For example, on July 5, 1678, John Barker complained against John Williams, who had agreed to "put him forth in a trade." Dissention between Barker and Williams has been discussed earlier, but on this occasion, Barker argued that when he did "arrive at man's estate," he was not prepared to take on a trade but had only been employed in "servile employment" by Williams. Apparently, the court was able to settle the matter without legal action.[57]

Adoption

In an early case of adoption, the child was completely separated from both parents. On January 30, 1649, an agreement was made between Thomas and Winnifred Whitney and John and Bennett Smith stipulating that four-year old Jeremiah Smith would "be with him [Whitney] as his own child." The Whitneys would adopt Jeremiah "without annoyance or disturbance from the said John Smith or Bennet his wife or any by from or under them." They promised to provide for

Jeremiah, "competent and convenient meat, drink, apparel, washing, lodging fit for one of his degree and rank."[58]

Jeremiah's birth parents agreed to "make over all their right title and interest which they have in the said Jeremiah Smith," to the Whitneys, who would have "the full disposing of him as aforesaid all due respects from son to parents." Should Thomas Whitney die, his wife, Winnifred agreed to fulfill the bargain. All four parents signed the agreement, which was witnessed by Nathaniel Morton.[59]

Very little is known about John and Bennett Smith. We do know that on November 8, 1638, John was ordered to appear before the court, "after the birth of the child begotten on the body of Bennet Moorecock." The record notes that he later married Bennet, but he was still sentenced to be whipped for fornication.[60]

Sometimes children were placed with other families, or "assigned," in a formal agreement that resembled an adoption, but which was not as permanent. For example, on April 12, 1667, an agreement was made between William Harlow and Nathaniel and Lydia Morton specifying that William's son Nathaniel would be "committed" to the Mortons. The child was two-and-a-half years old, born on September 30, 1664. His mother, Mary, had died five days later, on October 4, 1664.[61,62]

By 1667, when William entered into this agreement, he already had nine children by three wives; his tenth would be born on April 21, 1667, nine days after the toddler Nathaniel was placed with the Mortons. William Harlow had lost two wives just after childbirth, the above Mary, and his first wife, Rebecca, who died after delivering her fifth child on June 2, 1657. In all, he fathered fourteen children. In the settlement of his estate, dated September 9, 1691, he names four sons and seven daughters.[63,64]

The agreement was that Nathaniel would stay with the Mortons until he was twenty-one and would remain with "the longest liver of them." Should Lydia Morton be widowed, and the child be seven years old, his birth father would pay ten pounds, "to help her towards the more comfortable bringing up of the said child." If they were both to die before little Nathaniel became twenty-one, he would return to his natural father.[65]

It is unknown if <u>Nathaniel Harlow</u> stayed with the Mortons or returned to his father. On March 17, 1691, when he was twenty-eight years old, Nathaniel <u>married Abigail Buck</u>. They had three children: Abigail (who married Robert Cooke), Nathaniel (perhaps named after Nathaniel Morton), and James. Nathaniel Harlow died intestate on April 19, 1721, in Plympton, and his three children were named in the disposition of his estate.[66,67]

Not all cases of adoption were as agreeable as Nathaniel Harlow's. The case of Josias Litchfield is a sad example. Lawrence Litchfield died in 1649 or 1650 in Scituate, and on his death bed he requested that his youngest son, Josias, be placed into the care of John and Ann Allen, "if they would accept him and take him as their child." However, Litchfield's wife, Judith Dennis Litchfield, was still living. Understandably, she was unwilling to relinquish her son, who was under two years old. Eventually, and most likely after some prodding, she "consented to her husband's will in the thing," if "John and Ann would take the child for their adopted child." Everyone agreed that "Judith thereupon send the child unto them and desired her child might call them father and mother and yet own her for his natural mother as long as she should live." Judith wanted little Josias to know her as his birth mother, even though he was being raised by the Allens, who had no other children.[68]

Nine years later Judith had re-married, and took the opportunity to request that Josias' adoption agreement be reviewed. Apparently, never comfortable giving up her child in the first place, she wanted him returned to her. During the proceedings, Josias was asked by his "own mother," that is, his birth mother Judith, if he wanted to continue to live with the Allens. The boy "willingly answered yea." They were, after all, the only parents he had ever known.[69]

It has been speculated that there was some family relationship between Lawrence Litchfield and John Allen, but that has not been proven. In his will, dated June 2, 1663, John Allen named as his heirs his wife and Josias, who was then fifteen. Josias should have "a portion out of his estate, and that he should have the house and land where he then lived when he come of age." He left his wife "the other house and land of his," and added that the rest of his estate "should be in his wife's power to give to the said boy as she did see him carry himself." John Allen treated Josias as any son would have been, but he also made it clear that Josias, perhaps a difficult teenager at the time, be "beholding to my wife; and not my wife to the boy."[70]

Because he was underage, Josias was appointed two guardians by the court. On June 1, 1663, Josias chose Lieut. Torrey and Cornett Studson, who were paid twenty pounds from the estate, "to be improved for him, and soon after that time [he] be freed and to be put forth to a trade, and conveniently fitted out with suitable apparel and necessaries." Josias would receive his inheritance, "when he shall come to the age of twenty-one years, to be possessed of the farm and appurtenances given him by the said John Allen."[71]

Josias Litchfield grew up in Scituate and married Sarah Baker on February 22, 1671. They had six children. In 1687, Josiah named his newborn daughter Judith, presumably after his birth mother who had died in 1685. In all, over the next one hundred years, several descendants of Josiah Litchfield repeated the custom of naming a daughter Judith. No doubt the story of the distraught mother was passed on along with her name. Josias Litchfield died January 29, 1708, without a will, but left a large estate. An "apprizement" of all his lands totaled over eight hundred pounds.[72,73]

Problems with Servants

Once a child had been placed with a family as a servant, the child was expected to accept that family as his or her own. There was no running back home, as we have already seen with the Billingtons. On July 4, 1679, Robert Godfrey was sentenced to be whipped at the post, "for stealing a bar of iron and running away from his master, and for other misdemeanors."[74] Robert was nineteen at the time.[75,76]

Several years later, on July 6, 1686, Robert Godfrey and his new wife, Hannah Hackett, were "convicted in court of fornication before marriage but after contract," and fined five pounds and court fees. Their first child was born in April 1686, and while there is no record of their marriage date, apparently it was less than the requisite nine months.[77,78]

, the child who had been placed in service proved
ɔl. In those situations the courts intervened. Such was
ᴄ ɔf John Wade, who was in service to John Barnes. John
Wade was the eldest son of Nicholas and Elizabeth Hanford Wade,
and was about fifteen years old at the time. Barnes' complaint to the
court was against Edward Holman, "for entertaining John Wade,
his servant, and for carrying the said Wade to Duxbury in his boat,
without his master's consent." Holman was interfering with Barnes'
control over his servant. The characters in this story are a remarkably
interesting bunch.[79,80]

John Barnes arrived in Plymouth around 1632 and was a yeoman
by occupation. He married Mary Plummer in 1633, and after her
death married her sister Anne in 1636 (some sources list his second
wife as Joan Plummer). Barnes was a wealthy man who was engaged in
trading. He appeared before the courts on several occasions, charged
with various crimes, but his main problem was excessive drinking. He
was called into court on March 1, 1653, accused of drunkenness, and
he showed up in court so intoxicated that he earned himself a fine
of ten pounds and was ordered to post forty pounds for future good
behavior. In 1661, the court ordered that any tavern or inn keepers in
the town of Plymouth, "are hereby prohibited to let John Barnes have
any liquors, wine, or strong drink at any time."[81]

Barnes' death was the subject of a coroner's jury inquiry on March
5, 1672, when he was killed by his own bull who, "suddenly turned
about upon him and gave him a great wound with his horn on his
right thigh, near eight inches long." Barnes languished about thirty-six
hours before dying, apparently in great pain.[82,83,84]

Edward Holman, who was a friend of John Barnes, was a fellow
drinker and was considered a bad influence in Plymouth. He was
born in England about 1605 and came to Plymouth in 1623. Holman
was a seaman, married, and was one of the original Purchasers. On
November 30, 1640, Edward relinquished one-third ownership of his
boat to John Barnes for a land transaction that went bad.

In December 1641, Holman, along with three other men,
including Joshua Barnes, most likely a relative of John's, were charged
with stealing a trunk they salvaged from the "bottom of the bay about

Satucket," near Bridgewater It was the custom that any wreckage or cargo from a shipwreck that appeared on Plymouth shores would belong to the colony, not just to the individual who happened to discover it. Holman reported that he took enough canvas from the wreckage to make a main sail, a pair of drawers, a waistcoat and shirt from the flotsam. The rest he turned over to the colony. He then asked to be reimbursed for expenses he incurred, "for his pains about a chest of goods," in getting the chest to Plymouth. Expenses came to one pound, seventeen shillings, six pence. The court cleared Holman of wrongdoing and ordered he be repaid.[85,86,87]

Holman was also before the courts in 1652. It was ordered that "he henceforth do no more frequent or come at the house of [Thomas Shrive], nor that the wife of the said Shrive do frequent the house or company of the said Holman." Holman had been visiting Martha Shrive "at unseasonable times of the night," and was fortunate to receive only a warning. Should the couple continue in this behavior, the court cautioned that "either of them will answer it at their peril."[88]

Enticing young John Wade to leave his master and sail away with him to Duxbury was a more serious charge. Edward Holman was found guilty and was fined ten shillings. During the hearing it became known that this was not the first time this had happened, and Holman was further advised that if he did it again, he would be fined twenty shillings.[89]

John Barnes had other problems with young John Wade, so he took the opportunity in court to complain about his servant's bad behavior. He "ran up and down like a runagate," Barnes said, and "he [Barnes] could have no command over him." Barnes asked that he be freed "from any further care of inspection over him [John Wade]." The court ordered that young Wade remain with Barnes, "until he could send word to his [Wade's] father and take further order with him about him."[90]

John Wade last appears in the Plymouth Records in his father's will, dated February 7, 1683, when his father left him fifty acres of land in Scituate.[91] There is speculation that he is the same John Wade who lived in Lyme, Connecticut, but that connection has not been proven with any certainty.

American Indian Children Forced into Service

The story of King Philip's War certainly deserves much more attention than there is room for in this work, but the fates of the Native American women and children in the courts in the aftermath must be addressed. After King Philip's War, the Indigenous People, who had fought and been defeated, became wholly subject to the authority of the colonists. The Native Americans who peacefully surrendered during and after the war could settle into the towns that would accept them. On July 22, 1676, Plymouth's Council of War decided that they could stay where they had settled or be "sent to the several towns [within the colony] in some meet proportion of them, where they may have liberty at present to work for their livings, till some other place be assigned them."[92]

However, that same council ordered that "it shall be lawful for any of the magistrates of this jurisdiction to dispose of the children of those Indians that have come in and yielded themselves to the English, unto such of the English as may use them well, especially their parents consenting thereunto, during the time until such children shall attain the age of twenty four or twenty five years." With the parents' consent, or perhaps without, American Indian children were put into servitude until they were young adults. On March 6, 1677 the order was amended to require that these arrangements be formalized with signed agreements of indenture, "to prevent future differences." Later, on July 7, 1682, the courts ordered that any Native American servant who ran away to rejoin other Natives "shall be immediately apprehended," brought before the magistrates, and whipped before being sent back to his master. Any who broke the law could be sentenced into "perpetual slavery."[93,94,95]

The government of Plymouth struggled with what to do with the son of King Philip, an unnamed boy of nine. After the war, King Philip, also know as Metacom, the son of Massasoit, had been captured as a war criminal and was beheaded. His wife and son were captured and held in prison at Plymouth for several months in 1676. The fate of Metacom's wife is unknown; the fate of his son, however, raised a theological debate for the government. The colony was governed based on scriptural evidence, but there were conflicting Bible passages concerning the capture of an enemy. When the courts were unable to decide how to proceed, they sought the counsel of four of Plymouth's ministers. The question they were struggling with was whether the child should be executed because he was the son of a murderer.[96]

John Cotton, minister of Plymouth and son of John Cotton of Boston, and Samuel Arnold, minister of Marshfield, cited the passage from Deuteronomy, 24:16, which states that "fathers shall not be put to death for the children, nor the children put to death for the fathers, but every man shall be put to death for his own sin." And yet, they added, King Philip's crimes were so egregious, "horrid villainies," that some punishment was in order for his son, who "may [have been] involved in the guilt of the parents." Look at Psalm 137:8-9, they argued, which addresses the sorrow of the Jews in their exile and their longing for Jerusalem, where it does state that "Blessed shall he be that taketh and dasheth thy children [of their enemies] against the stones."[97]

Increase Mather then cited the Bible story of Joab, who killed all the males in Edom. Hadad, who was an Edomite child, escaped into Egypt. (1 Kings 11:17). Mather believed that this passage called for Metacom's child to be spared, as God had spared Hadad. James Keith, minister of Bridgewater, urged clemency, and cited 2 Chronicles 25:4, which says that when Amaziah became King of Jerusalem, "he slew his servants that had slain the King his father. But he slew not their children."[98]

With no clear decision coming from the ministers, Plymouth courts eventually decided to take the middle path. Metacom's son was spared execution but was sold into slavery. His fate is unknown, but he probably joined other American Indian slaves who were sold and shipped to the Caribbean, where they were forced to work on the sugar plantations. It is hard to imagine that a nine-year-old boy could survive for long under those circumstances.

This story demonstrates how the colony had changed in just over fifty years. Soon after arriving, the Pilgrims sat down with Massasoit and agreed on a treaty that was mutually beneficial.[99] Five decades later, Massasoit's son, Metacom, or King Philip, led a war to stop the English encroachment into the region, which was threatening the Native People's very existence. And now Metacom's son, Massasoit's grandson, had been captured by the colonists and sold into slavery as one of the outcomes of that war.[100]

Mistreatment of Servants

In many ways the master/servant relationship was similar to the relationship between a parent and child. As a result, the courts were reluctant to challenge a master's authority, just as they were unwilling to challenge that of a parent. However, sometimes the relationship between master and servant was not in the child's best interest. There are six cases of servant abuse in the court records wherein the child survived after being badly treated. In some cases, the master was not punished, but the child's service was transferred to another master.

For example, Roger Glass, a teenaged servant boy to John Crocker, was "corrected" by his master "in a most extreme and barbarous manner." The courts replaced Roger with his uncle, John Whitcomb, who paid Crocker three pounds for the boy's service. Nonetheless, Crocker was not fined or punished.[101,102]

Any complaint from a servant about mistreatment could backfire, as it did for Robert Ransom. On August 1, 1654, eighteen-year-old servant Robert Ransom brought a complaint before the court. Ransom claimed that he was "hardly used and unreasonably dealt with…by his said master," Thomas Dexter, Jr. The court heard testimony on both sides of the complaint but decided that the charge could not be proved. Ransom was warned to "carry himself better than he had formerly" or he would receive corporal punishment. He was also fined twenty shillings and spent "a night and part of a day" in jail. No charges were filed against Dexter.[103]

A father interceded in the treatment of his son by his master on June 8, 1655, when John Hall complained to the court that his son, Samuel, was being mistreated by his master Francis Baker. Hall accused Baker of "kicking [the child] and otherwise unreasonably striking of him." The child was sent home with his father on that date, but at the next court, August 7, 1655, the case was again taken up. John Hall was ordered to pay Francis Baker eight pounds "for the remainder of his servant's time unexpired." The court also allowed the child to remain with his father. Again, no charges were filed against Baker.[104]

In March 1654 Joseph Gray, servant to Thomas Gilbert, "received some hurt" and was sent to live with "Mr. Street's family" in Taunton. Some time later, Mistress Gilbert requested that Joseph be returned to her service while her husband was away in England. The courts denied her request, "until his case be heard." By 1657, the child Joseph was back in her care, and he came before the court on June 3 to complain "that he is ill-used, being decrepit, and is in want of competent and convenient clothing." Authorities in Taunton were ordered to investigate the boy's condition, and to assure that "he may be competently provided for," especially that he be provided shoes and stockings in the winter season. "We likewise desire you seriously to remember that some speedy course may be taken for the curing of the boy's foot, being in danger of perishing." The child's foot was probably frostbitten due to exposure. Even though it was clear that Joseph was being neglected, the authorities chided him "to carry towards his mistress as a servant ought to do, with all due respect and obedience."[105]

On June 6, 1654, the unnamed servant of Thomas Huckens (Huckins) complained to the court about his treatment by his master. In this case, the servant prevailed. Huckens was ordered to appear in court, and the authorities, "having heard what can be said in the case," admonished Huckens "to carry better towards his servant." He was fined four shillings for court costs.[106]

The case of John Walker is an extreme one in many ways. The fourteen-year-old servant died at the hands of his master and mistress, Robert and Susanna Latham of Marshfield. Justice in this case was sacrificed in favor of family connections and social status.

On January 31, 1655, a jury was appointed "to view the dead body of John Walker, servant to Robert Latham...to find the cause of how he came to his untimely end." The child's parents have not been identified, but he was engaged in service to Robert Latham and his wife Susanna Winslow Latham. Some sources claim that Robert Latham was the son of William Latham, who sailed on the *Mayflower* in 1620 as servant to John Carver, the colony's first governor. After Carver's death, Latham served out his term with William Bradford, and was in the second governor's household in 1627.[107,108,109]

The jury's report was read to the court on February 6, 1655:

> We, upon due search and examination, do find that the body of John Walker was blackish and blue, and the skin broken in diverse places from the middle to the hair of his head, viz, all his back with stripes given him by his master, Robert Latham, as Robert himself did testify; and also we found a bruise of his left arm, and one of his left hip, and one great bruise of his breast; and there was the knuckles of one hand and one of his fingers frozen, and also both his heels frozen, and one of the heels the flesh was much broken, and also one of his little toes frozen and very much perished, and one of his great toes frozen, and also the side of his foot frozen; and also, upon the reviewing the body, we found three gaules [galls or open sores] like holes in the hams [buttocks], which we formerly, the body being frozen, thought they had been holes.[110]

After examining the body, the jurors interviewed several witnesses:

> And also we find that the said John was forced to carry a log which was beyond his strength, which he endeavoring to do, the log fell upon him, and he, being down, had a stripe or two, as Joseph Beedle doth testify; and we find that it was some few days before his death; and we find, by the testimony of John Howland and John Adams, that heard Robert Latham say that he gave John Walker some stripes that morning before his death; and also we find the flesh much broken of the knees of John Walker.[111]

The jury concluded that the child:

> Did want sufficient food and clothing and lodging, and
> that the said John did constantly wet his bed and his
> clothes, lying in them, and so suffered by it, his clothes
> being frozen about him; and that the said John was put
> forth in the extremity of cold, though thus unabled by
> lameness and soreness to perform what was required;
> and therefore in respect of cruelty and hard usage he
> died.[112]

The jury held a "second review" of the case and administered
the trial by touch, as explained previously. Unlike the Batson case,
however, this time "the dead corpse did bleed at the nose." Robert
Latham was questioned by the court and held over for trial. At the next
court, March 6, 1655, he was indicted "for felonious cruelty done unto
John Walker, his servant, aged about fourteen years, by unreasonable
correction, by withholding necessary food and clothing, and by
exposing his said servant to extremity of seasons, whereof the said John
Walker languished and immediately died, the 15 day of January, anno
1655."[113]

Latham was judged guilty of "manslaughter by chance medley,"
meaning there was no malice aforethought, no plan ahead of time to
kill the child. But then things became even more complicated.

Robert Latham invoked his right to the ancient English custom
known as "benefit of clergy." Dating back to the twelfth century, the
custom held that clergy could only be tried in ecclesiastical courts. To
prove one was a member of the clergy, a literacy test was required;
the defendant had to prove he could read passages from the Bible.
Over time, lay defendants tried to claim "benefit of clergy" and in 1351
Edward III made it official that the privilege was available to all who
could read. Psalm 51 was traditionally used in the literacy test, and
on occasion a clever but illiterate person would memorize the psalm,
recite it, and claim benefit of clergy. The case could then be referred
to an ecclesiastical court, where judgment and punishment were
generally more lenient. Over time, this custom evolved and became a

way for an otherwise guilty defendant to escape hanging. On the other hand, under the severe laws in early England, reciting the "mercy psalm" saved many from unfair and unreasonable punishments. In Latham's case, it was clearly an attempt to escape justice.

Robert Latham read the "neck verse" before the courts at his trial, Psalm 51, verse 1, "Have mercy on me, O God, after thy great goodness, according to the multitude of thy mercies do away with mine offenses." After reading the psalm, his sentence was pronounced, "that the said Robert Latham should be burned in the hand, and his having no lands, that all his goods are confiscate[d] unto his highness the Lord Protector; and that the said sentence should be forthwith executed; which accordingly was performed the 4th of March, 1655." His life was spared, but he was branded, and all his belongings were confiscated.[114]

Three months after Robert was punished for John Walker's death, on June 8, 1655, the court addressed the guilt of Robert's wife, Susanna: "We present Susanna, the wife of Robert Latham, for being in a great measure guilty, with her said husband, in exercising cruelly towards their late servant, John Walker, in not affording him convenient food, raiment, and lodging; especially, in her husband's absence, in forcing him to bring a log beyond his strength."[115]

Kenhelm Winslow testified on the child's behalf, testifying that Joseph Beedle told him that he [Beedle] "came forth and took the log [off] of the boy...." While the jury found "this presentment a true presentment," no action was taken at that court, but Susanna's culpability in the crime was again addressed three years later.[116]

On June 1, 1658, the court record states, "Whereas Susanna Latham hath stood presented unto this court for sundry years for cruelty toward John Walker, servant to Robert Latham, these are to signify, that accordingly as it was manifested in the court, that if any will come in, they shall have full and free liberty to prosecute against her at the next October court, or otherwise that then the said presentment shall be erased out of the court records." The court was clearly reluctant to hold Susanna accountable, leaving it up to the colonists to decide whether or not she would be held liable for the child's death.[117]

Apparently, no one was willing to bring charges against her, and once again the issue came before the court three months later. "At the court held at Plymouth the 5th of October 1658, proclamation was made three times in the court, that if any would prosecute against Susanna Latham according to this order, they should be heard; but none appeared in the case, and according to this order, her presentment was erased out of the records of the court."[118]

Why was Susanna Latham so favored? Her father, John Winslow, Sr., had two brothers who sailed to Plymouth on the *Mayflower*; John himself arrived in Plymouth in 1621 aboard the *Fortune*. Her mother, Mary Chilton, was also a *Mayflower* passenger. Susanna's parents were well thought of in the colony and perhaps in deference to them no one pursued her guilt.

In 1657, Robert Latham was declared a freeman. Ironically, Robert Latham was before the courts on July 5, 1669, complaining against his son-in-law for the treatment of his daughter:

> In answer to the petition of Robert Latham, and his daughter, the wife of Isaack Harris, wherein he complained of great neglect of the said Harris in not taking care of his wife's comfortable subsistence, being departed the government, and hath left her, with her child, to be burdensome to the said Robert Latham, her father, and that, notwithstanding such order as the court hath formerly taken, she is neglected to be supplied with such necessaries for her subsistence as is meet, this court doth order and authorize the selectmen of the town of Bridgewater, viz, Lieut. Haward [also known as Hayward or Howard], John Willis, Sr., and John Carey, to take notice of what visible estate appertained unto the said Isaac Harris, and to take into their custody, and to improve it for the relief and subsistence of his wife, aforesaid, and that they be careful to keep a due account of their receipts and disbursements on that behalf.[119]

Even with his role in the death of young John Walker, Robert Latham was considered a worthy citizen of Plymouth. In 1667,

1668, and 1670, he worked on committees to lay out the highways in Bridgewater. In 1672 he served as Bridgewater's constable. On the other hand, on June 3, 1679, he was fined by the courts for "being twice drunk," and had to pay ten shillings.[120,121,122]

Chapter Eight

Notable Women of Plymouth

While we know a great deal about women's relationships with men in Plymouth Colony, mainly that they were subservient, we do not know much about women's relationships among themselves. Were some women regarded as having a higher social status than others? If so, what were the attributes that gave a woman prestige and position relative to other women? Were women ranked among their peers in accordance with the position of their spouses? Were women with wealthy husbands given more respect than those of the destitute? Unfortunately, these issues were not addressed in the records left by the Pilgrims.

We do know that there was no formal aristocracy in Plymouth, no privileged class that ruled through heritage. Edward Winslow wrote that the royal hierarchy was one of the things, "which we came from thence to avoid." There would be no lords or ladies in the new colony.[1]

As far as privilege for the wealthy was concerned, the Separatists downplayed the desirability of riches. It was believed that somewhere comfortable between wealth and poverty was the most desirable state. Robinson wrote that, "both poverty and riches, if they be in any extremity, have their temptations, and those not small,.... And, in truth, the middle state is freest from the greatest danger either of sin, or misery, in the world." The wealthy were at the most risk, he added; "for hardly doth anything cause the mind to swell more with pride, than riches...." It cannot be denied, however, that there were rich and poor among the passengers on the *Mayflower*. John Carver was perhaps among the wealthier as he was able to invest substantially in the venture from his own personal estate. He also brought five indentured servants and took in an orphan as well. Carver was elected the colony's first governor.[2,3,4]

Once the Pilgrims landed at Plymouth and began the hard, dirty work of building a settlement, wealth and social position may have become irrelevant. Everyone was in the same position, rich and poor, men and women. The illnesses that began to spread affected them all regardless of who they were. With social hierarchy somewhat flattened out, other attributes began to mark a man or a woman's reputation. The ability to work hard and get along was probably most desirable in the men; besides that, for the women it was character that became most important.

It was usually on the occasion of a woman's death that her character was commented upon, but even that honor was reserved for only a few. It wasn't that there were so few women of sterling character at Plymouth, but that it was not the custom to single someone out for praise during their lifetimes.

There were a few women who are notable in the history of Plymouth colony, not so much for their accomplishments, but for their uprightness. Their reputations were spotless; their piety unquestionable.

Mary Brewster

Only one woman was with the Pilgrims from the beginning—Mary Brewster, the wife of Elder William Brewster. William Brewster had been the postmaster at Scrooby Manor, and the leader of the original Separatist congregation. Little is known about Mary's early life; not even her parentage is certain. She was likely born around 1569, and married William in about 1592. She eventually bore him six children, one of whom died in Leiden.[5]

As his wife, Mary was the mistress of Scrooby Manor, responsible for directing many of the day-to-day activities of this stop on the Great North Road. When her husband became more involved in Separatism, Mary joined him in attending services at Reverend Clyfton's dissenting congregation in Babworth in defiance of royal decrees. Later, when William began holding his own meetings at the manor house for the nascent Separatist group, no doubt Mary served as hostess and

A view of Scrooby Village.

provided the table for her husband's fledgling congregation. When the orphan boy, William Bradford, joined her family, she became a mother to him, and most likely was the role model the future colonial governor sought in a wife and mother for his own family.

When the Pilgrims decided to separate from the Church of England so they could practice their religion freely, they also resolved to leave their home country. What Mary Brewster or any of the other Separatists' wives thought of this plan is nowhere recorded. But the women and their children were a necessary part of the proposal. This was to be an enterprise of families.

After several unfortunate attempts, in 1608 the Separatists finally made a successful escape from England, or at least some of them did. Most of the men had already boarded a ship ready to sail to Amsterdam. A few of the remaining men and all the women and children were some distance away, having come separately in a bark, a small sailing ship. They were on the Humber River, stuck on a sandbar, waiting for a rising tide to release them.[6]

At this most inopportune moment, the king's men appeared, determined to capture the law-breaking Dissenters. The captain of the ship, seeing the danger they all were in, quickly gave the order to weigh anchor, hoist the sails and set off, leaving the women, including Mary Brewster, to fend for themselves. Bradford writes that the men were in "great distress for their wives and children which they saw thus to be taken and were left destitute of their helps."[7] Undoubtedly the women were terrified and in great distress as well, both for themselves and their children.

The women were taken into custody by the local magistrates, and, Bradford reports, "pitiful it was to see the heavy case of these poor women in this distress; what weeping and crying on every side, some for their husbands that were carried away in the ship as is before related; others not knowing what should become of them and their little ones; others again melted in tears seeing their poor little ones hanging about them, crying for fear, and quaking with cold."[8]

What is not clear is if William Brewster, a wanted man, was with Mary and their children—Jonathan, about fifteen, Patience, about eight, and Fear, only two—when they were captured, or on the ship on its way to Amsterdam, or perhaps in custody himself. Bradford only tells us that the women and children were shifted about, "conveyed from one constable to another," until they were finally released. He does not relate the details, and gives only a veiled suggestion of their difficulties, the "many other notable passages and troubles which they endured and underwent in these their wanderings and travels both at land and sea." "In the end," he reports, "notwithstanding all these storms of opposition, they all got over [to Amsterdam] at length, some at one time, and some at another, and some in one place, and some in another, and met together again according to their desires, with no small rejoicing." There were about one hundred twenty-five members of the Scrooby congregation who ultimately reached Amsterdam and reunited.[9]

After a short stay in Amsterdam, the Pilgrim congregation settled in Leiden, where Brewster, then the ruling elder, began to publish books, setting the type himself and taking it to a local printer. He was soon in trouble for producing books about the dissenting movement and smuggling them illegally into Scotland. In 1619, to escape arrest, Brewster went into hiding, most likely in England. The unwelcome attention to the little Separatist congregation was probably one of the unspoken reasons the group began to consider relocating once again, this time to the New World.[10,11,12]

While the preparations were being made to pack up and leave Leiden, Mary was once again on her own, now a mother of five. She was fifty-two years old when the family left the city, and it probably wasn't until they arrived in Southampton, England, to board the *Mayflower* that she was reunited with William Brewster.

After a terrifying voyage of more than two months, the first winter in Plymouth was devastating for the Pilgrims. Half of the party died due to disease and exposure. While the men began to build houses on shore, the women remained on board the *Mayflower* nursing the sick and comforting the dying. Mary was one of only a handful of adult women to survive, but her health had been damaged. On December 20, 1623, John Robinson wrote to William of his hope that "Mrs. Brewster's weak and decayed state of body will have some repairing by the coming of her daughters." In 1623, her daughters, Patience and Fear, arrived at Plymouth aboard the *Anne*. Their presence must have been a comfort to her, as Robinson had hoped. All her living children were together, her son Jonathan having sailed to Plymouth in 1621 on board the *Fortune*.[13] On April 16, 1627, Mary Brewster died. She was about fifty-eight years old. Her husband lived another seventeen years and never remarried. He was one of the founders of Duxbury, incorporated in 1637, and continued to live there with their son, Love. William Brewster died on April 10, 1644.[14,15]

There is no mention of Mary Brewster in the Plymouth Colony records; nor is she mentioned in Bradford's history of the colony, not even in his lengthy memorial to Brewster on the occasion of his death in 1644. In that tribute, Bradford wrote that Brewster had "done and suffered much,…and bore his part in well and woe…[for more than] 36 years in England, Holland and in this wilderness…." Certainly, the same could have – and should have - been said of his wife.[16,17]

Katherine Carver

The first First Lady of Plymouth was Katherine Carver, wife of Governor John Carver, but their time at Plymouth was very short. John had been instrumental in getting the entire enterprise started and paid for. Nathaniel Morton wrote that Carver "being one … of a considerable estate, spent the main part of it in this enterprise." With his combination of both capital and experience, he became a chief organizer of the *Mayflower* voyage. Katherine White was John's second wife, and both were members of the Separatist congregation in Leiden, where John was a deacon. The couple had no children. Katherine was related to John Robinson through marriage; her sister Bridget was married to the Pilgrim pastor, who called John, "my dear brother," and Katherine, "my loving sister" in their correspondence.[18,19,20,21]

The couple sailed on the *Mayflower* along with Desire Minter, who was perhaps a relative, and four servants: John Howland, Roger Wilder, eleven-year-old William Latham, and an unnamed "maidservant" for Katherine. They also took in one of the More children, Jasper. The Carvers, probably the wealthiest of the *Mayflower* passengers, may have been given a more comfortable cabin on board, and enjoyed some deference, but that is unknown.[22]

John Carver fully participated in the first land expeditions once the *Mayflower* reached Cape Cod Harbor. As a major organizer of the venture, he may have a hand in writing the Mayflower Compact, but the agreement's authorship is unknown. Once all the signatures were secured, the company "chose, or rather confirmed, Mr. John Carver (a man godly and well approved amongst them) their Governor for that year." It seemed the choice of Carver as governor was a foregone conclusion, "confirmed" rather than elected, but he had shown full commitment to the venture, working alongside everyone else.[23]

Carver deserves much credit for the treaty that was signed with Massasoit on March 22, 1621. "With drum and trumpet after him, and some few musketeers," Governor Carver approached the American Indian sachem and kissed his hand. After refreshments of "strong" water and "a little fresh meat," the treaty of peace was negotiated. The treaty stood for more than fifty years.[24]

Only a month later, John Carver died. He was working in the fields in April during the Pilgrims' first spring at New Plymouth. William Bradford described Carver's death: "In this month of April, whilst they were busy about [planting] their seed, their Governor (Mr. John Carver) came out of the field very sick, it being a hot day. He complained greatly of his head and lay down, and within a few hours his sense failed, so as he never spake more till he died, which was within a few days after."[25]

Carver's death, most likely from a stroke, was a blow to the infant colony. He was well respected as a leader and highly esteemed as the primary investor in the whole venture. Bradford wrote that Carver's death "was much lamented and caused great heaviness amongst them, as there was cause. He was buried in the best manner they could, with some volleys of shot by all that bore arms."[26] Nathaniel Morton praised Carver after his death, writing that he was a man of "singular piety, and…humility."[27]

It was less than two months later that Katherine followed her husband in death. Bradford noted that "[Carter's] wife, being a weak woman, died within five or six weeks after him." Morton adds that her death was caused by "excessive grief for the loss of so gracious a husband." He further adds, in one of those rare instances of commenting on a woman's character, that Katherine, "his wife…was also a gracious woman." To the Pilgrims, the Carvers' demeanor was proof that they were the recipients of divine grace and among the chosen. [28,29]

The Carvers left no children; William Bradford, however, wrote about what happened to those who were in the Carver company on the *Mayflower*. His servant, Roger Wilder, and the child, Jasper More, died during the first sickness. Desire Minter returned to England, but she "proved not very well" and died there. Latham, the servant boy, lived for twenty years in Plymouth. Later, he returned to England, and then sailed to the Bahama Islands. "There with some others [he] was starved for want of food." Katherine's maidservant "married and died a year or two after." She remains unnamed. Servant John Howland married Elizabeth Tilley, daughter of John Tilley. They had ten children and left numerous descendants.[30]

Alice Carpenter Southworth Bradford

In 1623, the *Anne* and the *Little James* sailed into Plymouth Harbor carrying about ninety passengers eager to join the colony. Some were from Leiden, Separatists left behind when the *Mayflower* sailed in

1620. The colony was about three years old and expectations must
have been high among its newest arrivals. They were not prepared
for what they found as they came ashore, and, apparently, could not
hide their disappointment. Governor Bradford remarked that when
the new arrivals saw the colonists, they "were much daunted and
dismayed." Some "fell a-weeping...pitying the distress they saw their
friends had long been in...."[31]

The Pilgrims, seeing themselves reflected in the disappointment
in their friends' eyes, must have realized the pathetic nature of their
situation. "Many were ragged in apparel [with] some little better than
half-naked." Seeing their shocked faces, the colonists could not deny
that despite all their work and all their suffering, the settlement was
still a primitive and desolate place, barely inhabitable. "Only some
of their old friends rejoiced to see them," Bradford miserably wrote.
But it was the governor himself who must have rejoiced when he saw
among the stunned newcomers Alice Southworth. It was her reaction
that probably concerned him the most.[32]

When the *Mayflower* returned to England on April 5, 1621, there
were no Pilgrims on board; there were, however, several letters written
by them to loved ones in Leiden. William Bradford undoubtedly
wrote to family and friends about his wife's death. Surely, more
correspondence came to Plymouth late in the year when the *Fortune*
arrived, and on the *Sparrow*, which arrived in 1622. Among the news
from Holland, William Bradford would have learned of the death of
Edward Southworth, which was significant to him.

Edward Southworth was a member of the Leiden Separatist
congregation. He had married Alice Carpenter on May 28, 1613, the
same year that William Bradford had married Dorothy May. They
undoubtedly knew each other; they would have worshiped together,
and both William and Edward were fabric weavers. More important,
Bradford would have known Southworth's wife, Alice Carpenter.
Perhaps there was some correspondence between the governor and
the widow, perhaps Bradford expressed an interest in Alice, perhaps
he invited her to come to Plymouth to be his wife. We can only
speculate; no correspondence, if there was any between the two,
has survived.[33]

Alice Southworth left two sons in Leiden—Constant, born about 1612, and Thomas, born about 1617. Alice sailed on the *Anne*, which arrived on July 10; her sister, Juliana, with her husband, George Morton, and their five children, were on the *Little James*, which arrived about a week later.[34,35]

Alice had four sisters, all of whom were linked with Plymouth Colony. Besides Juliana Carpenter Morton, sister Agnes Carpenter married Samuel Fuller in Leiden, but died before the group left for Plymouth. Mary Carpenter never married, but she did join her sisters in Plymouth sometime between 1644 and 1646. Governor Bradford wrote and warned her not to expect too much when she came to Plymouth, but Mary came to the colony anyway. She remained very close to her sister Alice, and lived to the age of ninety-one. Priscilla Carpenter married William Wright and came to Plymouth between 1627 and 1633. Following the family penchant for longevity, Priscilla lived to be ninety-two.[36]

Despite any disappointment she may have felt about her new home, Alice Carpenter Southworth married William Bradford on August 14, 1623, just less than a month after arrival in Plymouth.[37] It was a celebration of "great cheer," according to a witness, Emmanuel Altham:

> Upon the occasion of the Governor's marriage, since I came, Massasoit was sent for to the wedding, where came with him his wife, the queen, although he hath five wives. With him came four other kings and about six score men with their bows and arrows - where, when they came to our town, we saluted them with the shooting off of many muskets and training our men. And so all the bows and arrows [were] brought into the Governor's house, and he brought the Governor three or four bucks and a turkey. And so we had very good pastime in seeing them dance, which is in such manner, with such a noise that you would wonder.[38]

And now to say somewhat of the great cheer we had at the Governor's marriage. We had about twelve pasty venisons, besides others, pieces of roasted venison and other such good cheer in such quantity that I could wish you some of our share. For here we have the best grapes that ever you saw—and the biggest, and divers sorts of plums and nuts which our business will not suffer us to look for.[39]

Their first son, named William, was born July 17, 1624. They had two more children, Mercy, born May 22, 1627, and Joseph, born about 1630. The Bradford home must have been a busy one. Alice's children with Edward Southworth—Constant and Thomas—came to Plymouth in 1628, probably resided with them. Her nephew, Nathaniel Morton, author of the Plymouth history, *New England's Memorial*, may have lived with the family for a while. John, Bradford's son with his first wife, Dorothy, came to Plymouth sometime in 1627, when he was about twelve, and likewise joined the family. It may be that Mary Carpenter, Alice's sister, lived in their home, too.[40,41]

William Bradford was governor of the colony for the better part of thirty years, with few interruptions. Many of the court's meetings were held in the Bradfords' home and Alice provided hospitality, "entertaining our honored governor and magistrates...." After the governor's death, on May 9, 1657, she continued to accommodate the court, and was reimbursed her expenses several times.[42,43]

Alice Carpenter Southworth Bradford died March 27, 1670; she was about eighty years old. It appears that she was ill during her later years, "afflicted much with heavy pain," according to her nephew, Nathaniel Morton. A reference to her death was written into the court record, an unusual entry for a woman: "On the 26 day of March 1670, Mistress Alice Bradford, Sr., changed this life for a better, having attained to fourscore years of age, or thereabouts. She was a godly matron, and much loved while she lived, and lamented, though aged, when she died, and was honorably enterred on the 29 day of the month aforesaid, at New Plymouth."[44,45]

In her will she stated that: "I bequeath my soul to God that gave it and my body to the dust in hope of a joyful resurrection unto glory, desiring that my body may be interred as near unto my deceased husband, Mr. William Bradford, as conveniently may be." She had been married to Bradford for thirty-four years.[46]

In an ode to his "loving friend, my aunt and mother," Nathaniel Morton wrote that she "lived a life in holiness and faith, …in reading of God's word and contemplation,…. Her life was never stained with any sin that anyone could tell." He added, "Her glass is run, her work is done, and she is happy unto all eternity."[47]

❧❧❧

Three other of Plymouth's women are famous today, their lives as Pilgrims embellished over the years in fictional accounts. The story of Plymouth Colony and the Pilgrims gained more popularity and attention during the mid-nineteenth century when several incidents revived interest in the settlement. Bradford's history, *Of Plymouth Plantation*, was published in Boston in 1856. In 1858, Henry Wadsworth Longfellow wrote "The Courtship of Miles Standish," which sold more than 10,000 copies on the day of its publication in London. In 1846, Sarah Josepha Hale, editor of the popular *Godey's Lady's Book,* wanted to make the local New England custom of a day of thanksgiving into a national celebration, a national Thanksgiving holiday. She campaigned vigorously, using her columns in what was one of America's most influential periodicals.[48,49]

While Hale did not witness an official declaration of Thanksgiving in her lifetime, she did contribute to a national interest in the Pilgrims. Families desirous of linking themselves to these early settlers unearthed legends and stories about their ancestors. Many of these stories became so well known that they came to be accepted as truth, as was the case with the next three women.

Mary Chilton Winslow

In 1815, an article appeared in *The Collections of the Massachusetts Historical Society,* which consisted of notations about Plymouth Colony that had been collected by Samuel Davis. Under "Forefather's

Mary Chilton stepping on Plymouth Rock.

Rock," he noted, "There is a tradition, as to the person who first leaped upon this rock, when the families came to shore, December 11, 1620: it is said to have been a young woman, Mary Chilton." His source was a story handed down orally through several generations, and was, admittedly, weak and unreliable.[50]

Davis himself admits skepticism about the claim, writing "We are disposed, however, to generalize the anecdote. The first generation doubtless know who came on shore in the first boats; the second generation related it with less identity; the third and fourth with still less: like the stone thrown on the calm lake, the circles, well defined at first, become fainter as they recde." Nonetheless, Mary's descendants remain undeterred, and the legend has persisted.[51,52]

Mary Chilton was the daughter of Leiden Separatists James and Susanna Chilton. She was baptized on May 31, 1607, in Sandwich, Kent, England. She was about thirteen years old when she boarded the *Mayflower* with her parents. Her father was the oldest passenger, at sixty-four. He died soon after arriving at Plymouth, in December 1620; her mother passed away in early 1621. Now an orphan, Mary would have been placed with another family, but it is not known which one it was. In 1623, at sixteen, she received a share in the

Division of Land, which was located just between the allotments to John Alden and Capt. Myles Standish.[53,54,55]

In about 1626 Mary Chilton married John Winslow, who came to Plymouth in 1621 on the *Fortune*. In the 1627 Division of Cattle, she was listed in the sixth lot along with her husband. Their first child was born that same year, and they eventually produced ten children, nine of whom survived. About 1671, the family moved to Boston, where John became very wealthy and bought a mansion—complete with beautiful gardens—for five hundred pounds.[56,57,58]

In 1674, John Winslow died. He left to Mary, "my dear and well-beloved wife,…the use of my now dwelling house with the gardens and yards thereunto [and] the use of all my household goods for her to dispose of as she shall think meet, [and] the sum of four hundred pounds in lawful money." He also noted that "my Negro Girl Jane," be freed, after she has served twenty years longer in the service of his wife, attesting to the fact that Winslow was a slave owner.[59,60]

Mary Chilton Winslow died in Boston on May 1, 1679. She died a wealthy woman, with several pieces of table silver and large furniture items listed in her estate inventory. She named six children and several grandchildren among her heirs. No mention is made of Jane; however, Mary left five pounds to the pastor of her church.[61]

Inspired by the stirring legend, many artistic depictions have been made of Mary Chilton at the moment of her first step onto Plymouth Rock. Like other fanciful aspects of the Plymouth Colony story, the myth of Mary Chilton has come to be accepted as fact by many. But it is rare that any recalling of the legend also includes the fact that in 1655, Mary Chilton Winslow's daughter, Susanna and her husband, Robert Latham, were indicted for the neglect and death of their servant boy John Walker, as discussed above.

Priscilla Mullins

Among the passengers on the *Mayflower* was the Mullins family—William, his wife, and two children, Joseph and Priscilla. A servant, Robert Carter, accompanied them. All of them died the first winter except Priscilla. She eventually married John Alden and had eleven children. Her story is similar to that of many other Pilgrim women, and she probably would have drifted into obscurity, except that in 1858 Henry Wadsworth Longfellow published a narrative poem entitled "The Courtship of Miles Standish."[62]

Longfellow was a descendant of John Alden on his mother's side. He probably grew up listening to family lore about his ancestor and that first cold winter, a time of adversity, suffering, and death. Out of that history came his poem, his family's own origin story.[63]

The poem relates the story of recently widowed Myles Standish, who asks the younger John Alden to approach Priscilla Mullins and tell her that, "a blunt old Captain, a man not of words but of actions, / Offers his hand and his heart, the hand and heart of a soldier." John Alden has feelings of his own for Priscilla, whom he has "loved, and waited, and worshipped in silence." Alden goes on his errand, "urging the suit of his friend," only to have Priscilla retort, in a tremulous voice, "Why don't you speak for yourself, John?" As the *Mayflower* sails back to England, Priscilla explains to John, "Certainly you can forgive me for speaking so frankly, for saying / What I ought not to have said, yet now I can never unsay it." "It was wrong," says Priscilla in the poem, "I acknowledge; for it is the fate of a woman / Long to be patient and silent, to wait like a ghost that is speechless."[64]

Standish feels betrayed by Alden, and Alden feels guilty for being disloyal to a friend. Anger breaks up their friendship. Standish goes off to fight the Native Americans and returns to Plymouth with the severed head of Wattawamat, shocking Priscilla and causing her to thank God "in her heart that she had not married Miles Standish."[65]

In the poem months pass, and Alden's love for Priscilla only grows. "Ever of her he thought as he went about his daily chores and read his Bible," wrote Longfellow. He visits her one day as she is spinning wool when word comes that Myles Standish has been killed in battle with the American Indians. With his friend dead, John realizes that he is now free to pursue Priscilla on his own: "pressing her close to his heart, as forever his own, and exclaiming: 'Those whom the Lord hath united, let no man put them asunder!'"[66]

John Alden and Priscilla Mullins.

On their wedding day, John and Priscilla are shocked to see the quite alive Myles Standish enter the house, "boldly there in his armor." He begs Alden's forgiveness, blames his "hot blood," wishes Priscilla joy, and lauds her new husband.[67]

Longfellow's poem was wildly popular, reportedly selling twenty-five thousand copies within the first two months of publication. The romantic story of Priscilla and John would be firmly and permanently planted into America's history. If only it were true.[68]

What is true is that in 1620 John Alden joined the Pilgrim adventure in Southampton at the age of about twenty-one. He was hired as a barrel maker, responsible for keeping the barrels of food and drink on board secure and leak-free during the voyage. He was not a Separatist, but when given the opportunity to stay in New Plymouth or return to England, he decided to remain with the colonists. It is also true that he did indeed marry the orphaned Priscilla Mullins.

With his carpentry and woodworking skills, John Alden made a very practical contribution to the building of the colony. In 1631, he was elected as one of the governor's assistants, a position he held for several years. Due to his many years of public service, John Alden became "low in his estate," and in 1660, the courts voted him a stipend of ten pounds to help cover his expenses. He apparently remained a friend of Capt. Standish, since both moved their families out of Plymouth town into the new village of Duxbury in 1632.[69,70]

There is only one entry in the Plymouth Colony Records for

Priscilla Alden, the 1627 Division of Cattle, where the Alden family is assigned to John Howland's Lot Number Four.[71]

John Alden died on September 12, 1687 and was eulogized in a long obituary that praises him for being "holy, humble, and sincere," a man who "honored God with much integrity." There is no mention of Priscilla, who is believed to have died sometime in 1680.[72]

In 1930 two memorial stones were placed at the Myles Standish Burial Ground in Duxbury. The stone for John Alden reads: "Near here lyes ye body of Mr. John Alden who died in Duxbury Sept ye 12, 1687, aged Near 88 years; erected by the Alden Kindred of America 1930." Priscilla's memorial simply reads: "In memory of Mrs. Priscilla Alden, wife of John Alden, who died in Duxbury. Erected by the Alden Kindred of America, 1930." The couple had ten children born between 1624 and 1642.[73,74,75]

Elizabeth Poole

In his journal, Governor Winthrop of Massachusetts Colony wrote: "This year [1637] a plantation was begun at Tecticutt [Titicut] by a gentlewoman, an ancient maid, one Mrs. Poole. She went thither, and endured much hardship, and lost much cattle. Called, after[ward] Taunton." Whether or not Elizabeth Poole was the founder of Taunton, previously called Tetticut and Cohanett, is still debated, but her influence on the town's settlement and growth cannot be denied.[76]

Elizabeth Poole was baptized in Shute, Devonshire, England, on August 25, 1588. She sailed from England in 1637, on the *Speedwell*, bringing with her two friends, fourteen servants, goods valued at one hundred pounds, and twenty tons of salt to preserve fish. Elizabeth was not yet fifty, hardly the "ancient maid," and unmarried. Her brother William, who was five years younger, was already in Taunton, and had been named a freeman there on March 7, 1637. Clearly, they came from wealth.[77,78,79]

On another ship right behind Elizabeth were "bullocks and heifers," cattle brought by the Pooles to start a livestock herd. Elizabeth and her brother must have realized the potential market for beef as they were undoubtedly aware of the immigrants pouring into Boston and the Bay Colony during the Great Migration of Puritans to New England. The cattle being brought to the colonies were bound for the Poole's farm, but they arrived during the cold season and barely survived. To protect the animals from the freezing weather, Elizabeth and her servants had to "excavate places for stalls in the side of a hill, which so far as possible were sheltered by limbs of trees." As Winthrop noted, many head of cattle were lost. Yet, some must have survived, and their livestock holdings grew.[80,81,82]

They and their neighbors needed more acreage to graze their growing herds, and as a result they appealed to Plymouth courts to obtain more land grants. On March 3, 1640, the inhabitants of Cohanett, "now called Taunton," requested more meadow land. The court "seriously weighed and considered" the request and found that "unless they be supplied of meadow land, they cannot comfortably there subsist." The court agreed to grant the land, "to them and their heirs, to have and hold…forever," but only if the residents there promise to "continue in a church estate," and live on the land for the next seven years. Special provisions were made for extra land for three residents, "Mr. Hooke, Mrs. Streete, and Mistress Poole,…competent meadow and uplands for farms laid forth for them."[83]

For Elizabeth Poole, "competent meadow and uplands for farms" meant two hundred acres of upland, as well as forty acres of meadow, "at her farm at Littleworth,…being at the end next unto her house," and for her home lot, an additional fifteen acres. Myles Standish helped lay out the land, but the boundaries were vague, a detail which would cause problems later on. This grant appears to be the source of Elizabeth's holdings, though that is still up for debate.[84,85]

What is not in question is that she made the most of her grant, improving her land, growing her herds, and planting an orchard. Not only did she improve her own holdings, but she also invested in the future of Taunton by becoming a shareholder in 1654 in the Taunton Iron Works Company, along with her brother and niece.[86]

In 1654, "being sick and weak, yet of perfect memory and understanding," Elizabeth Poole, at the "age of sixty-five or thereabouts," made her will. She bequeathed most of her extensive property holdings to her brother, William, including her house in Taunton with its orchard, the forty acres she owned at Littleworth Farm, the hundred acres on the further side of the river, her current dwelling house, the other house she bought from Robert Thornton, and the land that came with it, her fifty acres by Two Mile Meadow, and the adjoining meadow. This was quite an impressive legacy.[87]

She left to her "cousin John Pole [Poole] all my household stuff and goods within," and to cousin Mary Pole, "one cow at my decease and all my apparel and wearing clothes." Ever the practical Pilgrim, Elizabeth asked that if the clothes do not fit Mary, that she "make sale thereof and put it into some stock that may be to her benefit." Ever the devout Pilgrim, she also left to "the Church of God at Taunton for the furtherance of any special service thereof one cow which so ever the overseers shall like best to take for that end after my decease." Her shares in the proposed iron works, she left to her cousin John Pole, urging him to "attend unto and to show all due respect unto his parents." To her "kind and old friend Sister Margery Paule, widow, one yearling heifer...." The will was presented to the court on June 6, 1656. An inventory of Elizabeth Poole's estate, "besides her housing and land," added up to over one hundred eighty-eight pounds.[88]

Clearly Elizabeth was successful in managing her properties, and for that she deserves admiration and praise, but her legacy has become much larger than that.

Fifteen years after her death a dispute surfaced over property boundaries within Taunton and with neighboring townships which led to an examination of the original grants and purchases. In January 1669, the town of Taunton appointed a committee of ten residents to research property holdings and boundaries, "so that the town may be freed from future damages." On March 2, 1669, the Plymouth court confirmed the order and added that "some fit persons be appointed out of each of the said townships to run the said lines." If an agreement could not be reached, then the court would step in.[89,90]

By December it was clear that an agreement was still not forthcoming, and representatives of the towns were ordered to "agree the case between themselves," or the court would impanel a jury "to bring the said controversy to a final issue and settlement." By January, relations between the towns' agents had not improved. Bridgewater's representatives, for one, expressed their lack of cooperation by refusing to attend meetings. The court ordered a hearing on the matter. An official report would not be presented until 1680, over ten years later.[91]

"At the town meeting held May 25, 1680, this committee of ten, appointed January 10, 1669, or a major part of them, made their report." The report acknowledged that the settlers of Taunton received land grants from Plymouth, but that they also "made purchase and bought the said tracts of land for our money [from] the right proprietors and owners, the Indians' Sachem or Prince of that part of the country... bought with our money in peace."[92]

This is where Elizabeth Poole comes in. Elizabeth Poole is not listed among the original purchasers of the land that would later become Taunton, although her brother William is. However, another document shows that Elizabeth Poole, and only Elizabeth Poole, bought the property that would become Taunton from the Indigenous People in a land deal later called "The Tetticut Purchase."[93,94]

In 1686, as part of their efforts to settle the property boundary disputes, a quitclaim deed was recorded which stated that "Mrs. Elizabeth Poole formerly of Taunton in the Government of New Plymouth aforesaid did, for and in behalf of the said Town of Taunton purchase ye lands of Tetticut in the year one thousand six hundred thirty and seven, and that the right owners of the said lands did then make sale thereof to the said Mrs. Elizabeth Poole as abovesaid and received pay of her for it." The document was signed by Native Americans Joseph, Peter and David Hunter, who had personal knowledge of the transaction and claimed it was supported "both by Indian and English testimonies." The lands of the Tetticut were sold by its lawful owners, "those Indians or Indian Sachems that formerly were the right owners of those lands," and they were sold to Elizabeth Poole.[95] This may have been the purchase referred to by Governor Winthrop above.

Did Elizabeth purchase the land in her own name? No record lists her as the owner of more property than had been granted to her by the court. Was she acting as an agent for the town's settlers? She may have been the only resident with enough resources to cover the transaction. If so, how much did she pay? To the last question, a claim is made that she purchased the land "for a jackknife and a peck of beans." The proof of this story rests again in oral tradition, a tale that was supposedly passed from grandmother to grandmother dating back to 1710.[96]

Whatever the truth, Elizabeth Poole's story had become a part of the legacy claimed by the town of Taunton. A plaque exists in front of the Pilgrim Congregational Church depicting her with a cow and bearing the inscription, "Unto the Church of God in Taunton I leave one cow." Her grave in Plain Cemetery is marked with a large metal sign which calls visitors' attention to the gravesite and identifies her as the "chief promoter of Taunton and its incorporation." The Taunton town seal depicts Elizabeth making the purchase from two seated Native Americans, and the city's motto, borrowed from Vergil, is "Dux Femina Facti," or "A woman led the deed."[97,98,99]

The inscription on her tombstone reads: "Here rest the remains of Elizabeth Poole, a native of Old England, of good family, friends and prospects, all which she left in the prime of her life, to enjoy the religion of her conscience, in this distant wilderness; a great proprietor of the township of Taunton, a chief promoter of its settlement, and its incorporation in 1639-40; about which time she settled near this spot, and having employed the opportunity of her virgin state in piety, liberality, and sanctity of manners, died May 21, 1664, aged sixty-five."[100]

Chapter Nine

Slander, Defamation, and "Unnecessary Talking"

Clearly, the real power in Plymouth rested with the men; women were subservient. It was their lot to be quiet and obey. William Gouge, author of the seventeenth century advice book, *Domesticall Duties*, wrote that while in her husband's presence, a wife's words "must be few, reverend, and meek." "Too much speech," he continues, "implies a usurpation of authority." John Robinson advised that "words are like clothes, used first for necessity, after for convenient ornament, and, lastly, for wantonness." What Robinson called wanton speech the Pilgrims called "unnecessary talking." Yet, with so many constraints on their behavior, it was not unusual for a Pilgrim daughter or wife to express her feelings and frustrations using the best weapon she had—her voice.[1,2]

Women's verbal expressions of their frustrations had two main targets, as represented in the court records. Several women complained against those who were in authority, both in government and in the church. Women who challenged the authority of the colony were charged with misdemeanors under the same law that addressed violence in the home: "Any person or persons as tend to the hurt and detriment of society, civility, peace, and neighborhood be inquired into by the grand inquest and the persons [shall be] presented to the court that so the disturbers thereof may be punished and the peace and welfare of the subject comfortably preserved." Should they be convicted, they could possibly receive severe physical punishment as well as fines.[3]

The second most common target for verbal criticisms were against those who were in the same situation she was, her neighbors and friends. Those women who used their voices to exercise some agency

neighbors within the community could find themselves
n expensive civil lawsuit. Reputation was everything in
Plymouth, especially for a female, and there were many cases of a
woman defending herself.

Women who used their voices aggressively against the government,
the church, or other colonists, whether in the heat of anger or in quiet
gossip, could expect serious consequences. Any dissention among
these Dissenters was not tolerated.

Religious Rebels

As mentioned previously, Plymouth was a religious colony founded
by a group of Separatists who had left England seeking freedom of
worship. However, it must be said that theirs was not a venture to
further the ideal of religious tolerance; what they wanted was religious
freedom *for themselves*. Their goal was to establish a sanctuary where
they could live according to their interpretation of the scriptural model.
 It was women, specifically Quaker women, who used their voices to
challenge the Pilgrim church.

The Quakers represented an even more radical form of the Puritan
movement than did the Separatists. Like the Pilgrims, they wanted
to live by the scriptural model, but they took it even further. They
wanted to abolish not only the ministers, but all the magistrates and
any governmental authority. They refused to take the oath of allegiance
to Plymouth and rejected all formal ritual.

As the Quaker religious sect became more popular in Plymouth,
the government responded by establishing several rules supporting
the original Separatist church. In 1650, church attendance became
mandatory for all, and those who "shall neglect…frequenting the public
worship of God" were fined. Furthermore, "every one that is a master
or dame of a family," was responsible to see that everyone under their
care attended Sabbath meetings, or face a penalty of forty shillings.
Anyone who was "lazy, slothful, or profane," and neglected to attend
worship, would be fined "or be publicly whipped." Furthermore, the
laws said that no work was allowed on the Sabbath: "Be it enacted that

Calling the Pilgrims to church.

whosoever shall profane the Lord's Day by doing any servile work or any such like abuses shall forfeit for every such default ten shillings or be whipped."[4]

Behavior during Sunday services was also governed by law. Attendees could not sleep, play, or "jest" during services. Scofflaws would be admonished the first time, and then be set in the stocks should they continue to offend. Further restrictions were adapted in 1662, when it was made unlawful to drink "wine or liquor" on the Lord's day, "except in case of necessity for the relief to those that are sick or faint or the like for their refreshing." The fine was ten shillings. In 1665, a law was passed that prohibited colonists from being outside the meeting house during services, for "behaving themselves profanely by being without doors ... in time of exercise." Later, in 1669, it was made unlawful to sleep inside or play outside the meeting house on the Lord's Day, to ride horseback with "unnecessary violence," or to smoke within two miles of the meeting house. It was further unlawful to transact business on the Lord's Day.[5]

With such strict rules, there were bound to be those who ran into problems, intentionally or not. Women who broke the laws governing church attendance were called into court to explain themselves. For example, on October 7, 1651, Elizabeth Eddy, mentioned earlier, was presented before the court and charged with "laboring, that is to say, for wringing and hanging out clothes, on the Lord's day, in time of public exercise." She was fined ten shillings, but the fine was later canceled.[6]

Several years later, in 1660, Elizabeth Eddy once again had to answer for violating the Sabbath when she travelled from Plymouth to Boston on the Lord's Day. Eddy, who was fifty-three years old at the time, explained that Mistress Saffin (Martha Willett Saffin) "was very weak and sent for her, with an earnest desire to see her in her weakness." Martha's desperation may be explained by the birth and tragic death of her son John at about the same time. Attending to a grieving friend in need might seem like a valid defense, but the court ruled that her reason was "not a sufficient excuse." She was, however, only admonished and released without fines.[7,8]

Ann Hudson, John Hudson's wife, was called into court on October 5, 1663, "for sundry times doing several works on the Lord's day." Whatever she had been accused of doing on the Sabbath, the jury found her not guilty and she was released. Quarreling was also illegal on the Lord's Day. At the March 5, 1678, court, Ruhamah Nickerson, wife of Joseph, was given the choice of being fined forty shillings or being whipped for "fighting and quarreling twice" on the Sabbath. At the same court, Edward Cottle and his wife, as well as the wife of Nathaniel Covell, were also fined forty shillings or suffer a whipping, "for profaning the Lord's Day by quarreling and fighting."[9,10]

While the laws governing religion were enforced throughout the colony, they were applied with special vigor when it came to Quakers, especially Quaker women.

In a direct challenge to the Quaker movement, on June 10, 1650, it became illegal for anyone to "set up any churches or public meetings diverse from those already set up and approved." The official church of Plymouth was the church established by the Pilgrims, and they would tolerate none other. That same day, it became illegal to criticize the established church, to "vilify by opprobrious terms or speeches any church or ministry or ordinance…." Fines were ten shillings for every default.[11]

On October 7, 1651, several colonists from Sandwich were brought into the court, "for not frequenting the public worship of God, contrary to order made the 6th of June 1651." They were Ralph and Susanna Allen, George and Hannah Allen, William Allen, Richard Kerby, Peter and Lydia Gaunt, Rose Newland, Edmond and Elizabeth Freeman, Sr., Goodwife Turner, and Widow Knott. While they did not identify themselves as Quakers at that time, many of them would later be associated with the sect in Sandwich.[12]

In the case above, men and women were equally charged. One aspect of the Quaker religious sect that was especially worrisome to the government was that women had an equal role with men. They were permitted to become ministers and allowed to speak during meetings. In fact, Samuel Johnson's famous 1763 witticism that "a woman preaching is like a dog walking on his hinder legs. It is not done well; but you are surprised to find it done at all," referred to female Quaker ministers.[13]

Being forced to attend the Plymouth church did not deter the Quakers. On February 3, 1657, Jane Launder and Sarah Kerby, who were sisters, were charged "for a disturbance by them made in the public worship of God on the Lords day at Sandwich, by opposing and abusing the speaker amongst them." While they did attend a Pilgrim church meeting, according to the law, the two women apparently made a scene during the services by challenging the speaker. Both were sentenced to be whipped for their actions. Jane was offered the opportunity to apologize, "to offend no more," and escape the whipping. Sarah received no such offer, and the punishment was administered.[14]

Sarah Kerby was among the most outspoken of the Quaker women. The daughter of Richard Kerby of Sandwich, she had a history of insolence. On March 5, 1645, she was summoned to appear in court, "concerning diverse suspicious speeches by her uttered against Richard Bourne and Mr. Edmond Freeman, of Sandwich." Richard Bourne served as Sandwich's representative to the court's township committee; Edmond Freeman was an assistant to the governor. This was five or six years before her involvement with the Quaker movement, but the courts had long memories. Sarah may have had a

Woman preaching at Quaker meeting.

history of being too outspoken for the court's comfort long before she
became a Quaker. She was at first sentenced to be "severely whipped,"
but the punishment was "respited." This action was meant to be a
warning to her to curb her speech, "to offend no more of this kind," or
"the said punishment would be inflicted."[15,16]

On October 2, 1660, "diverse persons" were fined for attending
Quaker meetings; among them were several women. They were the
wives of Robert Harper, John Newland, Henry Dillingham, William
Newland, and Dorothy Butler, Joan Swift, Deborah Smith, and Lydia
Hicks. Each was fined ten shillings.[17]

Beginning in the early 1650s, as their numbers grew in the colony,
prosecution of the Quakers became relentless. One of the most
enthusiastic enforcers of laws against Quakers was the infamous George
Barlow, previously mentioned. By 1664 things had quieted down when
George Barlow was replaced by Thomas Burges, Sr. as constable of
Sandwich. Burges apparently had a more conciliatory manner.[18]

The sassy Sarah Kerby married on June 5, 1657, less than six
months after being whipped. Her husband Matthew Allen, also a
Quaker, was George Allen's son. The couple left Sandwich and settled
in Dartmouth, farther away from the Quaker persecution in Plymouth.
There they had at least six children.[19]

Slander and Defamation – Criminal Cases

Plymouth law allowed that anyone could report a suspected illegal action to the magistrates or the community's representative on the grand jury. The case would be investigated and, if warranted, brought before the court for trial. One of the effects of this practice was to discourage gossip among the colonists. Pilgrims were supposed to take their complaints to the authorities, not to their neighbors.

Anyone who "publish[ed] any matter of a scandalous nature, except unto a magistrate or grand juryman," could face defamation charges. Spreading rumors, or "publishing" them, brought many colonists, both men and women, into court as the objects of civil suits for defamation. Yet, it was also the law that once a complaint had come to the court's attention, there needed to be at least two witnesses to the act or "concurring circumstances" that proved the complaint. As a result, many cases evaporated due to lack of evidence. Yet, two women were charged, convicted, and punished for slander and defamation by the courts—Hester Rickard and Eleanor Billington.[20]

Hester Rickard

On October 2, 1660, Joseph Dunham sued Hester Rickard, "in an action of slander and defamation," for one hundred pounds. Hester had been telling people that Joseph Dunham, "did offer her money to be naughty with [him]." The suit was withdrawn, perhaps after the testimony of Hester's father-in-law, Giles Rickard, who explained that Hester's husband, John Rickard, "was away from home when this suit was commenced." It is implied that had her husband been home, he would have prevented Hester from spreading a scandalous lie.[21]

However, that was not the end of the matter. There must have been something going on between the two because six months later, on March 5, 1661, both Hester and Joseph Dunham were back in court. Hester was charged with "lascivious and unnatural practices" and Dunham with "diverse lascivious carriages." They both had to sit in the stocks with papers detailing their offenses affixed to their hats. Joseph also had to post a bond of twenty pounds to guarantee his continued good behavior.[22]

Hester, it seems, was a very vocal woman, and her outspokenness got her into trouble more than once. Three years later, on March 1, 1664, she was once again before the court, charged with "most obscene and filthy speeches," along with Anne Hoskins. The women got into a shouting match, were reported, and brought into court. Both were found guilty and fined either twenty shillings each or to sit in the stocks. They chose to pay the fines. But that did not settle things between Hester and Anne.[23]

On December 2, 1665, Hester complained against Anne Hoskins, saying Anne was guilty of "slandering her in saying the said Hester was drunk as a bitch, and found in private company in an ordinary with John Ellis, of Sandwich." Faced with the charge in court, Anne admitted that she had lied and that there was no evidence to support the claim. Hester accepted the apology and "rested satisfied, and so the matter was ended."[24]

Once more, on March 2, 1672, Hester was back before the governor and his assistants, this time for "her uncivil and beastly carriages and speeches to her said husband." There must have been witnesses, for the record states that the charge "was fully proved against her by sufficient testimony." She was sentenced to be publicly whipped at the post, but even with all her faults, Hester had loyal friends, and at "the earnest entities of herself and others, and her promise of amendment," the sentence was suspended.[25]

There was, however, a provision. If at any time in the future, she be charged again for uncivil carriages towards her husband or others, "she is to be forthwith…publicly whipped as foresaid." Furthermore, the court forbid her from brewing beer and selling it, "as formerly she had done." The court decided that brewing, selling—and most likely drinking—beer appeared to be a "snare to her to occasion[al] evil." The provision must have worked, for there is no further mention of Hester Rickard in the court records.[26]

Eleanor Billington

Eleanor Billington was the wife of John Billington and mother of Francis and John. The family were passengers on the *Mayflower*, and John Sr. had signed the Mayflower Compact. Despite this, the family had a poor reputation. William Bradford called them, "one of the profanest families among them." "They came from London," he continued, "and I know not by what friends shuffled into the company." As has already been discussed, John Billington, the older, had been hanged for murder in 1630.[27]

Yet, as one of the original colonists, Eleanor Billington was entitled to free land grants, and she also inherited her husband's property in Plain Dealing after his death. Additionally, she was eligible for the use of communal hay lands, which were portions of unallotted land from which she could harvest the hay. On March 14, 1636, hay land was assigned to her, "for her own use," a marsh that abutted land she already owned. "What is too much for her," the record stated, "is for Mr. Done." The ambiguity of that statement would result, not surprisingly, in trouble between the two.[28]

At the next court, June 7, 1636, John Done accused Eleanor of slander, suing her for one hundred pounds. What Eleanor said about John Done was not recorded, but it must have been significant. She was ordered to pay him five pounds and "adjudged to be set in the stock and be whipped." It was unusual for a suit for slander to result in punishment, let alone two forms of punishment. Why did Eleanor Billington receive such a serious sentence? What did she say about John Done, or anyone else, for that matter? The courts had wide discretion to interpret law and inflict punishment, and it may be that she spoke out in court and offended the magistrates. Or it may be that her position as matriarch of the disreputable Billington family, as well as a reputation for speaking her mind, were factors behind the more severe punishment.[29]

Eleanor was a clever woman, outspoken, one who stood up for herself and did not leave things to chance. On January 8, 1638, Eleanor gave her son Francis all her lands, meadow, and pastures in Playne Dealing. There were a few conditions. She reserved for herself a parcel of land large enough "as will make a thousand and a half of hills to set with Indian corn or sow with English grain." Furthermore, she wanted to keep a "small parcel of ground to make a garden place and erect a house upon," and some land in a new field, which she would "be at charge to manure" and would be hers throughout her natural life. The last provision was that Francis Billington never sell the property or any part of it during Eleanor's life without her consent.[30]

With her property legally passed on to her son, with house, garden, and fields preserved in her name, Eleanor then went on to remarry. But not before she made a similar legal agreement with her intended, Gregory Armstrong. On August 28, 1638, eight months after she gave her son the property in Plain Dealing, Eleanor entered into an agreement with Gregory Armstrong that might in our day be interpreted as a pre-nuptial contract. The agreement stated that if Eleanor should die before Gregory, he shall continue to "enjoy the house they now live in and the land they occupy during his life." On his death, he is to give "two heifers of a year old...to the benefit of the natural children of Francis Billington." Eleanor had provided for Gregory to live out his days in their house and asked that he make a gift from her to her grandchildren.[31]

Should Gregory die first, the agreement stipulated, Eleanor would have all rights to his personal property, "except some things to his friends at his death, according to his estate." As it happened, Gregory Armstrong died on November 15, 1650. He left no descendants. There is no further mention of Eleanor Billington Armstrong in the court records.[32,33]

Slander and Defamation – Civil Cases

Most of the time a charge of damage to one's reputation was treated as a civil case wherein one colonist sued another, and there were many such cases. Historian John Demos posits that, because of cramped living conditions, families were very restrained in the "expression of hostile impulses" within the household in order to maintain harmony. One way those frustrations were released was through "the enormous quantity of action [court cases] between neighbors." Many of those cases involved slander and defamation.[34]

In this community, where a woman was so dependent on her neighbors, her reputation was of great value to her, and it was a serious matter when her character was attacked. It was most often her husband or father who came to the woman's defense and brought the lawsuit against the slanderer. If the case involved a married woman, or *feme covert*, her husband was also named in the suit because as the head of the household he was responsible for everything that went on under his roof. Thus, any attack on his wife or daughter was also an attack on his ability to manage his family. If the woman was single, or *feme sole*, it was her father who represented her.

For example, on March 5, 1663, William Barstow sued John Palmer, Jr. in a civil case, complaining that Palmer was "reporting that Mary, the daughter of the said Barstow, had taken a false oath." Mary had been accused of lying, and her father was demanding forty pounds in damages. The jury decided for Mary's father, but awarded him only five pounds damages and court costs. Nothing was said about Mary's guilt or innocence in the judgment, but perhaps it was assumed that a guilty verdict on John Palmer also cleared Mary of lying.[35]

A husband was protecting his wife's reputation on October 5, 1663, when James Doughtey (perhaps Doty?) sued Peter Collimore. Collimore, according to Doughtey, was "reporting" that Thomas Ingham told him that Doughtey's wife was cheating in business transactions by wetting her wool before selling it. She was accused of telling Ingham, that he might make his cloth heavier by "laying it on a damp floor," causing it to absorb water and "hold weight," thereby increasing its worth. The jury found for Doughtey and awarded him five pounds damage and court costs. His wife was cleared of the charge.[36]

On March 2, 1669, Robert Latham, "in the behalf of himself and Susanna his wife," sued Arthur Harris for slander and defamation in the amount of one hundred pounds. Harris was spreading the rumor that Susanna bought fish from the Native Americans on the Lord's Day, strictly forbidden by the church. The jury, in this case, found no grounds for the suit and dismissed the whole matter.[37]

On March 1, 1664, Samuel Allen sued John Barnes for one hundred pounds, claiming that Barnes spread the rumor that Allen was the father of the child that one of William Newland's unmarried daughters was carrying. According to Barnes story, Newland's daughter "was with child, and that she laid it to three men, one a married man, and two young men," one of whom was Samuel Allen.[38]

This accusation was more serious than lying or gossip. Being accused of fornication not only exposed Newland's daughter to criminal charges; it would have ruined her reputation. While John Barnes acknowledged his guilt in spreading a rumor, he did not actually say the rumor was untrue. He made a statement to the court, claiming that he heard the story "from another man's mouth," and that he had "unadvisedly reported the above said premises, to the detriment and disparagement of the above said Samuel Allen; for the which I am heartily sorry for." Allen's reputation was repaired by the verdict and apology, but what about Newland's daughter? The suspicion was never disproven, but there is no mention in the record of her being charged with any crime.[39]

In another case, brought on July 7, 1668, John Dogged sued George Robinson for defamation "to the damage of a hundred pounds," complaining that Robinson was spreading a false story. Robinson was telling his neighbors that Dogged "did entice and persuade his daughter, Mary Robinson, and proffer her money to lie with him [Dogged]." Robinson was found guilty of slander and was ordered to pay Dogged five pounds and court costs, and furthermore, to make an acknowledgement of spreading untrue stories about him and Mary Robinson. George Robinson made a public apology, admitting that he lied about Dogged's behavior towards his daughter.[40]

The court investigated the matter again three months later, on October 25, 1668, this time as a criminal case. John Dogged was presented in court, charged with "uncivil carriages to Mary Robinson of Rehoboth." The court was following up on the charges from the civil case. Dogged, again insisting on his innocence, asked that the charges be judged by a jury, and both the court and the jury declared him innocent of all charges. No mention was made of Mary Robinson's reputation.[41]

There were at least three other occasions when an investigation of a lawsuit for slander led to criminal charges. The first was on October 29, 1669, when a case of slander turned into much more. Joseph Turner, Sr., sued Michael Peirse for one hundred pounds for spreading the rumor that Turner attempted "to commit rape with Abigail Peirse, the daughter of Michael Peirse." Turner was suing Michael Peirse for telling the story that he, Turner, had forced himself on Abigail, "striving with her until she was constrained to cry out for help." But the complaint was that Peirse slandered Turner; there was no criminal case against Turner for attempted rape. After the court heard what the men had to say, the suit was withdrawn. Perhaps there was not enough evidence to convince the court an actual crime had taken place. However, without a verdict, Abigail was left with the supposition of attempted sexual assault, which would affect her reputation in the colony.[42]

Joseph Turner, Sr., had no time to celebrate his victory, because at the same court meeting, Turner found himself on the other side of a lawsuit. In this case a wife joined her husband in defending her reputation. Charles and Abigail Stockbridge sued Joseph Turner, Sr., for slander and defamation in the amount of two hundred pounds, claiming that Turner was spreading the story that Charles was a "cockily rogue," arrogant and conceited. Furthermore, the Stockbridges charged, Turner was telling others that Abigail Stockbridge, "is as very a strumpet as any in New England,…a brazen faced whore." The court found for Charles and Abigail and ordered Turner to pay one hundred pounds damages and court charges. Turner exploded and what happened next was quite a scene.[43]

As reported at the March 1, 1670 court, there were several testimonies as to Turner's behavior on October 29, 1669, after he lost the case to the Stockbridges. His "horrid incivility in words and actions, and in the presence of several women," shocked everyone. Charges resulting from the outburst were so numerous and so serious that the court needed some time to sort them all out. Turner was ordered to appear at the June court to answer for "charges against him, being so many and of so heinous a nature." However, by the June court, no one knew where Turner was; he had "departed from this court without the court's leave or knowledge." An order for his arrest was issued.[44]

But before that could be addressed, Charles Stockbridge himself was the defendant in "an action of slander and defamation to the damage of one thousand pounds." Joseph Tilden brought the complaint that Stockbridge was gossiping, telling others that "Nathaniel Turner and Joseph Turner could kiss Elizabeth the wife of the said Tilden as often as they [liked] and do something else too." Furthermore, according to Tilden, Stockbridge was saying that "Nathaniel Turner knew her [carnally], the said Elizabeth Tilden, as well as her own husband knew her." After investigating, the jury found for the defendant; Stockbridge was found not guilty.[45]

On June 7, 1670, Joseph Turner, Sr., although still missing, was charged and convicted for his "most lascivious, obscene, and vile expressions and actions, spoken and acted towards several persons diverse times." For his bad behavior before the court and in general, Turner was sentenced to receive the severe whipping of thirty stripes, fifteen at Plymouth and fifteen more at Scituate on a public training day. There is no record of the outcome of this case.[46]

However, Turner was once again in Plymouth, and also once again in trouble, on July 4, 1673, when he was in court charged with leading a gang of eleven men who tore down Isaac Chittenden's fence in Scituate in an apparent property dispute. The men did, "contrary to law and in a riotous way, throw down a fence or great parcel of fence of the above said Chittenden's, by him set up on land laid out to him by...the authority of this government...." The men were found guilty and ordered to pay five shillings each in fees.[47]

Gossip and "Unnecessary Talking"

While there was no law against gossip, the court chided at least one woman for "unnecessary talking." On March 1, 1659, Mary Briggs, of Scituate, was presented for telling a lie. The court, "having examined particulars about it," cleared Mary of the charge. However, one of the governor's assistants, Timothy Hatherly, was ordered to counsel and admonish Mary "to be wary of giving occasion of offense to others by unnecessary talking."[48]

In a community like Plymouth Colony, rural, primitive, and sparsely settled, women were especially dependent upon each other. Women assisted each other during childbirth, shared advice, provided health care, traded produce and dairy products, and supported and encouraged each other. This web of inter-dependency demonstrates the existence of a distinctive women's culture among the female colonists, and gossip was one of its elements. One of the functions of gossip, idle conversation that might include talk about others, is that it binds women together with shared information, interests, and values. On the other hand, gossip can be a form of punishment or retribution that leads to isolating those who do not share community values.

The point is that gossiping was probably part of a woman's everyday interactions with her neighbors. She may have been astonished that a chat with a friend could have serious legal consequences. For example, on October 25, 1668, James Clarke sued Sarah Barlow and Marcy Bartlett for damages in the amount of two hundred pounds. The two women were gossiping with others, saying that they saw James "kiss his maid and use other uncivil carriages that he acted towards her in the field upon the Lord's day." What Sarah and Marcy had "reported" to others was a case of "unseemly familiarity between [Clarke] and his maid," which was a serious criminal charge.[49]

The court "fully considered the matter," heard and compared testimony, and decided that James Clarke had indeed been "defamed and slandered...because the thing charged by them doth in no measure appear by testimony." The court also noted that the women's "way of divulging" this untruth, implying they used gossip to spread the rumor, "was manifestly scandalous." Nonetheless, since there were some "appearances of truth in their report," they were fined only ten shillings apiece for a misdemeanor. In other words, the two women may have seen something suspicious, but their allegations could not be verified, and they certainly should not have told others until the accusations were proven.[50]

John Sutton sued both Abraham Sutliff and his wife for slander on December 6, 1659, even though it was Sarah Sutliff who was the gossip. John Sutton complained that Sarah "hath reported that the said John Sutton was basely begotten and basely borne," that he was illegitimate. Sutton wanted his reputation—and presumably his mother's—cleared. The court found Sarah guilty and ordered her to apologize in writing to the court. In addition, she was also required to make a verbal apology "at the Scituate meetinghouse" during morning meeting the first Sunday in October. Sarah's apology read: "I, having no ground nor cause so to speak, neither know any such thing [about] him, and am very sorry I wronged the said John Sutton in so saying."[51]

Perhaps there was a chuckle in the courtroom on May 7, 1662, when Rose Morton stood before the court charged by Abraham Jackson of abuse, "by calling of him [a] lying rascal and rogue." There was a witness, Jonathan Pratt, who supported the charge. Rose denied calling Abraham a rogue, but "she owned that she called him lying rascal." Rose apologized and "promised to be more careful of her words for the future." The court accepted her apology and let her go, "passed it by," without any punishment.[52]

Some cases seem to have arisen out of misunderstandings that could not be resolved without the intervention of the courts. Nathaniel and Abigail Thayer sued John and Lydia Smith for slander and defamation for two hundred pounds, a sizeable amount. On March 5, 1668, the Thayers charged that the Smiths were reporting that Abigail Thayer had stolen five pounds of goods from them. This may have been a trade or a purchase that went bad, because the four of them settled the case among themselves after the jury was impaneled.[53]

In the following case, a rumor needed to be traced back to its source, which proved to be complicated. Anthony Dodson sued John and Rebecca Cowin for one hundred pounds on March 4, 1673. Dodson claimed that John and Rebecca were spreading the rumor that Dodson was spreading rumors. The Cowins, according to Dodson, were gossiping that Dodson said that John Williams said that William Rogers "broke up his house." (This suit was probably another chapter in the saga of the marriage problems between John and Elizabeth Williams, already discussed.) By spreading this lie, Dodson argued, he had been "wronged, reproached, and defamed, and so comes to be damnified." The jury disagreed and found for the defendants.[54]

These slander hearings could become very heated; often they lead to vengeful countersuits. For example, on March 1, 1653, John Bower sued Joan Barnes for one hundred pounds for slander and defamation. The jury found for Bower and awarded him five pounds and court costs. Immediately thereafter, Joan's husband, John Barnes, sued John Bower for one hundred *and ten* pounds for trespass. The jury probably saw this action for the vindictive act it was, and found for Bower, but awarded him only court costs.[55]

Accusations of Witchcraft

Probably the most dangerous of rumors were those accusing a woman of witchcraft. Plymouth law in 1636 stated that any "solemn compaction or conversing with the devil by way of witchcraft, conjuration or the like" was a capital crime. A woman accused and found guilty of witchcraft could be executed. As Englishmen, the Pilgrims knew about witches. Between 1580 and 1680, Great Britain executed at least four thousand witches. There were two charges of witchcraft in Plymouth colony, neither of which resulted in an execution. One was in 1661, the other in 1677, both incidents well before the infamous Salem Witch Trials of 1692.[56,57]

Dinah Silvester Accused Elizabeth Holmes

On March 5, 1661, Joseph Silvester was required to post of bond of twenty pounds to guarantee that his sister, Dinah, would appear before the court the following May to answer a complaint by William Holmes of Scituate. Holmes had charged that Dinah had defamed his wife, Elizabeth Holmes, accusing her of being a witch.[58]

William and Elizabeth Holmes lived in Scituate and had at least eight children. William was sixty-nine years old at the time of this case; Elizabeth was forty-seven. Dinah was the daughter of Richard Silvester and was born on April 2, 1642, in Weymouth. At the time of this case, she would have been just nineteen years old.[59,60]

In her statement to the court in 1671, Dinah reported that she had seen a bear. She concluded that the animal was the wife of William Holmes practicing witchcraft. The court, understandably skeptical, asked her more questions, inquiring about the exact location of the bear, and "what manner of tail the bear had." Dinah responded that it was "about a stone's throw from the highway," and "she could not tell [what kind of tail it had], for his head was towards her." Whether it was her answers themselves, or the manner in which she answered the questions, her responses to the court made them very suspicious of her story.[61]

At the next court, May 7, 1661, William Holmes of Marshfield brought a formal suit against Dinah Silvester, "for accusing his wife to be a witch." After considering all the evidence, the court found Dinah guilty and sentenced her to "either be publicly whipped or pay the sum of five pounds to the said William Holmes." She was later given the choice to pay the fine or "make a public acknowledgement of her fault." She chose the latter. While offering the excuse that she did not remember the incident the same as the witnesses have sworn, "I do rather mistrust my own memory and submit to the evidences."[62]

Dated May 9, 1661, Dinah's apology read:

> To the honored court assembled: Whereas I have been convicted in matter of defamation concerning Goodwife Holmes, I do freely acknowledge I have wronged my neighbor, and have sinned against God in so doing; though I had entertained hard thoughts against the woman; for it has been my duty to declare my grounds, if I had any, unto some magistrate in a way of God, and not to have divulged my thoughts to others, to the woman's defamation. Therefore, I do acknowledge my sin in it, and do humbly beg this honored court to forgive me, and all other Christian people that be offended at it, and do promise, by the help of God, to do so no more....[63]

The statement was signed with the mark of Dinah Silvester.[64]

In her statement, Dinah acknowledges that she should have reported her "hard feelings" and the reasons behind them to the magistrates for investigation, instead of gossiping about her neighbor.

Here is yet another example demonstrating the role of the grand jury in managing the peace of the community.

Overall, 1661 was not a good year for Dinah Silvester. Six months later, on October 1, 1661, Dinah and her father, Richard, were both in court complaining against John Palmer, Jr., "for acting fraudfully against the said Dinah, in not performing his engagement to her in point of marriage." Dinah had been forsaken by her intended, and she and her father were awarded twenty pounds and the cost of the case, one pound, eight shillings, six pence. One month later, Palmer paid Dinah Silvester the full amount, and the Silvesters signed an agreement that he was free "from all dues, debts, and demands upon what account so ever, from the beginning of the world to this day."[65]

Dinah's father died in 1663, when she was twenty-one years old, leaving her fifteen pounds in his will; however, she had to collect the money herself from Daniel Bacon, who owed it to her father. The family's problems with the court continued. On October 31, 1666, John, Naomi, and Dinah Silvester, brother and two sisters, were charged by the Marshfield constable, William Ford, "for molesting and abusing him in the execution of his office." Ford had arrested their mother for some unknown offense, and the children "rescued" her away from the constable. The court found for Ford and fined the Silvesters forty shillings.[66,67]

On July 2, 1667, Dinah Silvester was charged with committing fornication and fined ten pounds. Two years later she was back in court again, this time accusing Elkanah Johnson of fathering her child. There is no further mention of the charge in the Plymouth court record; in fact, this was Dinah's last appearance in the colony's records.[68,69]

Mehitable Woodworth Accused Mary Ingham

In 1677, Mary Ingham, wife of Thomas Ingham, was charged with bewitching Mehitable Woodworth, daughter of Walter Woodworth, all of Scituate. On March 6, 1677, the court record was nearly biblical in its language, and foretold what would be happening in Salem in fifteen years. The charge read:

Mary Ingham, thou art indicted by the name of Mary Ingham, the wife of Thomas Ingham, of the town of Scituate, in the jurisdiction of New Plymouth for that thou, having not the fear of God before thy eyes, hast, by the help of the Devil, in a way of witchcraft or sorcery, maliciously procured much hurt, mischief, and pain unto the body of Mehitable Woodworth, the daughter of Walter Woodworth, of Scituate,…and some others, and particularly causing her, the said Mehitable, to fall into violent fits, and causing great pain unto several parts of her body at several times, so as she, the said Mehitable Woodworth, hath been almost bereaved of her senses, and hath greatly languished, to her much suffering thereby, and the procuring of great grief, sorrow, and charge to her parents; all which thou hast procured and done against the law of God, and to his great dishonor, and contrary to our sovereign lord the King, his crown and dignity.[70]

Mary was married to Thomas Ingham, who was a weaver. In his *History of Scituate*, Samuel Deane claims that the Inghams were "old and solitary," which made them easy targets for witchcraft charges. Mehitable Woodworth was known to be "unfortunate as to her health." She had a nervous disorder, "which in those superstitious days was synonymous with being possessed with the devil." Nothing further is known about either woman's personal circumstances.[71,72]

Mary requested a jury trial, "of God and the country." Twelve men found her innocent, "and so the said prisoner was cleared as abovesaid.[73]

No further cases of witchcraft have been found in the Plymouth Colony records. How to explain fewer accusations of witchcraft among the Pilgrims than in other New England colonies? There were superstitions among the Pilgrims, along with a belief in omens and signs, but the colony did not engage in the hysteria associated with the Salem Witch Trials. One historian explained that what happened in Salem was "a perfect storm," caused by a combination of factors.

These included "declinism [a decline in prosperity], inexperienced judges interpreting Scripture, Indian wars, denominational strife, socioeconomic tension, general pre-scientific superstition, petty jealousy, and paranoia."[74]

Things were much simpler in Plymouth. While there were rules and laws and customs governing expectations and behavior, the Pilgrims also were very practical and judged all the cases they tried with an element of common sense. Perhaps the two charges of witchcraft that came before the authorities were simply not believable to them. Whatever the reasons, this community avoided the horrors of the Salem executions.

Chapter Ten

Unclean Carriages and Lascivious Acts

Pilgrim sexuality was governed by laws that were based on religious beliefs. Ideally, according to their precepts, any sexual relations would be between one man and one woman and would take place within a married union only. The success of the colony depended on men and women mating and producing children, who would in turn, mate and produce more children. Ideally, all this coupling would occur within the institution of marriage, but sexual drives are very powerful, and at times Plymouth's young men and women lacked self-control.

The average age for a woman to marry was about twenty; for men it was closer to their mid-twenties. This meant that it was several years after puberty before they could lawfully engage in sexual activity. As a result, it was not uncommon for couples to willingly participate in illegal dalliances. Even with all the laws and standards and community expectations, it has been estimated that up to fifty percent of the colonists engaged in sexual activity before marriage.[1]

How were these offenses discovered? There was no privacy in Plymouth as we understand it today. Neighbors entered each other's homes casually and unannounced as a matter of custom. Any suspicious activity discovered under those circumstances was immediately reported to the local authorities. As William Bradford wrote about evils committed in Plymouth: "they are here more discovered and seen and made public by due search, inquisition and due punishment." Plymouth historian James Deetz observed that "This was a society where everyone's conduct was the business of their neighbors."[2,3]

Flirtations and Playfulness

Some crimes were obliquely referred to in the court records as "light behavior," "unclean carriages," "lascivious acts," and other terms. These terms, writes Deetz, "appeared to cover everything from improper flirtations to a flagrant display of wanton sexual behavior." To the Pilgrims, these terms meant interactions of a sexual nature that did not include intercourse.[4]

Fines for these breaches were less than other sexual infractions. For example, on July 7, 1681, Hannah Lennet was called into court accused of "light behavior" with Joseph Randall in Barnstable. She was fined only twenty-five shillings (which if paid in corn, would amount to about four bushels), but if she did not pay her fine, she was to be whipped. The circumstances, of course, can never be known, but there was no fine or corporal punishment given to Joseph Randall. In the court's view, whatever she was doing with Randall was illegal and she was to blame.[5]

Henry Samson reported what appears to have been a noisy party to the authorities. On June 8, 1651, he gave evidence to the court that John and James Shaw, Samuel Cutbert, and Benjamin Eaton, all from Plymouth, and Goodwife Gannett, Martha Haward, and William Snow, all of Duxbury, were engaged in "vain, light, and lascivious carriage… at an unseasonable time of the night."[6]

The court addressed the charges on October 7, 1651 and found only some of them at fault; James Shaw and Mistress Gannet were fined thirty shillings each, with the warning that if they did not pay, they would be whipped. The others, except for John Shaw, "who would be liable for punishment when the opportunity serveth," were released. However, Martha Haward (also known as Hayward or Howard) and the rest were admonished "to take heed of such evil carriages for the future." Was Goodwife Gannett singled out for greater responsibility because she was a married woman and should have known better?[7,8]

Even the suspicion of illicit behavior could land a woman in court. On May 4, 1652, Martha Shrive, wife of Thomas Shrive (or Sheriff), was brought before the court and warned to avoid the company of Edward Holman. He had been observed visiting her home at "unseasonable times of the night." The visits were "feared to be of ill consequence." One year later, on June 9, 1653, they were apparently still seeing each other. Another warning was issued by the court that they "keep out of the company of each other." This time the court added that if they did not abide by the court's order, they were in "peril of suffering corporal punishment by whipping."[9,10]

Edward Holman "clearly existed on the fringes of Plymouth society." He had married Amy Glass in 1644 but was widowed by the time his attraction to Martha Shrive was addressed by the courts. He was never made a freeman, and never held a position in the colony. Holman died in 1675.[11]

In 1652, Martha Shrive was the mother of at least three boys. After her husband's death in 1675, she married Thomas Hazard, who made an unusual declaration: "This is to satisfy all men, whom it may anyway concern, whereas there is a promise of matrimony betwixt Thomas Hazard and Martha [Shrive], yet I the foresaid Thomas Hazard do take the said Martha [Shrive] for her own person, without having anything to do with her estate or with any things that is hers." Apparently, Martha was wealthy, but may not have had particularly good judgment. After Thomas Hazard's death, she married Lewis Hues, who within six or seven weeks of marriage left her, "taking a great part of her estate." Martha's son, John Shrive, took over his mother's "estate real and personal," and put her on an annual allowance.[12]

Fornication

Fornication, that is, having sexual relations, including intercourse, outside of marriage, was taken very seriously by the courts. Not only were these acts unlawful and against religious principles; they threatened the community financially. A child born out of wedlock to an impoverished couple would most likely become a ward of the community, a financial responsibility for everyone.

Punishments were significant. Often a woman who was found guilty of fornication was fined, but if she could not pay the fine, she was sentenced to be whipped. Singling out those who may have been unable to pay a fine for a harsher punishment implies that the courts wanted to especially discourage the poor from engaging in illicit sex. An unwanted pregnancy among the destitute could result in the community having to step in and support the unwed mother. Therefore, not only were there religious precepts at work in these fornication laws, but there were also economic considerations as well.

Variance in Fines

The law against fornication set the fine at ten pounds, but actual fines varied, presumably due to the circumstances surrounding each case. For example, Sarah Smith was in court on July 2, 1667, and was fined ten pounds for committing fornication. However, "on some considerations," the court reduced her penalty to five pounds. The circumstances of the incident are lost to history, but even reduced by half, the fine would have been substantial for Sarah. She was the daughter of Rev. John Smith of Barnstable, and one of twelve children. Surely a minister with such a large family could hardly afford the fine.[13,14]

Penetration was one of the court's requirements for a case of fornication, and it may be that in cases with unusually low fines the couple did not go that far. Perhaps it was a case of fondling and not fornication when Abisha Marchant and Mary Jones were discovered in bed together. On August 11, 1670, the court fined him only forty shillings. Another case with an unusually small fine was heard in July 1681. James Mayo was charged with "uncivil lying on a bed with Martha Harding." He was fined only twenty shillings.[15,16]

In at least one case, the community stepped up in defense of the charged woman. On October 4, 1664, Ruhamah Turner, who was about nineteen at the time, was fined five pounds for committing fornication. However, a marginal note reads: "Several of the neighbors of Sandwich engaged to pay this fine on the behalf of Ruhamah Turner." The following March, John Ewen (Ewer) was named as her partner. He was fined only three pounds.[17,18,19]

While the court record is somewhat ambiguous, it appears that Ruhamah and John each tried to pay off their fines, albeit in very small

Fines could be difficult for families to pay.

amounts. Ruhamah paid fifty shillings on June 7, 1665. This amount was officially "abated" from her fine two days later. A few years later, on October 29, 1669, John Ewen paid twenty shillings toward his fine. As a result, this one occasion of fornication resulted in five separate court records, the initial case and the ensuing records of payments towards the fines. Sadly, some researchers have misinterpreted these multiple records as evidence that Ruhamah had many sexual offenses, thus attributing to her a scandalous reputation she does not deserve. Ruhamah later married John Jennings of Sandwich, on August 29, 1667. They had several children.[20,21,22]

The case of Jonathan Higgens is a curious one. On July 4, 1679, he was charged with "committing fornication with his wife's sister after his wife's death." He was fined twenty pounds; there is no mention of a fine for her. Jonathan's first wife was Elizabeth Rogers, who died in 1678 at thirty-nine years of age. He then married her sister, Hannah. Both sisters were granddaughters of Thomas Rogers, a *Mayflower* passenger.[23,24]

Was the fine larger than usual because she was considered by the court to be a relative of Jonathan's, even though not a blood relative? Or, given that Sandwich had a large Quaker community, were the couple married in the Quaker way, which was considered unlawful? What is evident is that his friends did not consider this relationship as scandalous as the court did. The record states that, "At the earnest petition of some of his friends," the court reduced the fine to ten pounds.[25]

While some couples were punished only with fines, others were punished only with whipping. David Linnet and Hannah Shelly, for example, were found guilty of "unclean practices each with the other," on June 3, 1652, and were "sentenced by the court to be both publicly whipped at Barnstable where they live."[26] Why they were not given the less painful option of paying a fine is not known.

Risks of Fornication

Any woman who engaged in sexual acts outside of marriage put herself at great risk. Not only did she risk pregnancy and the possibility of contracting a sexually transmitted disease, but if she were charged and found guilty of fornication she would be humiliated before her friends and family in public court. She would have to pay a substantial fine or incur painful physical punishment, and her reputation would be ruined.

Reputation

James Deetz remarked that "A woman's reputation among her neighbors was often the most important possession she had in the close-knit, small world in which she lived." A public scandal, wrote John Robinson, is like a scar, which "they carry to their graves with them." Once tainted, a woman's reputation was difficult to repair. In the case of Thomas Bonney and Elizabeth Farniseede, Thomas tried valiantly to repair the damage he had done to Elizabeth's reputation.[27,28]

On March 3, 1646, John and Elizabeth Farniseede sued Thomas Bonney for slander claiming that he "hath said that Mistress Farniseede did justle [jostle] him in her house, and that he took it as a temptation of him unto lust." Thomas further accused her of "coming bare legged unto

him, speaking unto him, Thomas Bonney, will you mend my shoes?"
Elizabeth denied "that ever she came to him in any such manner." What
really happened between Thomas Bonney and Elizabeth Farniseede will
never be known for certain; she denied everything, and he apologized
that "he might be mistaken" about her intentions.[29]

In court Thomas Bonney made a long apology to the Farniseedes,
admitting that "it was his own base heart that caused him to make
that construction thereof,...that he had no sufficient reason so to
conceive, but that evil suspicion arose from the corruption of his own
heart." Trying to repair her reputation, he went on to say that Mistress
Farniseede "is a very honest, modest, and chaste woman, both in heart,
word, and deed."[30]

Even so, Thomas was ordered to "put into the hand of the deacon
of the church of Duxbury five shillings," to be distributed to the poor.[31]

Pregnancy

Primitive forms of birth control were practiced in colonial America;
folk techniques brought over from Europe were known and shared
among women. For married women, it was believed that breastfeeding
inhibited conception, which is actually true. While a woman can
get pregnant while nursing, there may be a period of diminished
fertility for some. But, for the unmarried there was only abstinence,
withdrawal, and crude condoms fashioned from the intestines of
animals. However, these forms of birth control depended on the man's
willingness to cooperate. On her own, a woman might use honey or
lemon juice soaked onto a sponge or small cloth and inserted into her
vagina as a crude early form of spermicide.[32]

There is no evidence in the records that any form of pregnancy
prevention was used at Plymouth, although some may have used the
methods mentioned above. For Pilgrim women, having unmarried
sex was very perilous. It is estimated that about one out of five sexual
encounters—in or outside of marriage—resulted in a pregnancy.[33]

The courts were careful to identify the father of the illegitimate
child, since he would be ordered to pay support. For example, when
Susanna Turner was convicted of fornication with John Williams, of

Barnstable, on June 5, 1672, she was fined eight pounds. Williams, the father, was ordered to pay to her "two shillings by the week towards the keeping of the said child," payable quarterly. This child support was to continue until the next court meeting, "the first Tuesday of March next." Apparently, the child was sickly because the court added the cryptic provision, "if the said child live so long." Williams was warned not to leave the colony, "without license."[34]

Richard Bennett was sentenced to be whipped on June 6, 1681, for "his lascivious and light behavior with Deborah Woodcock," and telling "sundry lies" about it. He was also sentenced to pay "one and twenty pence a week for the space of three years...for and towards the keeping of the child born of the said Deborah." Deborah was sentenced to pay a fine of ten pounds. Their daughter, Jane Woodcock, was born March 11, 1681.[35,36]

Poor decisions seemed to run in the Woodcock family. Six years earlier, on March 1, 1675, Israel Woodcock, Deborah's brother, was charged by Rebecca Littlefield that "he hath begotten her with child." Woodcock "stiffly denying it," could not convince the court he was not the father. He was ordered to pay child support and fined five pounds. Rebecca was ordered, "to suffer according to the law against this her fact [her own doing]."[37]

A child whose father was either unnamed by the mother, or was too poor to pay child support, posed a problem for the courts. To avoid having to support the child with public funds, the courts employed creative solutions. Consider the complicated case of Dorothy Temple, servant girl to Stephen Hopkins. This was a situation where the community needed to decide how the child would be taken care of.

On February 4, 1639, the court ordered that Stephen Hopkins keep his servant, Dorothy Temple, and her illegitimate child, for the remaining two years of her indenture. If he should refuse to do so, then "the colony [will] provide for her, and Mr. Hopkins to pay it."[38]

Hopkins apparently refused, and was jailed for contempt of court the same day. He was ordered to remain in custody until "he shall either receive his servant, Dorothy Temple, or else provide for her elsewhere at his own charge during the term she hath yet to serve him." Hopkins did not want to support Dorothy and her child, and neither did the colony.[39]

A few days later, more details were revealed, and the father of the child was named. He was Arthur Peach, who had been executed for murder and robbery before the child was born. With the child's father dead, there was no one left to pay child support. John Holmes stepped forward and agreed to assume the rest of Dorothy's indenture—but for a price. He wanted three pounds from Stephen Hopkins. Hopkins agreed, and the three pounds and "other considerations" released the community and Hopkins, "of the said Dorothy Temple and her child forever."[40]

With that obligation settled, the court turned to how Dorothy would be punished. On June 4, 1639, Dorothy was formally charged with "uncleanness and bringing forth a male bastard." She was sentenced to be whipped twice for her crime, but "she faint[ed] in the execution of the first, [and] the other was not executed."[41]

Sexually Transmitted Diseases

Any woman who engaged in sexual intercourse outside of marriage risked contracting disease. In the 1686 divorce case of John and Mary Glover, already discussed, Mary Glover was infected with a sexually transmitted disease when she committed adultery. She then infected her husband, "with that filthy, annoying disease called the pox, to his great sorrow and pain, ruin of his estate, and hazard [to] his life." It was probably syphilis, a most dangerous disease that could eventually be fatal. Not surprisingly, for the colonists, "there was tremendous shame associated with contracting a venereal disease."[42,43]

Bestiality

At Plymouth, the practice of bestiality was considered an offense against the Law of God. Two passages in the Scriptures forbid this act. According to the Pilgrims' Geneva Bible, the law was from the book of Leviticus, 20:15, "the man that lieth with a beast, shall die the death, and ye shall slay the beast." Furthermore, the story of Onan, from the

Book of Genesis, 38:9, who refused to father a child with his widowed sister-in-law, and instead spilled his seed on the ground, confirmed to the Pilgrims that a man's seed has only one acceptable receptacle.

The most notorious case of "buggery" in the early New England colonies occurred at Plymouth and involved a teenage boy. On September 7, 1642, Thomas Granger, Jr., who was a servant to Love Brewster in Duxbury, was indicted for "buggery with a mare, a cow, two goats, diverse sheep, two calves, and a turkey." The court record is brief. Thomas, who was probably about sixteen or seventeen years old at the time, was found guilty, and "received the sentence of death by hanging until he was dead." That simple account was expanded upon by Governor William Bradford in his history of the colony.[44,45]

Thomas was a servant "to an honest man," wrote Bradford, meaning Love Brewster. Granger's mother and father lived in Scituate. The teenager was "detected of buggery" with several of Brewster's animals. Someone accidentally came upon him engaged "in lewd practice towards the mare." After being questioned, Granger confessed to the act, and went on to admit that he also had relations with several more animals. He confessed several times, privately to the magistrates, to ministers, "and others," and later to the whole court and jury. During his investigation, Bradford asked Granger where he learned such behavior, and the boy replied that "he was taught it by another that had heard of such things from some in England."[46]

Despite his young age, the jury found him guilty and he was condemned to hang. Then he was ordered to identify the animals he violated, "and whereas some of the sheep could not so well be known by his description," when "they were brought before him...he declared which were they and which were not." This was important because the court, following biblical law, was soon to execute all of the animals.[47]

On September 8, 1642, wrote Bradford, there was a "very sad spectacle." A sad spectacle, indeed. At Granger's execution, all the animals were killed, "before his face," "first the mare, and then the cow, and the rest of the lesser cattle." After the animals had been slaughtered, Thomas Granger was hanged. The animals were buried in a large pit, and "no use was made of any part of them." Because the animals had been defiled, they were considered unsuitable for human consumption. The loss to Brewster must have been substantial; the animals killed probably included most of his livestock. There is no record of any reimbursement.[48]

The case only gets worse. On January 3, 1643, letters of administration were granted to Timothy Hatherly and Edward Eddenden to account for the "goods and chattels" of Thomas Granger, Sr., "in the behalf of his wife and children, and to pay debts, as far as it will go, and to provide for her and her children." Apparently, Thomas, Sr., died shortly after the execution of his son, leaving his wife and two children. Among his outstanding debts were charges of six pence for a latch on the prison door, apparently for the incarceration of his son, one pound for food for the ten weeks Thomas Jr. spent in jail, and two pounds, ten shillings for the execution of the boy and Brewster's livestock.[49]

Homosexuality

The 1636 statutes made sodomy and buggery capital offenses punishable by death. While the courts in Plymouth instituted laws against male homosexuality, there was no mention of same-sex relations between women. Leviticus, 18:22, in the Geneva Bible, addresses only male homosexuality: "Thou shalt not lie with the male as one lieth with a woman, for it is abomination." However, since there is no penetration with a penis during lesbian activities, those acts were not considered sodomy.[50]

There is only one case of presumed lesbian sexual relations in the Plymouth court records, and it appears to have made the court more than a little uneasy. On March 6, 1649, the Grand Inquest presented the case of "the wife of Hugh Norman and Mary Hammon, both of Yarmouth, for lewd behavior each with other upon a bed." Mary Hammon, who was about fifteen years old and newly married, was cleared of the charge, "with admonition."[51]

On October 2, 1650, eighteen months later, the court revisited the charge against Sarah Norman, since she was unable to appear earlier "by reason of some hindrances." Besides the "lewd behavior," she was also charged with "diverse lascivious speeches," and ordered to "make a public acknowledgement…of her unchaste behavior." Perhaps it was her "lascivious speeches" that drew the attention of the courts to Sarah, and they took the opportunity to address her earlier "unchaste behavior" and issue an admonishment. She was further warned to "take heed of such carriages in the future, lest her former carriage come in remembrance against her to make her punishment the greater." No corporal punishment was ordered.[52]

Both Mary Hammond and Sarah Norman lived in Yarmouth where they most likely became friends. Women were so dependent on one another in this culture, and there can be little doubt that deep friendships with real affection were quite common among otherwise heterosexual women. The court's hesitation and seemingly reluctance to address the issue of lesbianism in Plymouth may reflect their uncertainty about classifying female intimacy and their hesitation to categorize such activity beyond "unchaste behavior." It should also be noted that Sarah Norman's six-year-old daughter had drowned in a well less than a year before this incident on May 28, 1648. Perhaps the court considered the effects of that tragedy in their decision.[53]

Nonetheless, the courts considered Sarah Norman to be the aggressor, shown by the lighter admonishment given to the younger and less-experienced Mary Hammond, who had been married only six months earlier, in November 1648. The admonishment was apparently taken seriously by Mary since there is no further mention of her in the court records. She and Benjamin went on to have at least six children, four sons and two daughters, both of whom died young. Her husband was a respected man in the community; he was named constable of Yarmouth in 1652, served on the Grand Inquest in 1669, and in 1675 was named constable of Sandwich. The family later moved to the Plymouth town of Rochester, newly incorporated in 1686. Benjamin died there in 1703, aged 82, and Mary joined him in death two years later.[54,55,56]

Sarah White had married Hugh Norman in 1639, and she did not marry well. During her trial and sentencing, her husband abandoned her and their children and returned to England. The government of Plymouth, and, presumably, her father, "Goodman White," tried to locate Hugh Norman in England and force him to pay child support.

Thomas Allyn was travelling to England on other business in 1649 when the courts asked him to try to find Hugh Norman. He did, but his report must have been a disappointment to the magistrates.[57,58]

Allyn reported that he found Hugh Norman in England, in the village of Orchard, about two or three miles from Taunton. He was living in an abandoned house, and "he kept there two or three whores and non-else in the house." Allyn added that he could not speak with Norman because "[Norman] had not clothes to wear fitting [appropriate] to company [meet] with men." Hugh's mother had died and left him sixty pounds and a tenement building. He sold the building for a hundred pounds, "all which he spent in less than a year's time." When asked to provide for his wife and children, Norman replied "that he had no wife and would not own her nor would go more unto her."[59]

More information came to light in 1654 when another investigator, Thomas Richard, shared what he knew about Hugh Norman. It seems that Norman had spent all his money "upon a naughty woman whom he would have married as they pretended." The couple "kept company… under hedges and other base places." After his money was gone, the woman left him and "is gone to Barbados."[60] This is the last reference to Hugh and Sarah White Norman in the Plymouth Colony records.

Adultery

As has already been discussed in the section on divorce, adultery was considered a dreadful crime, punishable by death in Plymouth's early years. Adultery threatened the stability of the entire colony and when a charge was filed, the couple were fully investigated by the courts. Punishments were severe.

In 1639, the colony's first case of adultery heard in court was between Mary Mendame, wife of Robert Mendame of Duxbury, and an American Indian named Tinsin. Both were found guilty. Mary was sentenced "to be whipped at a cart's tail through the town's streets and to wear a badge upon her left sleeve. If she was seen without the badge, the letter "A" for adulteress, "then [she is] to be burned in the face with a hot iron." Tinsin was sentenced to be whipped at the post, "with a halter about his neck." The halter, or noose, was probably used to remind Tinsin, and all who viewed the whipping, that the court could have ordered him hung for his crime. His punishment was lighter than Mary's because it was determined that she lured and enticed him.[61]

In 1641, Thomas Bray, single, and Anne, the wife of Francis Linceford, all from Yarmouth, were charged with adultery. Thomas and Anne were accused of having "committed the act of adultery and uncleanness, and have diverse times lain in one bed together in the absence of her husband." Both confessed to the crime and were sentenced to be severely whipped "at the public post," and that both "shall wear…two letters,…AD, for adulterers, daily, upon the outside of their uppermost garment, in a most eminent place thereof."[62]

That same day, Francis Linceford had some other business to clear up with Thomas Bray—the return of goods left in his care. Apparently, Francis Linceford made a trip to the West Indies and left several items in Bray's care. Linceford requested that Bray, "shall deliver all the rest of the goods of the said Linceford which are in his hands." The deal was complicated. Some of the items, which were mainly household goods, were given to Bray, apparently to sell, so that he could "pay four pounds to several persons the said Linceford was indebted unto" when he left Yarmouth. Linceford wanted the remaining items back.[63]

Thomas Bray wasn't the only man with his eyes on Anne Linceford. Just three months later, after having moved about fifteen miles westward to the town of Sandwich, on March 1, 1642, Thomas Tupper, of Sandwich, was charged with a misdemeanor, "lascivious and unclean carriages towards Linceford's wife, late of Yarmouth." "Linceford's wife" was also presented, "for the same miscarriage." Thomas Tupper was in his mid-sixties at the time, one of the original founders of Sandwich, long married to his wife Anne, and well remembered as a Christian missionary to the Native Americans. No further mention is made of this charge in the court records but undoubtedly there was gossip in the neighborhood, given Tupper's otherwise stellar reputation.[64,65]

Chapter Eleven

Children's Deaths

Historian John J. Navin wrote that the children of the Pilgrims, "were the silent victims of religious enthusiasm and far-flung schemes that shifted them among households, towns, nations, and continents, dooming many in the process. Pawns in a world of adult conflict and enterprise, the sons and daughters of Plymouth's founders paid a high price for their parents' ambitions." It is, of course, impossible to know how their lives would have played out had they stayed in England or in Holland, but even William Bradford was moved by the sight of "poor little ones…crying for fear and quaking with cold" during one of their attempts to flee England.[1,2]

Among the passengers of the *Mayflower*, there were fourteen young adults and nineteen children. During the voyage, only one young adult died—William Butten, whom William Bradford listed as a "youth." During the first winter sickness seven children died, nearly one-third of all the children. In many cases, those who survived were orphaned. Seventy-five percent of the adult women died and fifty percent of the men, many of them parents. Of the five surviving teenaged girls, four were orphans. As their parents perished, the children were assigned into new families for their care.[3,4,5,6]

Those who survived had a life of toil ahead of them. By the terms of the agreement with their investors, the Pilgrims would be indentured for seven years, building the colony and "fishing, trading, etc.,…and not a day's freedom from task." This included the children. We know from Bradford that women "took their little ones [into the fields] with them to set corn" from the very beginning.[7,8,9]

Official Records of Children's Deaths

It is difficult to determine an accurate death rate for children in Plymouth Colony. The court records reveal only those deaths that required investigation—those of a sudden or suspicious nature. The deaths of fifteen children under the age of eighteen were recorded by the courts between 1620 and 1684. However, no record exists that tells us exactly how many more children died from other than suspicious circumstances; for example, those that may have succumbed to disease. What we do know is that without benefit of birth control, Pilgrim mothers on average became pregnant every two years, and yet most families had fewer than three children living into adulthood. Many children remain unaccounted for.[10]

Some effort was made to record the births, marriages, and deaths of Plymouth colonists. In 1646, a law was passed addressing the registrations: "There shall be in every town within this government a clerk or someone appointed and ordained to keep a register of the day and year of the marriage, birth, and burial of every man, woman, and child within their township." Some town clerks were more diligent than others, and while these registers give us important information, they are far from complete.[11]

No record exists of miscarriages, but there are a few records of full term stillbirths. The first such record is that of Sarah Allerton's child, a son, born February 22, 1620, "dead born" on board the *Mayflower*. On December 16, 1648, "a son of Peter Wright [was] stillborn." In 1650, "a daughter of Nathaniel Morton's [was] stillborn on the 23rd of November 1650." Undoubtedly, there were many more.[12,13]

Those records of a child's death that do exist rarely give the cause. One of the first births recorded in the colony's Miscellaneous Records register was the birth of Sarah Hull, the daughter of Trustrum Hull, born October 18, 1647 in Yarmouth. The very next page records her death. Little Hannah Glass, daughter of James Glass, was born June 2, 1647, and died just two weeks later, on June 15, 1648. Hester Templer was "aged five years and a half" when she died, buried on September 13, 1649." No reasons for any of these deaths are given.[14]

Newborns and Their Risks

For newborns, historian John Demos estimates the mortality rate of children was about one in ten. Pregnant women were expected to continue with their daily tasks. They did not receive pre-natal care as we know it, and probably suffered from poor and limited diets. Compared to modern standards, sanitation practices were inadequate, if they were practiced at all. No doubt having multiple pregnancies, and having them within two years of each other, contributed to the risk for the mother as well as the newly born.[15]

With no way to control conception, women lived in a cycle of childbirth, breast feeding, conception, childbirth, breast feeding, conception, over and over throughout their fertile years. For example, consider the family of Joseph Rogers of Sandwich. Baby Sarah was born August 6, 1633, and died on the fifteenth of the same month. Next came Joseph, 1635, Thomas, 1638, Elizabeth, 1639, John, 1642, Mary, 1644, James, 1648, and Hannah, born in 1652. The family of Nathaniel Warren of Plymouth produced at least ten children in less than twenty years. In quick order came Sarah, 1649, Hope 1651, Jane 1652, Elizabeth 1654, Alice, 1656, Mercy 1657, Mary, 1660, Nathaniel 1661, John, 1663, and finally James, born in 1665.[16]

Almost every family experienced losing a child, and tragedies of an intimate nature abound in the records. John Morton's wife, Lettice, delivered their first child, named after his father, on December 11, 1649; the child died just over a week later, on December 20. Only one year later, they had another child, another son they named John. They went on to have six more children, including twin boys born on June 7, 1653. The twins, named Manasseh and Ephraim, apparently also died, since there is no further mention of their names in the historical record. Jonathan Bangs and his wife Mary Mayo Bangs had a son they named after his father on May 11, 1670. Sadly, the child died the same day. Little Jonathan was the third of twelve children born to the couple between 1665 and 1689.[17,18,19,20,21]

other example is the Dean family. Bethiah Edson married Ezra n December 17, 1678. Just ten months later, their first child, her 's namesake, was born on October 14, 1679. The baby died on

Public worship at Plymouth.

November 27, only six weeks old. Their first son, Ezra, was born October 14, 1680, one year later to the day. Samuel was born on April 11, 1681, probably prematurely. He lived to be almost two years old and died on February 16, 1683. Still mourning the death of Samuel, Bethiah delivered Seth on June 3, 1683. Then came Margaret, in 1685, and finally Ephraim, in 1687.[22] There is no further mention of Bethiah Dean in the colony records after 1687. There may have been more pregnancies and more lost children for Bethiah, or she may have died. There is no Plymouth record of Ezra Dean remarrying. What we do know is that Bethiah had six children in a space of eight years, two of whom died.[23,24,25]

That women survived as many pregnancies and childbirths as they did is remarkable given the circumstances. John Demos estimates that in Plymouth Colony a mother would die in about one in thirty deliveries; with multiple pregnancies for each woman, that means that about one out of five women died during or shortly after experiencing a childbirth. For example, William Briggs' wife delivered a son, her ninth child, on March 19, 1680. She died the following day. The child, named John, apparently survived. Why William's wife died was not noted. Contributing factors to a new mother's death might have been exhaustion and dehydration from long labors, blood loss from hemorrhage, or infections known as "childbed fever."[26,27]

Twins

Twins were not uncommon in the colony. According to the register of "Births, Marriages, Deaths, and Burials," nine sets of twins were born between 1633 and 1689. In many cases both infants survived. Twins were just another pregnancy to many families in the colony. For example, Isaac Chittenden married Mary Vinall in April 1646. Their first pregnancy resulted in twins, Sarah and Rebecca, born Feb. 25, 1647, after which came Mary, 1648, Israel, 1651, Stephen, 1654, and Elizabeth, 1658.[28]

Twins born into the Bangs family not only survived; they thrived. Edward Bangs' wife, Lydia, delivered twin girls on October 15, 1651 in Eastham. These girls were her eighth and ninth children, and her last. Apphia and Mercy went on to marry—both on the same day, December 28, 1670—and had families of their own. Likewise, Thomas Gilbert's wife, Ann Blake Gilbert, delivered twin girls on August 11, 1679. They were named Sarah and Mary. Both lived and had children of their own.[29,30]

In some cases, the twins survived birth, only to succumb within a year or two. For example, the first set of twins in the colony records, Thomas and Hannah Smith, were born on April 23, 1647, to Richard Smith and his wife in Plymouth. Thomas died the next year. Hannah survived and grew up to marry Francis Curtis and produce five children. Samuel and Elizabeth Watson, the twin children of George Watson, were born January 18, 1647. Samuel died on August 20, 1649. Elizabeth survived, and later married Joseph Williams of Taunton on November 28, 1667.[31,32,33]

In at least one case, both infants died. The record states that Samuel Dunham's wife delivered twin boys on February 25, 1652. Sadly, the record also states that "a son of Samuel Dunham, being a twin, died soon after the birth…, and the other twin died six days later."[34]

Apparently, the Pilgrims were not superstitious about the birth of twins. No record has been found indicating that the mother or the children were treated any differently in the colony. There is no way of knowing how many twins were miscarried before birth as the Pilgrims did not record those instances.

Disease

In the year 1633, Plymouth experienced "an infectious fever," which was probably the smallpox. This epidemic killed more than twenty colonists, "men and women, besides children." The outbreak also took the life of their doctor, Samuel Fuller, before "it pleased the Lord the sickness ceased." Smallpox was a horrible disease. The next year it spread to the Native Americans who lived near the trading post at Windsor, and William Bradford wrote at length about the suffering of those who "died most miserably; for a sorer disease cannot befall them."[35,36]

> For usually they [Native Americans] that have this disease have [the sores] in abundance, and for want of bedding and linen and other helps they fall into a lamentable condition as they lie on their hard mats, the pox breaking and mattering and running one into another, their skin cleaving by reason thereof to the mats they lie on. When they turn them, a whole side will flay off at once as it were, and they will be all of a gore blood, most fearful to behold.[37]

So ill were the Indigenous People that "they were in the end not able to help one another, no not to make a fire nor to fetch a little water to drink, nor any to bury the dead." A few of the "English house… had compassion of them, and daily fetched them wood and water and made them fires and buried them when they died." The Pilgrims, who had already experienced their own epidemic of smallpox, escaped this disease, perhaps due to an immunity, even though they helped cared for the afflicted.[38]

On June 10, 1641, the Pilgrims participated in a Day of Humiliation, a day set aside for fasting and prayer, appealing to God "for the healing of a bloody cough among children especially at Plymouth." Whooping cough, also known as "chin cough," afflicted both adults and children. Copious bleeding accompanied the coughing, and it was a terrifying disease. The colony was visited again with the disease in 1649; November 15 of that year was set aside for another Day of Humiliation for the "children in the Bay dying by the chin cough and the pox and we [Plymouth] being also many visited to sicknesses or diseases." The epidemic worsened and another day of prayer was scheduled for December 19, "very many amongst us being visited with colds and coughs in a strange manner especially children their coughing constraining [and] casting [ejecting] and bleeding at the nose and mouth...."[39]

Dysentery was hard on children, who could succumb quickly to the dehydrating and weakening effects of diarrhea, but the "bloody flux" was especially violent. Dr. Ernest Caulfield commented that "from the evidence on hand one may conclude that bloody flux was one of the most formidable and widespread diseases of the seventeenth century." Its causes can be traced to infectious viruses, bacteria, protozoa or even worms, and symptoms include fever, abdominal pain, and bloody stools. Bloody flux often infected entire families and close communities because the cause of the disease could be a shared food or water source combined with poor sanitation and hygiene. In 1671, Jane Sharp also blamed "corrupt air" for spreading disease. The colony of Virginia, for instance, experienced an epidemic in 1621 that killed more than 600 colonists out of an estimated population of 2,000.[40,41]

Besides epidemics of contagious diseases, there were the more common childhood illnesses to endure. Many children had worms, for example. Some were afflicted with "convulsion fits." There were poisonous berries and mushrooms all around, and wild animals lurking in the surrounding environment. How they survived common colds and fevers is remarkable, considering that medicines, or "physicks," consisted mainly of plants and potions.[42]

As the population of New England grew, there were more episodes of contagion. In 1657, and again in 1687, there were measles outbreaks in Boston which affected both adults and children. Whooping cough and diphtheria hit Boston hard in 1659. Rev. Danforth of Roxbury noted that "the Lord sent a general visitation of children by coughs and colds, of which my three children, Sarah, Mary, and Elizabeth Danforth died, all of them within the space of a fortnight."[43,44]

Death in Suspicious Circumstances

While we do not find records of children dying from disease in the court records, we do find the details about the fifteen deaths of children that were investigated as suspicious, and they are sad stories indeed. By today's standards, these deaths were predictable and preventable, and we may question how closely parents watched over their children. For example, in this seaside community, why were children not taught how to swim? But this was a rather unforgiving environment and children were sometimes engaged in dangerous work, much of which may have been unsupervised. Siblings watched over each other, but there were times when an adult was the only one who could forestall danger.

Death by Drowning

Most of the "untimely" deaths of children, in fact over half of those investigated, were attributed to drowning. Unfenced wells were a known hazard. Little Thankful Pakes fell into the family's well and drowned on November 15, 1655. Her father, William Pakes, was chastised by the court, who found his well "to be very dangerous, as both in that it lies at the foot of a hill, and also having no fence about it to preserve a child from shooting or tumbling in." The jury's verdict was that "the child's falling or tumbling in the water was the cause of the death of Thankful Pakes." No charges were filed against her father. Another similar accidental death by drowning was that of the unnamed child of Daniel Doane's, "who was drowned in a well" in 1667.[45,46]

Elizabeth Walker was only two-and-a-half years old when she drowned in the river in Rehoboth in 1665. The daughter of Phillip Walker, she was walking to school alone when she accidentally fell into the water. Her body was found by two other children. They notified adults who pulled her body from the river. A subsequent jury found the death an accident. Phillip Walker lost another child to drowning nine years later. In 1677, Michael Walker, just ten years old, "came accidentally to his end by his falling through the floor of the sawmill upon the water wheel, or just by it, when it was going." Michael was "carried away with the stream" and ended up under the ice, where he perished.[47,48]

In 1672, Richard Lake's daughter fell into a stream and drowned. "We all do judge," the jury claimed, "according to what light we can gather, that the child came to its end by falling into a brook of water, and so was drowned." That same year three-year-old Peter Trebey, visiting from Newport with his mother, was "near the riverside" when "by some accident" he fell into the river in Taunton and drowned. Only one year later, Edward, the son of Samuel Jenkens, two years old, drowned in his father's well.[49]

Even as homely a task as washing clothes was fraught with danger. No charges were filed in 1676, when little Bethiah, namesake daughter of Bethiah Howland, jumped into a washtub and was drowned, "stifled [smothered]" among the clothes and water.[50]

Ten-year-old William England was in service to Joseph Wilbore of Taunton in 1651. One evening he had taken a "great canoe" to fetch firewood "from the further sides of the river called the Great River," as he often did. When he failed to come home, "his dame called to him" but there was no response. When Wilbore returned home and learned the boy was missing, he "immediately sought for him." About a quarter of a mile down river, Wilbore found the canoe, but not the boy. The search continued the next morning. "Being the Lords day,"

James Walker and Richard Burt found the child floating in the water while on their way to meeting. The jury found that the child struggled with "the ordering of his canoe," lost control of the boat, and "did fall over the said vessel, and so perished in the water."[51]

Death from Exposure

Freezing winter weather presented another danger for children, their small bodies being especially vulnerable to dying from exposure. There were four children's deaths from exposure at Plymouth, all boys. One of the earliest deaths from exposure occurred in 1648, when the son of John Wing "drowned [suffocated] in the snow" on December 11 in Yarmouth.[52]

A few years later, another child, little John Slocome, died as a result of being outdoors in winter weather. In 1651, a large group of persons, "to the number of twenty," travelled two miles from Plymouth Town to Fowling Pond to gather cranberries. Among them was John Slocome, nine years old. This was in February, when it was very cold, and on the way home, John could not keep up with the others. "About a mile from his home, upon confidence of his knowledge of the way home,... but missing the path, strayed in the woods, and returned not again." For three days his father "raised the town, and with a considerable company the whole night following, with drum, guns, and loud voices" they searched for the child.[53]

The following January, a farmer herding his cattle found John's skull, "other parts of the corpse," and shreds of clothing "scattered in small pieces," near the head of Mill River, which was three miles from town and two from Fowling Pond. The jury found that John, "when he strayed away, wandered with much labor, and being spent with weariness and cold, perished among the brushy shrubs, and was devoured and torn [by animals], and the parts of his carcass dispersed with ravenous creatures."[54]

Another child who became lost in the woods was an unnamed servant child, "which was kept by John Smalley." His body was found about six or seven miles from Smalley's house. "We all do judge," a jury decided, "that it came to his death by straying away, lost its right path to get home again, and was killed by the cold."[55]

Work Related Deaths

Children and teenagers often did the type of work in Plymouth Colony that today would be performed by adults; some tasks were arguably beyond their ability. In 1661, John Bond, servant to George Watson, was killed while bringing a load of wood home to his master. While unloading the cart, John, "someway touching the mare," startled the animal who ran away with the cart with the boy still in it. John jumped off the cart, landing "before the wheel" and was run over. The ensuing jury found the death accidental.[56]

Thomas Fish was probably a teenager when he died at the mill dam August 19, 1664. He had mixed feelings about working that day, "being not willing to go." A co-worker agreed, saying to Thomas, "It is too late to go to work today to Goodman Burges." But Fish took up his wheelbarrow and went anyway, and began to work at shoveling a bank. During the digging the bank collapsed, burying Thomas. Co-workers "hastened to take the clods from him," but he was badly bruised and "he was got to bed." Four and a half pain-filled days later, Thomas died from his injuries.[57]

Accidental Deaths

Even with the best of care, accidents happened. On October 14, 1667, the unnamed child of Nicholas Nickerson died. It was discovered that a piece of pumpkin shell had become lodged in his windpipe, and the child had choked to death. No charges were filed.[58]

In Scituate in 1680, the child of Thomas Hatch's, who was about eighteen months old, was found dead in bed the morning of July 1. The child had been ill with a cold a day or two earlier, which may have contributed to his death. However, it was determined by the jury to be a case of suffocation. A jury decided that the child, "according to our information and best understanding, judge, that either it was stifled by lying on its face or accidentally over laid in the bed, as a cause of its death." Several people were apparently sharing the bed with the toddler, "in the absence of its parents." In the house that night were Waitstill Elmes, about twenty years old, and perhaps a servant, Sarah

Hatch, the child's sister, and Daniel Pryor, who would later marry Thomas Hatch's daughter Mary. Sharing a bed was not unusual in the Colonial Era, and perhaps someone rolled over during the night onto the child and suffocated it. No charges were filed.[59]

In what may have been one of the first cases of a child killed while playing with his father's gun in the colonies, Richard Sylvester's son shot himself in the head and died. The tragedy took place in 1642 in Weymouth, just before Sylvester moved his family to Plymouth. In September, Richard Sylvester and his wife Naomi had gone "to the assembly, upon the Lord's day, [and] left their children at home." The oldest, who was about seven years old, had gone outside tending to their cattle. The two youngest, one about five and another around three, were indoors. As Governor Winthrop told it:

> The middle-most…son…seeing his father's fowling piece, (being a very great one,) stand in the chimney, took it and laid it upon a stool, as he had seen his father do, and pulled up the cock, (the spring being weak) and put down the hammer, then went to the other end and blowed in the mouth of the piece, as he had seen his father also do, and with that stirring the piece, being charged, it went off, and shot the child into the mouth and through his head. When the father came home he found his child lie dead, and could not have imagined how he should have been so killed, but the youngest child, (being about three years old, and could scarce speak,) showed him the whole manner of it.[60]

By 1650, Sylvester sold his property in Weymouth and moved to Marshfield, Plymouth Colony. It was in Plymouth that his daughter, Dinah, was charged with accusing the wife of William Holmes of being a witch, as already discussed. When he died, Richard Sylvester named eleven children in his will. No doubt, however, he and Naomi still mourned the loss of the toddler who shot himself with his father's gun.[61]

By His Own Hand

On February 23, 1660, a jury was assembled to investigate the death of a servant by the name of William Day who was found dead in his master's barn. There was an investigation and after "the jury have heard what any person or persons could evidence," it was unanimously determined "that the forenamed William Day was a self-murderer." The reasons why William Day took his own life have been lost to the centuries since the day he was discovered. Nothing further is known; this is the only Plymouth record under the Day surname.[62]

Infanticide

After King Philip's War, the Indigenous People were under the complete authority of Plymouth Colony courts. They did not even have a separate-yet-equal power over their own affairs, governed by a tribal court. Many had surrendered during the war, or shortly thereafter. They lived and worked in the colony, and any crimes they committed were addressed by the colony courts.

For example, in 1683, Awashunkes, her daughter, Betty, and her son Peter, were brought into court "on suspicion of their having a hand in the murdering of a young child." Awashunkes was known as "Squaw Sachem of Saconett," and was a respected leader of the community. She and her daughter "solemn[ly] affirmed that the said child [was] dead before it was born."[63,64]

While Awashunkes was an important woman in the community, there was more to this case that troubled the courts. Yet another woman, "Sam's wife," had reported earlier that Betty was with child, but Awashunkes and Betty denied the charge of fornication. The court ordered two other Indigenous women to examine Betty and they reported that "she was not with child." As a result, Sam's wife was whipped for making a false report. Now, the court learned, the pregnancy "appeared to be really so," and the whipping had been administered without just cause.[65]

The two women who examined Betty and lied about her condition were ordered to pay ten shillings each to "the said Sam's squaw," for the whipping she suffered. Furthermore, Betty was likewise ordered to pay her twenty shillings." Awashunkes, Betty, and Peter were charged twenty shillings each "for the charge of their bringing [arrest] and imprisonment."[66]

As for Betty, she was ordered to be whipped by the Native Americans at Saconett for fornication. They were ordered to investigate the child's death, "to find out any further grounds of suspicion of the said murder." There is no further record to confirm or deny that Betty or Awashunkes or Peter murdered the newborn.[67]

There was another case involving an American Indian woman named Betty before the court on March 5, 1685. She may have been the same Betty referred to in the above proceedings. "An Indian squa[w] named Betty, was indicted for killing her husband, named Great Harry." Under questioning, she denied that charge, but later admitted that while she did not intend to kill him, she did throw a stone at him. Actually, she testified, she was throwing the stone at the bottle of liquor he was drinking from, but missed and "hit the said Indian, her husband, on the side of his head, whereof he died."[68]

The case being put to the grand jury, they found it is true bill and referred it to the petty jury. The petty jury found "the said Betty, Indian squaw, for the said fact, guilty of homicide by misadventure." Yes, she threw the stone that killed her husband, but his death was ruled an accident. Betty was released.[69]

Chapter Twelve

Danger and Desperation

By the 1640s life in Plymouth Colony had become easier, at least when compared to the earlier years. The residents had learned to live with the icy winters, and had erected warm and somewhat comfortable homes. Thanks to Squanto's help, they had adapted to farming in Plymouth, and if food was not actually in abundance, it was adequate. Diseases occurred now and then, but casualties were limited compared to the first winter. A treaty was in place with the Native Americans that somewhat lessened day-to-day anxiety. Overall, life was tolerable, and perhaps occasionally enjoyable.

Nonetheless, the work required to sustain this existence was grueling for everyone. Except for seasonal changes that dictated when certain chores needed to be done, each day was typically like the one before, a monotonous drudge. Women had additional hardship. Their domestic tasks had to be completed while they were pregnant, nursing, or watching over small children. In the midst of all this, there were still real dangers to be found, and everyone needed to be vigilant. Some coped better than others.

Dangers in the Environment

In 1674, John Josselyn wrote *An Account of Two Voyages to New England,* wherein he stated that within a stone's throw of his house, snakes were found, "some of them as big as the small of my leg, black of color, and three yards long, with a sharp horn on the tip of their tail two inches in length." Rattlesnakes were so prevalent in Plymouth that they were a part of the Indigenous Peoples' lore and legend. For example, when the Narragansett threatened the colony in 1621, they did so by sending a messenger with a "bundle of arrows tied about with a great snakeskin." The rattlesnake skin was their symbol of a challenge. Undaunted, the colonists sent the skin back "with bullets in it," flaunting the colonists' superior weaponry.[1,2,3]

Wolves were a threat, so much so that beginning in 1633 the court offered a bounty for the heads of these "ravenous creatures," that had been caught in traps. The threat was mainly to sheep and goats and other smaller animals. By 1642, a law was passed ordering that "all towns within the government shall make wolf traps and bait them and look unto them daily upon the penalty of ten shillings a trap that shall be neglected." The number of traps each town was required to make varied from two to five. In 1654 alone, the account of "wolves killed by the Indians [and] brought into this court," numbered almost twenty animals, plus a number of "young ones." By 1665, the threat of wolves had apparently lessened, and each community was required by law to set only two traps.[4,5,6]

Aside from the risk of dangerous animals, other hazards existed in the wild. Women often gathered berries and roots in the forest to add to their meals, an innocent activity that caused at least one death. Mary Totman's demise in 1666 was ruled accidental by the courts on April 24 of that year. As was her habit, Mary had been gathering roots in the forest, and she had "gathered, dressed, and did eat a root, which we judge, she mistaking it, thinking it to be the same which she had formerly often eaten of." The root, however, was poisonous, and "was the sole cause and occasion of her death." But there is more to this already sad story.[7]

The year before, on March 7, 1665, Thomas Totman appeared before the court to answer the charge that he had "carnal copulation with his now wife before marriage." He testified that he and Mary were under contract, that is, they were formally engaged at the time. The court was not convinced. It fined him ten pounds, but if he could prove they were engaged at the time, the fine would be reduced to five pounds. There is no further record of this charge.[8]

The couple had a son they named Stephen in early 1666, just before Mary died. After her death, Thomas did not remarry. In 1678,

Wolves were a serious threat to both people and livestock.

when Stephen was about fourteen, his father died. The court investigated and on June 5, 1678, determined that "we find no other thing or cause [for Thomas' death] but only willful absenting himself from food to be the cause and means of his death." Was it a longing for Mary that caused Thomas to stop eating? The record is silent.[9,10]

Thomas and Mary's son, Stephen, grew up and married in 1691, but he had his own heartbreaks. His first child, also named Stephen, born October 11, 1691, died in infancy. Another son born in 1693, again named Stephen, apparently died, because on May 27, 1695, a third son they named Stephen was born, and he, too, died young. The couple had two more children, Mary, named after her late grandmother, born in 1696, and Christian, born in 1699. After the birth of Christian, Stephen Totman's wife died. He relocated to Plymouth with his two motherless children and remarried. In 1711, he and his new wife Dorothy named their fourth child Stephen, the only one of his father's namesakes to survive.[11]

Fire, a constant danger

All cooking was done over the household fire, which was also the only source of heat in this seaside colony. Considering that in every household there was a fire constantly burning in the hearth, it is a wonder that there were not more disasters than there were. The chimney was framed in wood and lined with mud and clay to prevent wayward sparks from starting a fire. Buckets of water were kept by the open hearth to put out any sparks that flew into the room. By law, thatch roofs were a thing of the past. Yet, fire was a constant concern.

The first fire in the colony, on January 14, 1621, was while the *Mayflower* was still in the harbor. A small fire inside one of the new houses released a spark "that flew into the thatch, which instantly burnt it all up, but the roof stood and little hurt." John Carver and William Bradford, "who then lay sick in bed," were inside the house. Fortunately, they quickly escaped and only their belongings were lost. Three years later, on November 7, 1623, there was "a bad fire." The fire "did considerable damage" to several buildings at Plymouth. Three or four houses were destroyed, along with "all the goods and provisions in them." So terrifying was the event that "several of the inhabitants through discontent and causalities removed to Virginia."[12,13,14]

Fire was such a concern that by 1636, it was a capital crime to willfully set fire to a house or a ship. It was further ordered that should a fire break out in a house, the colonists were required to fire three shots into the air, Plymouth's signal for an emergency, followed immediately by two shots, indicating the emergency was a fire.[15]

There is one court case of a fire set accidentally. On June 4, 1645, Roger Cooke and William Latham appeared before the court to "complain against John Barker, and Ann, his wife, in an action of trespass upon the case, to the damage of twenty pounds, for the said Ann's burning of their house accidentally." Even though the fire was called an accident, Ann was still responsible to make restitution. The jury could not decide whether there was fault, and "the matter was ended." There was, however, a settlement. John Barker agreed to "give the plaintiff twenty shillings towards their losses." It appears from the amount of the award that the damage was minimal.[16]

Medical emergencies

Medical treatment was very primitive in Plymouth Colony, when compared with modern medicine. Illnesses and accidents were routinely treated by women in the home. Even with her rudimentary medical knowledge, the Plymouth housewife could stitch a wound, apply herbal poultices and tend to children with fevers. Physicians, such as there were, were few and far between, but she could always call on a neighbor for help. When a professional health care provider was summoned, perhaps to set a broken bone, the doctor expected to be paid. Once the patient was well, fees were sometimes forgotten.[17]

In one case, on October 6, 1657, the local "chirurgeon" filed suit for payment of his overdue fees. Ann, the wife of John Williams, Sr., had for several years been "grievously afflicted" with a "desperate, dangerous sore" on her left thigh in the hip area. The sore had for some years been "breeding or growing" and Williams requested the aptly named doctor, Comfort Starr, to treat her. Starr made several journeys to the Williams home, performing surgery and applying medicines externally. Apparently, he ceased making house calls there, so it can be assumed that the sore eventually healed. But he had not been paid, and as a result he was suing Williams. The jury decided for the plaintiff and awarded Starr fourteen pounds and court costs, which amounted to ten shillings.[18]

That an untreated, and presumably infected, sore could continue to fester for years and not cause the woman's death is remarkable. The remedies that Comfort Starr applied could have been an ointment of bark, herbs, leaves, or maybe even turpentine tar.

Some women were not so fortunate. After Mary Chase of Yarmouth died in October of 1659, there was an investigation. After making "search and inquiry," the jury decided that Mary "died a natural death [due to] inward sickness." With a calm acceptance the jury noted that such an illness is "evident to all men naturally." In other words, such is life.[19]

Impoverished women

Poverty was a fact of life in Plymouth, but some situations were so serious the courts intervened. For example, on October 27, 1674, Mary Wyatt's condition was discussed in court. She was the widow of James Wyatt, and "hath several times supplicated to this court for relief" of her debts. She owed Joseph Leonard eleven pounds, and the court's reaction was to award him eight acres of her property to cover the debt.[20]

Four years later, on October 30, 1678, the court learned that Mary was still "in great necessity and a very low condition, in want of maintenance, notwithstanding the estate of her deceased husband [that] came [to] her." The court then appointed James Walker, William Harvey, Sr., and Walter Dean, "or any two of them," to lease some of the lands and meadows that James Wyatt had left to his family. The income from the leases was to "be improved for the relief of the said widow." Basically, the colony took over managing her assets for her benefit, and also to protect the town from having to provide public funds for her support. On October 27, 1685, Mary Wyatt died. She left a will to dispose of her remaining assets, assets that probably would not have been there except for the intervention of the community.[21,22]

Women Behaving Strangely

Now and then, a woman—or a man—might develop emotional problems that required the courts to intervene. Life in Plymouth Colony was a real challenge, especially for women who were trapped in a cycle of childbearing. Some coped better with the pressures than others. As they did with cases of women living in poverty, the community and the courts stepped in to see that women with emotional issues received the help they needed.

Goodwife Thomas, "The Welsh Woman"

Referred to only as "Goodwife Thomas, the Welsh woman" in the court records, it is difficult to connect her to any other Plymouth family. Apparently she was living alone, and for unknown reasons was in great personal difficulty, although she owned property in the colony.

In 1658, three of the colony's leaders were requested to investigate the situation of the Welsh woman, who was living "disorderly." The community was concerned that "she be not for the future endangered to come to misery and extremity, as formerly she hath been." On September 29, Mr. Collier, Mr. Alden, and Constant Southworth were to "take some speedy course" to address the situation of a woman living alone near North River.[23]

But by March the following year, a complaint was filed by William Tubbs of Duxbury, stating that Goodwife Thomas was living on his land without his permission. On March 1, 1659, Mr. Collier and Mr. Alden were again requested "to take some speedy course to remove her unto her own land."[24] A few months later the court had to intervene. It appears that someone was helping her build a house. On June 7, 1659, it was ordered that "Goodwife Thomas, the Welsh woman, shall not be assisted by any in setting up any house or cottage anywhere except it be on her own ground." Apparently, she insisted on living some place other than on her own land. Or perhaps there was confusion over the boundaries of her property.[25,26]

With the colder weather quickly approaching, on October 6, 1659, the court ordered Goodwife Thomas to report to Mr. Collier and Mr. Alden in Duxbury, to discuss her situation and determine a solution. After considering the problem, Collier and Alden made arrangements with Robert Barker for her care. The arrangement was finalized on August 7, 1660. Barker would "take possession of such goods or chattels as are belonging to the said Welsh woman." He would also take possession of Goodwife Thomas herself, taking her "into his custody, that she may live in his house." He was charged to "see that she do not live extravagantly [unrestrained] as formerly, and to perform the conditions made with the town of Duxbury on that behalf." If she should leave Plymouth, Barker would "return her estate again to her, and in the meantime not to make [take] any of it away or dispose of any part thereof unless he be necessitated thereunto to provide clothing for her, or in case of sickness or the like, and shall be ready to give an account of what he expends or not of when required by the court."[27]

For her own safety and to protect those whose land she was squatting on, the solution was to have her move in with Robert Barker and his family, who would gather all her possessions, and take care of her, provide for her, and keep exact records of his spending towards her care. How that turned out is not known; there is no more mention of the "Welsh woman" in the court records.

Susanna Perry

A mystery surrounds the case of Susanna Perry. On January 7, 1645, William Perry of Scituate acknowledged before the court that he owed the colony a fine, details of which would be worked out later. The issue was that his wife, Susanna Perry stood accused of "spoiling and defiling a well of water in Scituate." She was ordered to attend the next general court to answer to the charges. However, the case was "respited until she is able to come." She may have just given birth.[28]

Susanna Perry, the daughter of Richard and Margaret Carver, was twenty-seven years at the time of this charge. She married William about 1640, and there may have been several failed pregnancies; their first child was born sometime in 1645. There is no further mention of the case in the Plymouth Colony Records. Whatever Susanna did to the well is unknown, although her husband assumed responsibility and paid a fine. The Perry's went on to have five children. Susanna died before 1693, the year her husband died.[29,30,31]

Alice Berry

Alice Berry, the wife of Richard Berry, engaged in a spree of breaking, entering, and stealing from her neighbors between 1653 and 1655. On May 3, 1653, she was presented in court "for stealing of a neckcloth from William Pearce his wife of Yarmouth." Two months later, on June 9, 1653, she was again brought into court, "for going into the house of Samuel Arnold, and taking bacon and eggs when there was no body at home." A side note in the record reads, "Alice Berry sentenced for this and other doings of like nature, sentenced to sit in the stocks for the space of an hour at Yarmouth in some public place."[32]

Two years later, Alice was back in court. On March 6, 1655, she was charged with "going into the house of Benjamin Hammond, when nobody was at home, and feloniously took away a woman's shift, that was new made, but without sleeves, and a piece of pork." Two months later, on June 8, 1655, Alice was charged with "thievishly milking the cow of Thomas Phelps of Yarmouth." She was charged ten shillings, "or refusing to pay, then to sit in the stocks at Yarmouth an hour the next training day."[33]

Richard Berry (Beere) and Alice (last name unknown) of Barnstable and Yarmouth, were married in 1652. Alice was probably in her early twenties. Their son John was born that same year, followed by an unnamed child in 1654, and Elizabeth in 1656.[34,35,36]

It was between 1653 and 1656, with three small children to care for, that Alice took to thievery. She stole from several households, never the same one twice. She must have been an inept burglar since she was caught so often. Most of the items taken were food. These cases of theft (and there were probably more as the record referred to "other things of like nature"), earned Alice relatively light punishments, fines and time sitting in the stocks. Why was the court lenient on her? Did she steal food because she was in need?

Sadly, Alice was another Pilgrim woman who did not marry well. Richard Berry was a troublemaker who appeared several times in the colony records. On October 29, 1649, Berry accused Teague Jones of attempting to sodomize him, and the courts decided to hold them both over for further questioning. Berry also accused Jones of unclean practices with Sarah Norman, wife of Hugh Norman. These were very serious charges, and at the March 6, 1650, court, Berry recanted the whole story, "in both the aforesaid particulars," admitting he lied and was ordered to be whipped for his perjury. Apparently, Berry and Jones had been spending a lot of time together and the court may have suspected them of homosexual behavior. On June 9, 1653, the court ordered that "Teague Jones and Richard Berry, and others with them, be caused to part their uncivil living together, as they will answer it." This was about the time that Alice began stealing things.[37,38]

There may have been more cases of thievery that were not addressed as such in the courts. For example, on March 6, 1655, William Chase, Jr. entered the Berry house and took away "by violence a parcel of flax and a small parcel of hose yarn." If this was a case of Chase retrieving something that was stolen from him, the court showed no sympathy. Chase was sentenced to sit in the stocks an hour on a military training day at Yarmouth.[39]

In 1659, Berry testified in a stolen property case. He was in possession of stolen property, of "sundry goods and calves" that actually belonged to William Nickerson. Nickerson first sued Edward Sturgis, and then Anthony Thatcher, for the theft of those goods and animals in the amount of twenty pounds. The complex case consumed court time for six months until the settlement was finalized. In the final reckoning, Thatcher was ordered to pay Nickerson twenty shillings for his loss. Berry was awarded costs for his testimony and travel, but something must have come up during that hearing, because once that case was settled, the court's attention—and fury—turned to Berry himself.[40]

On October 6, 1659, the court came down hard on Richard Berry, calling him "a grossly scandalous person, debauched, having been formerly convicted of filthy, obscene practices." He was "sentenced to be disfranchised of his freedom of this corporation," meaning that his status as a freeman, including his voting rights, were revoked.[41]

Although no longer a freeman, he and Alice eventually went on to have eleven children. Not surprisingly, the family was impoverished. On January 19, 1660, shortly after being disfranchised, and "with his wife's consent; and other friends," Richard Berry "hath given unto George Crisp of Eastham and his wife, their son Samuel Berry, to be at the ordering and disposing of [them] as if he were their own son." One less mouth to feed.[42,43,44]

Samuel was a handful himself. In his will, George Crisp noted that the child had become "stubborn and rebellious and went away." As a consequence Crisp left instructions that Richard Berry be paid "the small sum of twelve pence and no more," to cover the time Samuel was out of Crisp's indenture.[45,46]

Berry continued to be a scoundrel. On October 5, 1663, he was fined forty shillings for "playing at cards," along with William Griffin and his wife, and Richard Michell. The fines were remitted by the court five months later. Zachariah Ryder accused Berry of stealing his axe on June 3, 1668. Less than a year later, while exhibiting amazing impudence, Berry was observed smoking tobacco just outside the meeting house on the Sabbath in clear violation of Plymouth law. He and his friends were each fined five shillings.[47,48]

In 1675, Richard and Alice's daughter Elizabeth, twenty years old, was the recipient of unwanted attention from Nathaniel Hall. For his "uncivil words and carriages towards Elizabeth Berry, and also for giving writings…to entice her, although he had a wife of his own, was sentenced by the court to pay a fine of five pounds to the use of the colony or be publicly whipped." (This record tempts us to assume that Elizabeth Berry was able to read the mash-notes Nathaniel Hall was giving to her. However, the literacy level of Plymouth's women remains debatable. There is simply not enough evidence).[49]

Richard Berry's will was dated 1681. A subsequent inventory names his widow, Alice Berry. Richard did not have enough of an estate to pay his debts and the court ordered that "Mr. John Miller and Jeremiah Howes, of Yarmouth, to make sale of the house and lands of the said Berry's to pay his just debts." His widow and children were not completely forgotten, as the court ordered that if there was anything left over, "after such debts are paid, the said remainder to be at the court's dispose for the use and benefit of the children."[50,51]

The long-suffering Alice Berry delivered her last child on December 12, 1677. Between 1652 and 1677, she had borne at least eleven children. When Richard's will was read, the oldest was twenty-nine, the youngest four years old. Her death date is not known.[52]

Women Under Attack

Under the umbrella law that prohibited any actions that interrupted the king's peace in the colony, cases of assault—whether verbal, physical, or sexual—were prosecuted by the courts. Women were the most frequent victims.

A case of verbal abuse in 1670 is a good example. On June 7, 1670, John Dunham was called into court to answer "for his abusive speeches and carriages towards Sarah, the wife of Benjamin Eaton." He was ordered to post the hefty sum of forty pounds, with the conditions, "that if the said John Dunham be of good behavior towards our sovereign lord the King and all his liege people, and in special towards Sarah, the wife of Benjamin Eaton, and appear at the court of his majesty to be holden at Plymouth aforesaid the last Tuesday in October next, and not depart the said court without license," his bond would be released. No further record exists.[53]

The court records are often frustrating in their lack of detail, especially in cases of abuse and assault. Such is the case with the beating of Katherine Winter. On October 7, 1651, George Russell of Scituate was charged with "his uncivil and unreasonable beating of Katherine Winter." He was ordered to pay twenty shillings "to be employed for the good of the said Katherine." While they had his attention in court, the governor and his assistants addressed some unfinished business with George Russell. He was charged with "encroaching on the undivided lands of Scituate," and ordered to take down a fence he constructed that "stopped the highways." No fines were imposed.[54]

The case of Samuel Norman demonstrates that violent outbursts of anger would not be tolerated in the colony. Norman was charged on June 7, 1670, with "breaking the King's peace" by striking Lydia Taylor and throwing a hoe at Hannah Davis. Norman was fined three shillings, four pence, for hitting Lydia, and ten shillings for endangering Hannah's life. He was further ordered to post sureties of twenty pounds to ensure his "good behavior towards our sovereign lord the King and all his liege people, and in special towards the parties wronged by him as aforesaid." He was ordered to appear in court in October. Little is known about Samuel Norman. Five years earlier, on June 9, 1665, he was fined ten shillings for telling a lie. That fine was carried in the treasury records for two years before being cleared.[55,56,57]

In a case dated March 2, 1652, Rebecca Palmer's father-in-law, John Willis, complained on her behalf against Tristram Hull and his wife. He claimed that Rebecca was "molested and hindered in performing faithful service unto her master Samuel Mayo of Barnstable" by Tristram's wife. What John meant by "molested and hindered" is not clear, but an order was sent by the court to the grand juryman of Barnstable to "warn the wife of the said [Tristram] Hull to desist from such practices any further." Furthermore, the court wanted to know why Tristram Hull's wife did not appear in court; without the defendants, the case could not proceed. Since the defendants did not show, the case was dropped.[58,59]

The punishments for assaults of a sexual nature were much more serious; an offender was often whipped, at times severely. For example, on August 21, 1637, John Bundy attacked Elizabeth Haybell, servant to William Brewster, in Brewster's own home. Bundy was "examined and found guilty of lewd behavior and uncivil carriage," and was sentenced to be severely whipped. This case appeared to be straightforward, but attacks on women at Plymouth were difficult cases to prove.[60]

First, the court required two witnesses to validate a claim. For example, on March 1, 1670, Michael Peirse of Scituate was before the court for "unseemly carriages" towards Sarah Nicolls, of Scituate. But, since there "appeared but one testimony to the presentment, and that the testimony was written and not read unto the deponent," the court decided not to proceed. It could be argued that Peirse got off on a technicality.[61,62]

Secondly, the law laid the responsibility on the woman to cry out for help and to report the crime. The source for this legislation was Mosaic law, specifically Deuteronomy 22:23-25, which the Pilgrims interpreted that if a woman cried out for help during an attack, it was possible someone would come to her aid; if she did not scream, it was assumed the act was consensual.

One example was in 1642, when Lydia Hatch was brought into court "for suffering [tolerating] Edward Mitchell to attempt to abuse her body by uncleanness." Apparently, the crime was reported by an unknown person in the community, and the court reproached Lydia because she did not report the crime herself. At the same court she was also convicted of "lying in the same bed with her brother Jonathan," and it is unclear which action earned her a sentence of whipping.[63]

The court then addressed Edward Mitchell's crimes. He was charged with the attempted sexual assault on Lydia Hatch, but also accused of "lewd ... practices tending to sodomy with Edward Preston." It is not known which crime the courts found more offensive, but Edward Mitchell was sentenced to be whipped twice, once in Plymouth and again in Barnstable, as was Edward Preston.[64]

Another case when blame was shared between the victim and the offender, was heard on March 5, 1655. The Grand Inquest reported

John Gorum for "unseemly carriage towards Blanch Hull at [an] unseasonable time, being at night." He was fined forty shillings. But Blanch Hull was fined fifty shillings "for not crying out when she was assaulted by John Gorum in unseemly carriage towards her."[65]

Attacks on women could take various forms. "Lascivious carriages" is the term the Pilgrims used to cover any behavior that violated the community's standards of sexual activity, save the crime of rape. These acts could include playfulness, flirting, dalliances, and the like; they could also include acts with more sinister intentions, such as obvious displays of sexual intention.

Lotharios like George Wright were not tolerated in Plymouth. On March 1, 1647, he was charged "for attempting the chastity of diverse women by lascivious words and carriages." He was found guilty by a jury, but the court, after "maturely consider[ing] the matters and circumstances," decided to request a bond of forty pounds for good behavior, and his appearance at the next court.[66]

Those most vulnerable to sexual abuse were female servants. Some men considered them as fair game for their lustful intentions. The court did not. For example, on March 6, 1655, the Grand Jury presented John Peck of Rehoboth. He was charged with "lascivious carriages and unchaste in attempting the chastity of his father's maid servant." "To satisfy his fleshly, beastly lust," he had been molesting her for over a year, "without any intent to marry her." The servant always resisted, she testified, and Peck was fined fifty shillings.[67]

Another servant, Elizabeth Doxey, charged her master's son with a serious crime. Once again, it was concern over the illegitimate child's financial support that influenced the judgment. On July 5, 1670,

> Elizabeth Doxey, late servant to Mr. Joseph Tilden, deceased, being delivered of a child, and charging of Nathaniel Tilden to be the father of it, the said Nathaniel Tilden appeared at this court to answer to it, and being examined, denied it; notwithstanding, the court saw cause to take security of him to save the town of Scituate harmless from any damage that might accrue unto them by the said child until another father

appear; and a warrant was directed to the constables of Scituate to cause her, the said Doxey, to be sent as soon as she is capable to Plymouth, to receive punishment according to her demerits.[68]

As for Nathaniel, on March 8, 1671, he was charged with "uncivil carriages with Elizabeth Doxey," and fined forty shillings. He was not named as the child's father, and there is no further record of any punishment for Elizabeth Doxey.[69]

In one case, the abuse of a young woman resulted in a fine payable to her mother, rather than to the victim. The widow Elizabeth Ensign brought a charge against Thomas Summers, "to the damage of five hundred pounds." On October 3, 1665, Summers, Elizabeth alleged, was guilty of "enticing and drawing away her daughter unseasonably [inappropriately], and by unlawful means, against her will, and abusing her said daughter." The charges were very serious, and the amount of the suit amazingly large. After investigation, the jury decided the charges were not quite so serious and the amount preposterous. Summers was ordered to pay Elizabeth fifty shillings and court costs. The full details of what really happened between Elizabeth and Thomas were not recorded, and perhaps this was a case of exaggeration or miscommunication among the parties involved. (This was the same Thomas Summers who was in a long-term feud with John Williams, already discussed).[70]

The case of assault on Ann Hudson involved not only physical assault, but also exposure. Richard Turtall was charged with lascivious carriage towards Ann Hudson, John Hudson's wife, on March 5, 1656. Turtall assaulted Ann, "in taking hold of her coat and enticing her by words." He didn't stop there. He took out "his instrument of nature that he might prevail to lie with her in her own house." Despite the serious charges, there is no further mention of the charge or of Richard Turtall in the court records.[71]

Attacks against American Indian women were taken just as seriously. Lieut. Peter Hunt's servant, who was not named in the record and may have been a Native American, was charged with having "hath attempted the chastity of an Indian woman, by offering violence to her."

The outcome was an unusual one in Plymouth courts. On December 6, 1659, the court decided to turn the boy over to Captain Willett, who was in charge of the trading post in Maine, and who had previous experience with the Native American language and culture. He was charged to further examine the servant, and if found guilty, Willett alone would decide on what "due correction to be given [the servant], and determine also otherwise about the said fact as he shall judge meet."[72]

On October 29, 1672, William Makepeace, Sr., "living at Taunton River," was also charged with attempted sexual assault on a native woman. He was sentenced to be publicly whipped at the post for "lascivious attempts towards an Indian woman."[73]

"Lascivious attempts" against any woman were quickly addressed by the courts. On March 2, 1641, John Russell, of Dartmouth was accused of "attempting the chastity of Hannah, the wife of William Spooner." John was fined twenty pounds and released. On March 4, 1650, Robert Waterman of Marshfield was charged with "offering an attempt of bodily uncleanness to Sarah Pittney." He was fined fifty shillings, "or to suffer bodily punishment." In another case, "we have information," the record states on June 9, 1653, "of John Marchant, of Yarmouth, his attempting the chastity of Annis [Agnes], the wife of Thomas Phillips,…but have not as yet oath of it." By August, the courts had the confirmation they earlier lacked. "We present John Marchant… for misdemeaning of himself in words and carriages with and towards Agnes, the wife of Thomas Phillips." John Marchant was fined fifty shillings. Giles Richard (or possibly "Rickard") was also fined fifty shillings, charged and then convicted on June 9, 1653, for "lascivious carriages towards Mary, the daughter of Barnard Lumbard, of Barnstable."[74,75,76]

On occasion, the court ruled against the accuser in cases of assault. Jaell, the wife of John Smith, accused Nicholas White and Thomas Jones of "hav[ing] committed uncleanness with her," at the court dated March 4, 1673. Jaell made the accusation "to their faces" in court. After investigation, each man was required to post of bond of twenty pounds. But Jaell was also fined ten pounds "for committing fornication," the court apparently finding the act consensual.[77]

A woman's reputation was her currency in Plymouth.

The Capital Crime of Rape

Rape within the family has already been addressed, but there were other cases of rape in Plymouth that deserve attention. Rape was considered a capital crime in Plymouth, punishable by death. However, rape was difficult to prove, and it is possible that many cases went unreported. It was assumed that the sex was consensual unless the woman cried out for help, as discussed above, and there had to be two witnesses to the act. Since rape was technically punishable by hanging, it was critical that the crime be proven without a doubt.[78,79]

Two cases of rape were addressed by the courts in Plymouth, neither resulting in an execution. The first, the rape of Lydia Fish, has already been addressed. The second, the rape of Sarah Freeman by "Sam, the Indian" raises several interesting questions. On October 31, 1682, Sam appeared before the court "for his rape committed upon an English girl, being found guilty by the jury, who found him guilty by his own confession, in wickedly abusing the body of Sarah Freeman by laying her down upon her back, and entering her body with his."[80]

The court admitted that "in ordinary considerations he deserved death," however, "considering he was but an Indian, and therefore in an incapacity to know the horribleness of the wickedness of this abominable act," sentenced him instead to be severely whipped and banished from the colony. There were "other circumstances considered," circumstances unexplained in the record, that must have influenced the governor and his assistants in their highly unusual decision on the lesser punishment. Perhaps one of Governor Hinckley's assistants, John Freeman, who was also Sarah's uncle, had some information to share that was not recorded.[81,82]

Sarah was twenty years old when the rape occurred, born to Edmond Freeman and Margaret Perry on February 6, 1662. She married Richard Launder on January 6, 1696, fourteen years after the rape, when she was thirty-four years of age. This is rather late for a woman to marry in the colony, and her waiting so long may have been related to the attack. The first of five children were born to the couple on November 20, 1698.[83,84,85]

Suicides

Just as in any other society, there were those who did not adjust well to life in Plymouth Colony. Some could not cope with the pressures in the community, or their families, or the never-ending childbearing. There were two cases of women committing suicide in Plymouth, one in 1665, the other in 1677. Both women hanged themselves, which was the preferred way to execute criminals in Plymouth. The acts were considered as "self-murder" by the Pilgrims, sins against the sixth commandment. Their deaths were also considered a failure within the community because someone should have noticed that the women were desperate, and taken the initiative to report it.

Rebecca Sale

At the court meeting on March 7, 1665, the death of Rebecca Sale, wife of Edward Sale of Rehoboth, was addressed. The report of the Jury of Inquiry read: "We, whose names are hereunder subscribed, do hereby signify to all persons whom it may concern, that, according to our best light and apprehension, Rebecca Sale, the late wife of Edward Sale, was her own executioner, viz., she hanged herself in her own hired house."[86]

Rebecca was the second wife of Edward Sale. His first wife was named Margaret, whom he married before 1637. Margaret had a problematic history. On September 19, 1637, "Margaret Sale, the wife of [Edward], confessed adultery, and was found guilty" in the Massachusetts Bay Colony court. Along with John Hathaway and Robert Allen, Margaret was sentenced to be "severely whipped, and banished, never to return again, upon pain of death." On March 30, 1638, Governor Winthrop wrote in his journal that "Edward Sale of Marblehead [was bound in] twenty pounds for his wife's appearance when she shall be called for after her delivery." The child referred to was her firstborn, Ephraim, born May 6, 1638. Margaret must have died before 1642, when Edward married Rebecca.[87,88,89]

Rebecca and Edward's first child, also named Rebecca, was born into the family sometime in 1642. Two more children, Miriam and Nathaniel, were born in 1644 and 1646. When Rebecca hanged herself in Rehoboth in 1665, her youngest child was eighteen years old. Nathaniel lived to be sixty-eight years old, and never remarried.[90]

Why Rebecca Sale hanged herself remains unknown.

Abia (Abigail) Claghorn

The second suicide, that of Abia Claghorn, is more fully explained. The record of the court meeting on November 1, 1677, reads:

> The verdict of us, a jury impaneled by the constable of Yarmouth, to search into and view...what might be the occasion or cause of the untimely death of the wife of James Claghorn, of Yarmouth. We made enquiry who were the persons which first found the woman, and we found that it was her daughter Elizabeth, and her son Robert, who, upon examination, declared to us that they, missing their mother, and had made search and enquiry for her, they sent up into the chamber

by one of the children, who cried out that his mother is hanging herself; whereupon the said Elizabeth and Robert ran up, and found her hanging and dead. They thought, however, that she might have life, and therefore presently unloosed the rope or halter, and took her down; and seeing no life in her, they presently made outcry abroad, and there came to them Jabez Gorum and Jonathan White, who declared to us that they went up and found the woman under the rope dead and cold, and they took her up and brought her down into the lower room....

The above-said Elizabeth said that her mother was missing, as she judged, two hours or more before they found her. Having thus far proceeded, we went to view the place where she was hanged, as they told us, and found there a hair rope or halter, fastened very firm to the collar beam, in which the above said Elizabeth and Robert said she hanged; then we viewed the corpse, and found an apparent strake [line] on her neck, where the blood was settled; so that it is apparent to us that she strangling herself with a cord was the cause of her death, and by all our search and inquiry, we judge that she hanged herself, and have no cause, by all our examination and observation, to suspect any other to have a hand in it.[91]

James Claghorn and Abia Lumberd were married in Barnstable on January 6, 1654. Abia was the daughter of Bernard Lumberd, and James was an indentured servant of Lumberd's who had been transported to New England as a prisoner of war in 1650 during the Scottish Rebellion. Their first child, James, was born on January 29, 1654. The couple came before the court on March 6, 1655, to answer the charge of "carnal copulation before contraction."[92,93,94,95]

Five live births were born to the couple in Plymouth. Besides James, there were Mary, October 28, 1655, Elizabeth born in April 1658, Sarah, January 3, 1659, and Robert, October 27, 1661. Elizabeth and Robert were nineteen and sixteen when they discovered the lifeless body of their mother. The Barnstable Town Records list another child, Shubael, whose birthdate was not recorded.[96,97]

But there is more to this already tragic story. In a diary kept by Captain Hammond of Charlestown, Massachusetts, he records that on October 20, 1677, "Mr. [Increase] Mather this day informed me, that in Plymouth Colony, about a month ago, an English woman, said to have had nineteen children, and with child of the twentieth,... murdered [herself]."[98]

Surely this was Abia Claghorn he was referring to, given the dates and circumstances. As has been discussed earlier, Increase Mather sometimes exaggerated, and since the couple had been married only twenty-three years, it is doubtful that they had nineteen pregnancies during that time. However, there is a significant gap between 1661, when Robert was born, and 1677, when she hanged herself. Were those years counted by miscarriages and stillbirths? Was it possible that discovering herself pregnant yet again, and facing the possibility of another tragedy, was more than she could bear? Was she so despondent that she did not realize the effect of finding her hanging body would have on her own children? The records remain silent.

Chapter Thirteen

Growing Old in Plymouth Colony

If she survived to the age of fifty, a woman living in Plymouth Colony might expect to live another twenty-three years. The highest percentage of women's deaths, over twenty percent, occurred between seventy and seventy-nine years of age; sixteen percent lived into their eighties. Like today, the age of menopause could vary considerably, but usually their prime years for bearing children ended by a woman's mid- to late-forties. With pregnancy behind them, how did these older women fill those years? Basically, with more of the same, minus childbearing.[1]

There was no concept of retirement at Plymouth. Women kept up their daily routines as long as they could physically perform the work. Their lives were still very full, and they enjoyed the respect of the community. John Robinson wrote that "the younger sort" should be brought up to "a bashful and modest reverence towards all, and chiefly towards their ancients." A woman past fifty had produced as many children as possible, but was usually still engaged in childcare, either tending to her children or grandchildren.[2]

Besides the inevitability of increased physical limitations, there might be other changes in older women's lives. Very often their husbands died before them, leaving them alone to carry on.

Widows

Women of a marriageable age in Plymouth Colony, around their early twenties, were expected to do just that—get married. As James and Patricia Deetz put it, "The majority of women would have been married, living out their lives in the context of the recognized authority of their husbands, and working extremely hard to feed and clothe families that could include foster children as well as indentured servants."[3]

The key words here are "recognized authority of their husbands," because, at Plymouth, control and order began and ended in the home. The husband was the authority in his house and was responsible for the conduct of all within. He, in turn, was answerable to the governor and the courts. Wives' subjection to their husbands was the basis of all orderly conduct.

But what about widows? Basically, they had four choices open to them. First, they could remarry, which many of them did. Second, they could go to work, that is, add another job to the already fulltime responsibility of keeping a house. Third, a widow could depend upon her older children for her care. Last, and most desperately, she could appeal to the town for public assistance. But her first step was to get her inheritance in order.[4]

Laws of inheritance at Plymouth were unclear, and often the courts used their discretion to allow for special circumstances. Between her husband's death and her remarriage, overseers were often named to manage a widow's estate. They were usually friends of her late husband, men he trusted while he was alive. The overseers would see that the decedent's last will and testament, along with a full inventory of the man's estate, were submitted to the court to be proved within one month of his death. If her husband died intestate, i.e., without a will, it was the wife's responsibility to conduct the inventory.[5]

Widows at Plymouth Colony were entitled by law to have "the widow's third"—"a third part of his lands during her life and a third of his goods to be at her own disposing." She could have the "use or profits of one-third of the land owned by her husband at the time of his death and full title to one-third of his movable property." Even if her husband died without a will, her right to her inheritance was upheld by the courts. It wasn't until 1685 that the law clearly stated how the remaining two thirds of the estate was to be distributed. After a man's debts had been paid, "the widow shall have one third part of her late husband's personal estate to be at her own absolute dispose, and the other two-thirds to be disposed amongst the children as the law is provided." This may have been the custom in Plymouth before 1685, but this is the first legal reference to how the remaining two thirds were distributed.[6,7]

Children were not automatically considered heirs. Men would often name and leave their children specific assets in their wills, preserving their inheritances based on the male blood line. For example, on October 31, 1666, Grace Halloway was awarded the ten pounds her father left her, "the said Grace Halloway being now of age to receive the said sum as her portion." The court made sure that the money would not be squandered. "Major Winslow" was appointed to advise Grace "in reference unto the future way of her livelihood."[8]

To their credit, the courts recognized that women participated in the hard work—and associated hardship—in the establishment of the colony from the beginning. In the original agreement with the investors, women got equal shares in the colony. It appears that this was the same theory they applied to a marriage; for her work and sacrifice, she deserved her equal share.

In many cases, the courts could be further involved in estate issues, especially if the holdings were large. Debts needed to be settled, belongings inventoried. Sometimes widows had to demand what was legally theirs. The widow Elizabeth Glover sued John Combe (Coombe) on May 5, 1640, for a debt of twelve pounds he owed to her late husband. Combe was ordered to pay the debt out of his corn, wheat, and rye crops. In 1669, Penninnah Linnett (Linnitt, Linnel) widow of Robert Linnett, sued Robert's brother, David, charging that he "hath possessed himself of her house and land given her by the will of her deceased husband." Furthermore, David had given Penninnah "no satisfaction for the same." If he did not pay her a reasonable sum between this and the next March court, then "the court will take course that he shall be disposed thereof." Apparently, David did the right thing for his sister-in-law; there is no further record of this case.[9,10]

The disposition of Samuel Annabel's estate is a good example of how a husband could control what happened to his estate after his death. Anne, his widow, was before the court on October 30, 1678. After her husband died, his land holdings, after verification of ownership and title, were to be divided among his three children—Samuel, Jr., Anna, and John—once they became of legal age. In the meantime, their mother would have "all the profits of all the lands" until they reach twenty-one. Thereafter she would have "the thirds in the profits of the lands during her natural life." The widow Anne was also awarded, "all the movables and all the stock forever, to be at her own dispose for and towards the bringing up of the children." With his will, Samuel made certain his children would inherit his property. Should Anne Annable remarry, her late husband's property was already legally assigned to his children. Her new husband and any children they might have together would not have any legal claim. The court, ever paternalistic, added its wish "that she will have a care to bring [the children] up in a way of education as the estate will bear."[11]

The court's chiding of Anne to properly educate her children was probably reflective of misgivings about her character. One year before the settlement of her husband's estate, on October 30, 1677, Anne Annable was before the court charged with "selling of beer to English and Indians without license." She was fined twenty shillings and ordered to post a bond of twenty pounds. It may be that her son, Samuel, was also involved. He was likewise ordered to post a bond of ten pounds.[12]

When called upon to settle an estate, the courts sometimes stepped in to protect the widow from becoming impoverished. For example, when Joan Tilson's husband died without a will, the court awarded her "thirty pounds sterling of the said estate as her own property, to her and her heirs forever." They recognized that "she hath been a true laborer with him in the procuring of his estate." The reminder of the estate was distributed equally to the couple's children.[13]

Another example of the court taking care of the widow was the case of Sarah Ormsbey. It might have been that her husband Richard Ormsbey owed more debts than his estate could pay. On October 3, 1665, the court awarded to Sarah "the best bed that she hath, with a bolster and a pair of pillows, a pair of sheets, a pair of blankets, and the best rug or coverlid that was left, and curtains and valence to the bed, and all her own wearing apparel." Then the court appointed "John Pecke, John Allin, and John Woodcocke, of Rehoboth, to administer on the estate of Richard Ormsbey, late deceased at Rehoboth." They were to pay all his debts, and report to the court. A proclamation was issued stating that anyone who had claims against Ormsbey's estate should come to the court within a month.[14]

The goods of Richard Ormsbey sold for twenty pounds, which was paid to John Godfrey to settle Richard's debt. Left over from the estate sale were "a mare, and a colt, and a gun, and a little linen cloth, and a sow, and three pigs." The administrators were ordered to deliver the animals to the two youngest of Richard Ormsbey's sons. But Sarah's best bed, linens, and clothes were safe; where she moved them is unknown.[15]

In another case the court intervened to protect a widow and her small children. In 1670 Elizabeth (Billington) Bullocks was left with a large family to support after her husband died. She was Richard Bullocks' second wife, and he brought six children from his first marriage into the marriage with Elizabeth. Then they had four more children together. Richard's debts, "for the most part," had been paid, but there were three cows and a mare left in the estate. In a rare complimentary comment of a woman's behavior, and a Billington at that, the court noted that Elizabeth "hath with care and industry brought up diverse small children hitherto since the decease of her husband, and still is careful and industrious to bring them up, some of them being yet small." They decided that she could keep the cattle, "unto the bringing up of the said children."[16,17,18]

In 1685, laws were again revised which made the rules of inheritance somewhat more clear. If a woman's husband died, and the couple had no living children, the law stated that she was to receive half of their personal estate, once outstanding bills were paid. The remainder would go to the deceased's brothers and sisters, "brethren on the whole blood." The eldest brother would receive a double share, unless he was the only brother, in which case he would get the entirety. If there were no brothers, then the deceased sisters would "shall inherit alike."[19]

Remarriage

Most women of Plymouth lived out their lives with their original spouses. Seventy-four percent of women over fifty in Plymouth had been married only once; the rest had been widowed and remarried at least once. By the time they were over seventy years old, sixty-nine percent were still in their first marriages; thirty-one percent had been widowed and remarried.[20]

Widows were expected and encouraged to remarry, especially the younger ones who had small children. Thus, it was common for a widow to marry within a year or so of losing her husband. The colony's leadership believed that settling everyone into a patriarchal family encouraged social stability. Younger widows with small children to care for were the most likely to remarry and begin second families. It may be recalled that the first marriage in Plymouth was between widow Susanna White, the mother of two sons, and widower Edward Winslow.[21]

At least one husband discouraged his wife to remarry upon his death. Richard Silvester named his "loving wife" to be his executrix of his will, written on June 15, 1663. After leaving cash gifts to their children, he stipulated that "all the rest of my goods and chattels not given and bequeathed; I do give unto my wife together with all my lands." However, there was a catch. She would receive this inheritance only "as long as she remains a widow." If she should remarry, "she shall have but only five pounds out of my estate," the rest "shall be equally divided amongst all my children that shall then be alive."[22]

Naomi Silvester did not remarry, and the amount that her husband left her proved to be insufficient. On October 5, 1663, the court took up "the condition of Naomi Silvester, widow, her deceased husband having by his last will and testament left, in an absolute way, but a small, inconsiderable part of his estate unto her." The court took steps to remedy the situation after being assured she was a "frugal and laborious woman" by the "testimony of some of her neighbors."[23]

Take on a Second Job

Plymouth Colony was basically a farming community; everyone worked to provide food for the family. There was plenty to do just managing a household without taking on other responsibilities outside the home. Besides, there were very few opportunities open to women, and those that were possible were mainly extensions of their role as wives and mothers, as caregivers and homemakers.

Midwives and Healers

In *The English Housewife*, written by Gervase Markham in 1615, the section on "physic" makes it clear that women were the primary providers of health care in the family home. While the author claims that "the depth and secrets of this most excellent art of physic is far beyond the capacity of the most skillful woman, as lodging only in the breast of the learned professors," he argues that "one of the most principal virtues which doth belong to our English housewife... [is the] preservation and care of the family touching their health and soundness of body...."[24]

Plymouth housewives would have been willing and able to use their needle skills to staunch bleeding, stitch up wounds, and apply poultices to prevent infection and ease pain. Many of the ingredients in Markham's herbal concoctions were not available to the Pilgrims; they had to depend mostly on herbs they grew themselves or gleaned in the nearby woods and fields. Used also for flavoring food, herbs that were more commonly used were angelica, basil, dill fennel, hyssop, marjoram, parsley, rosemary, savory, tansy, and thyme. For more serious situations, housewives often turned to other women or the community's healer for advice.

Some women worked as both healers and midwives, administering "physicks," or medicines, derived from a variety of plant, animal, and mineral sources. From Plymouth Colony's wills and inventories, we know there were a number of books on medical care in personal libraries. Samuel Fuller, Plymouth's first "physician and surgeon," owner a number of "phisicke books." These books were likely also consulted by his wife, Bridget, who was the most well-known female healer at Plymouth.[25,26]

Samuel Fuller was a member of the Separatist congregation in Leiden and became a deacon in their church under John Robinson. Bridget Lee was Samuel's third wife; they were married in Leiden in 1617. His previous wives had both died before they had children. Fuller was one of the leaders of the Leiden Separatists who helped arrange the finances with the merchant adventurers for the voyage to America. Along with his brother, Edward Fuller, who brought his wife and son, Samuel sailed on the *Mayflower.* It was Samuel's servant, William Butten, who was the first of the party to die. Both Samuel and Edward signed the Mayflower Compact.[27,28,29]

On July 10, 1623, Bridget arrived in Plymouth on the *Anne*, along with Alice Carpenter Southworth, who was to become Governor Bradford's bride. The Fullers were awarded land and lots described as those that "lye on the South side of the brooke." Samuel served as the Pilgrims' doctor, a deacon of the Pilgrim church, and was also active in government. He was an original Purchaser. He was often called to treat not only his fellow colonists, but also Indigenous People and those passing through the colony.[30,31,32]

Samuel Fuller was "a good man and full of the holy spirit," wrote William Bradford.[33] When Fuller traveled to Salem to help those who were sick, Governor John Endicott of the Massachusetts Bay Colony was moved to express his deep appreciation to Governor Bradford: "I acknowledge myself much bound to you for your kind love and care in sending Mr. Fuller among us...."[34]

All of Samuel Fuller's community activities and services aside, there was still a farm to run, and during her husband's absences Bridget must have helped to manage it. Yet, she had community responsibilities of her own. She, too, was a health care provider. In one year alone, 1633, the court records and inventories of the deceased mention several instances of debts due her for "physick," attesting to her busy schedule. Richard Lanckford owed her six shillings, eight pence "for physick," Peter Browne owed her "one peck malt and purgac," apparently referring to a purgative for cleansing the bowels. Godbert Godbertson owed Mrs. Fuller two pounds, ten shillings, "for physick in sickness." Francis Eaton paid ten shillings to "Mrs. Fuller for physick." John Thorpe owed her one pound, sixteen shillings.[35]

In 1633, sometime between July 30 and October 28, Samuel Fuller died, having contracted "an infectious fever," which killed more than twenty colonists. Governor Bradford wrote that Samuel had died, "after he had much helped others...and had been a great help and comfort unto them. ...[also] being a deacon of the church, a man godly and forward to do good, being much missed after his death."[36,37,38]

Bridget was ill, too, at the time of Samuel's death, probably with the same malady that her husband had suffered. It was questionable whether she would survive. In his will, Fuller covered both outcomes: "If it shall please God to recover my wife out of her weak estate of sickness, then my children [shall] be with her or disposed by her." Should she die, Fuller had made careful plans for their two children; Will and Priscilla Wright would become the guardians of Samuel, four years old, and Mercy, who was about six. Sarah Converse was a foster child living with the Fullers; Will Wright and Thomas Prence were named as her guardians. Two other children were in Samuel's care, "committed to my education," Elizabeth Cowles and George Foster; his wishes were that both be returned to their parents. At his mother's death, Andrew Ring was also committed to Samuel for his care, and the will transfered guardianship of Andrew to Thomas Prence.[39]

Once he had addressed the needs of his wife, children, and those youths in his charge in his will, Samuel Fuller remembered his church. He willed the "first cow calf of his brown cow" to the Church of God at Plymouth, the offspring of which would become a welcome source of income as time went on. He then remembered several friends with small bequests in his will: gloves, or the money to buy them, were to go to Alice Bradford, Governor Winthrop, John Jenney, John Winslow, and Rebecca Prince; suits of clothes went to Brother Wright; his best hat and band, "which I never wore," went to "Old Mr. Brewster," along with his cloak and another suit. Mrs. Heeks, who taught his children, was left twenty shillings. Samuel named his son as his executor, but because his son was so young, Fuller established three overseers for his estate: Edward Winslow, William Bradford, and Thomas Prence, "and for their pains, I give to each of them twenty shillings a piece." His daughter Mercy got his Bible, and his son Samuel all his books, except his "book of physick," which was left to Roger Williams.[40]

After Samuel died, Bridget did recover from her illness. Once she recuperated, she went back to attending to her medical practice for the colony. On top of that she took over the management of the farm. In 1634, she paid taxes of nine shillings. She owned a one-acre plot of land in her own name, awarded to her as a "first comer," a passenger on the *Anne*. While Samuel's land holdings were willed to his son, the boy was only four years old, and it was up to Bridget, with the advice of the overseers, to manage the property.[41]

Three years after her husband's death, on March 14, 1636, mowing rights were granted to Bridget Fuller: "the ground from the Smelt River to Mr. Allerton's creek, and on the other side, the Smelt River to the point of trees." Later that year, on November 18, 1636, she recorded her cattle mark: "Mistress Fuller a half cut out behind the right ear." Another six acres of land was granted to her, "to belong unto her house in Plymouth, and be therewith used so long as the same shall be inhabited, or be fit to dwell in." On May 7, 1638, she requested another four acres "of lands at the New Field." Later that same year she asked for more meadow ground. In 1641, on September 16, Bridget Fuller was granted "one hundred acres upland to her meadow at Lakenham [today's North Carver], and to abut upon her meadow there, as near as it can be conveniently be laid forth."[42,43,44]

Bridget Fuller continued to run her farm while enlarging her holdings, and engaged with her neighbors in trading and breeding stock. On April 5, 1641, she entered into an agreement with Nehemiah Smith, promising to deliver four ewe sheep to Smith, which he would keep and breed for two years; at the end of two years, they would share the increase by dividing it in half. The agreement was to be renewed on June 24, 1643, with Smith keeping the original four ewes again, as well as her half of the increase for six more years and "the said Bridget shall have the one half of the wool sent to her yearly to Plymouth."[45]

Bridget also faced her share of problems associated with her business activities. In 1636, she took in a servant child. On January 5, Benjamin Eaton, "the son of Francis Eaton, of late deceased, was by the Governor and Assistants, with his mother's consent, put to Bridget Fuller, widow, for 14 years, she being to keep him at school two years, and to employ him after such service as she saw good and he should be fit for; but not to turn him over to any other, without the Governor's consent." For some unknown reason, this indenture did not work out. As already discussed, the boy returned to his parents, Francis and Christian Billington.[46]

A land dispute brought Bridget into court in 1640. She had enlarged her holdings with a grant of ten acres of meadow, "to be laid forth for her of that which lyeth next to Edward Doty's meadow, and parcel of upland to it." However, there was some dispute as to the exact location and boundaries of the grant. On September 1, 1640, Bridget sued Edward Doty for an action of trespass, requesting thirty pounds. She was awarded "three pounds damages, and charges, of the court; but the plaintiff is to perform her bargain to the defendant for wintering her cattle." Later, on January 3, 1643, there was a disagreement between Bridget and Josias Winslow regarding a boar, but the issue was dismissed "for want of better evidence."[47,48,49]

On March 16, 1649, "with the consent of his mother, Mistress Bridget Fuller," Samuel Fuller, who was then about twenty years old, sold property, two acres near Strawberry Hill, to Lieut. Matthew Fuller, who was his cousin. Samuel Jr. was beginning to come into his own. He was also now known as Dr. Fuller, following in his father's— and mother's—footsteps and serving as the community's physician.[50]

His reputation was a good one, so good that another town tried to recruit him - and his mother - away from Plymouth. On July 3, 1663, the town of Rehoboth voted to send a letter to Samuel Fuller asking if he would move to their town and serve as their physician. They also requested that his mother accompany him, to "come and dwell among us, [and] to attend on the office of midwife, to answer the town's necessity, which is at present great." Samuel Fuller requested permission to settle in Rehoboth and received it but did not move there after all.[51,52]

Mother and son also continued Samuel Senior's philanthropy. In 1664, Bridget and her son Samuel, granted a half-acre parcel of land, "a garden plot," to the church of Plymouth. This land was given with the stipulation that it be used only for the "proper use of the Church of Plymouth,…and to the said Church successively for ever…." Their generosity is still celebrated to this day in the form of the Samuel and Bridget Fuller Society, sponsored by the Pilgrim Hall Museum.[53,54]

Bridget Fuller died sometime after May 2, 1667. Her daughter Mercy was still alive in 1650, but there is no record in her name thereafter. Samuel Jr., however, married Mercy Eaton in 1686; they had eleven children, and he lived to be seventy years old.[55,56]

Running Ordinaries

For many widows, the hospitality business seemed like a sensible option. It was not difficult to open an ordinary, also known as a public house, a tavern, or an alehouse. The widow needed a license, a few extra tables and chairs, and a welcoming demeanor. It was not unusual for wives to help their husbands run taverns, and in at least one case they were necessary to the venture's success. James Leonard, of Taunton, was licensed to run a "public house," but when his wife died, the court determined that he was "not so capable of keeping a public house." It is not clear if it was the shock of her death that incapacitated him or if her help was essential to the success of the business, but since there was already another tavern in town, the courts recalled his license.[57]

On July 1, 1684, Mary Combe was licensed to keep an ordinary at Middleborough. Her husband, Francis, ran the ordinary from 1678 until his death in 1683, leaving a large estate of more than 329 pounds. Mary was granted her husband's license, permitting her "to provide lodging and victuals for men, and provender for horses," and warned her to "keep good order in her house, that she incur no just blame by her negligence in that behalf."[58,59]

Ordinaries were established and licensed mainly to attract travelers and designate the town as destination point. Many not only provided alcoholic beverages, but also served meals and offered sleeping accommodations. A woman could add a large room to her home, furnish it with mattresses and blankets, and open an inn. Besides the cooking, cleaning, and laundry, traditional chores of any housewife, there were many regulations to be aware of and obey. Ordinaries were often scenes of drunkenness, and being drunk in Plymouth was prohibited by law. Should anyone have any doubt what was meant by drunkenness, the law made it clear: "By drunkenness is understood a person that either lisp or falters in his speech by reason of over much drink, or that staggers in his going or that vomits by reason of excessive drinking, or cannot follow his calling."[60]

The laws were stringent. In 1638, a law was enacted that due to the "great inconveniences...occasioned by young men and other laborers who have dieted in Inns and Alehouses," no one should take meals in

A typical tavern.

the ordinaries located in the same town in which they lived. Nor should they "haunt them,…nor make them the ordinary place of their abode." The local tavern, in other words, was not to become a hangout for the town's young men. The law was relaxed slightly in 1646, allowing townsmen to drink at the ordinary, but only for an hour at a time. It wasn't only the drinking that bothered the courts. Taverns were the place for socializing and sharing ideas and complaints. Any opposition to the government or the church was to be closely monitored.[61]

In 1663, it was further enacted that single persons, "either children or servants," could not buy strong liquor or wine in the ordinaries. By 1671, ordinary keepers were required and empowered to report to the government "any person or persons [who] do not attend order, but carry themselves uncivilly by being importunately desirous of drink when denied, and do not leave the house when required." Not reporting offenders could result in fines for the innkeeper. More stringent laws followed.[62]

When the colony's laws were rewritten in 1671, a whole chapter was devoted to the keeping of ordinaries, "because there is so much abuse of that lawful liberty, both by persons that entertain, and by such as are entertained." Besides the regulations already cited, "victualing houses" were to be licensed by the court. Those licensed to keep "public houses of entertainment," should provide bedding, have pasture and provender for horses, and "not be without good beer." Prices were standardized, two pence for a quart of beer, eight pence for strong liquor or wine. Ordinaries would be inspected, "to take notice of such abuses as may arise in reference to the premises or otherwise, and make return thereof to the court." Unless it be for the relief of pain, no children or servants were allowed to "to buy or sit drinking any strong liquors or wine" in the tavern.[63]

In 1674, "to the restraining of abuses in ordinaries," it was made unlawful to sell drink to residents of the local town on the Lord's Day or to keep the inn open at night. Furthermore, all ordinary keepers were required "to clear their houses of all town dwellers and strangers that are there on a drinking account except such as lodge in the house." In 1682, it was only with the town's approval that an ordinary could be kept, and on lecture days, it was up to the ordinary keeper to "clear their houses of all persons able to go to meeting during the time of the exercise," except for extraordinary cases.[64]

These laws made being an innkeeper much more difficult, and the government seemed slightly unsure whether women could keep order in an ordinary. Even if they were issued licenses, they were often given special warnings, precautions not always mentioned when men received licenses. For example, On March 4, 1674, Timothy Williamson was licensed to keep an ordinary at Marshfield, "for the entertainment of strangers for lodging, victualing, and drawing and selling of beer." Four years later, after Timothy's death, the license was transferred to his wife, Mary Williamson. On October 30, 1678, she was permitted "to draw and sell beer, wine, and liquors." But further instructions were given to Mary that were not given to Timothy, that she "keep good orders in her house, that so there be no just cause of complaint in that respect."[65]

One of the most famous inns in Plymouth was that operated by James Cole, Sr., assisted by his wife, Mary, and namesake son, James, Jr. The Cole family settled in Plymouth in 1633, and that same year James was admitted as a freeman. There is no record of a license being issued to Cole, so it may have been on a casual basis that he began serving customers in his home. The first record concerning the tavern was in 1640, when on May 5 the court ordered him to stop selling liquor. There had been a brawl at Cole's, and a guest, John Kerman, testified that "there was such disorder in James Coles' house, with stools being thrown,...until the early morning hours when they finally fell asleep by the fire."[66]

Cole's must have been the only inn during Plymouth's early years, the only public place visitors could stay overnight. This was an important service he provided to the community, "the entertainment of strangers," so much so that in 1659 the court awarded him ten pounds of public funds to remodel his house, "so as it may be fitted as an ordinary."[67]

But Cole's tavern presented the court with many problems. In 1661, Cole was fined ten shillings for selling wine to the Native Americans. A few years later, in 1665, he was fined five shillings, "for suffering Richard Dwelly to be drunk in his house."[68,69]

James' wife Mary assisted him in running the inn, but she occasionally made bad business decisions. Mary was charged on March 2, 1669 with selling strong liquors to a Native American and fined five pounds. Even worse, she had "suffered diverse persons... to stay drinking on the Lord's day, at the house of James Cole, in the time of public worship." She was fined another three pounds. Her guests were each fined ten shillings.[70]

Besides the innkeepers, there were women who produced alcohol in Plymouth. The case of Hester Rickard, forbidden by the courts to brew beer, has already been discussed. In John Rickard's will, dated July 4, 1678, we see that the Rickards had been running a brewery in their outhouse (or out-building). Among some miscellaneous items listed were a cooling tub and a sieve, two bushels of wheat and four of malt, and some molasses. The "stilling of liquors" was licensed in Plymouth, but there were laws governing its distribution. For example, in 1686, Margaret Muffee was granted the license to "retail strong liquors" in Scituate, with the stipulation that her customers would only "buy it, and carry it out of door, or from her house, and not drink it there." She was further warned to "be careful whom she sells it to." On August 4, 1663 Lydia Garrett, a widow in Scituate, was licensed to sell "strong liquors...always provided that the orders of court concerning selling of liquors be observed, and that she sell none but to house keepers, and not less than a gallon at a time." This was not a license to run a tavern, but just to sell liquor. It is not clear if these women were running their own stills, but it is quite likely.[71,72,73]

These retailers also paid an excise tax to the government; a 1661 law ordered that for the "strong waters" that were distilled in the colony, six pence a gallon was charged in excise tax. For liquor brought in, the tax was twelve pence a gallon. Receivers of this excise tax were named for each town.[74]

Widows Dependent on Adult Children

Once the aged became too ill to work and care for themselves, they were frequently moved into their grown children's households. It was often the widowed grandmothers who helped their adult children with chores and taking care of the young children. They were the fortunate ones. The situation of an abandoned mother was considered so pathetic that her condition was the metaphor William Bradford used to describe Plymouth's church after many colonists moved out of the town and into outlying villages: The church, he wrote, is "like an ancient mother grown old and forsaken of her children, though not in their affections yet in regard of their bodily presence and personal helpfulness...."[75,76]

Appeal for Public Assistance

If the elderly could not depend on grown children to care for them, the community would help. In 1642 a law was passed that "every township shall make competent provision for maintenance of their poor according as they shall find most convenient and suitable for themselves by an order and general agreement in a public town meeting." However, eligibility for public welfare was carefully monitored. The law also provided that any children who came from

one township to another, "to be nursed or schooled or otherwise educated, to a physician or surgeon to be cured of any disease or wound, etc.," and they fell into poverty and "came to stand in need of relief," their original township would bear the burden. "They shall be relieved and maintained by the Townships whence they came or were sent from and not by that township where they are so nursed, educated or at cure."[77]

The first mention of public assistance for the poor was in 1624, when Edward Winslow returned from England with the first cattle for the colony. Poor relief was funded in part by the offspring of a heifer presented to the colony as a gift by James Shirley, one of the original adventurers who invested in the colony. In 1638, at a town meeting, the boundaries of Plymouth Town were described in order to establish who would be entitled access to the public welfare.[78]

On June 2, 1646, William Halloway of Taunton complained to the court that "an old woman which he brought out of England was chargeable to him," and he wanted relief from this expense. It is not clear how she came to be in his household, but the court agreed "to take order for her maintenance." Halloway was directed to "deliver her to the town, or whom they shall appoint to receive her, with her clothes and bedding, and such things as she hath." There is no further record of who took over this responsibility.[79]

Widows Who Remained Independent

Some women who were widowed were not interested in remarrying or taking on a job outside the home; they apparently wanted to remain independent and manage their own farms and finances. There were very few of them, but these women became landowners in their own right. While they were respected, they made the leadership of the colony somewhat uncomfortable because they existed outside of male control. Nonetheless, a few of these widows became very prosperous. Freed from the exhausting routine of repetitive childbearing, they proved astute businesswomen. One of the most successful was Elizabeth Warren.

In 1626, a deal was negotiated with the original investors in the Plymouth venture. For 1,800 pounds the investors from London, who had originally funded the colony, sold "said stocks, shares, lands, merchandise, and chattels" back to the colonists. On the list of purchasers was Richard Warren. After his death in 1628, his widow Elizabeth Warren was listed as a Purchaser, the only woman so designated. This was important because the Purchasers were favored above all others when land grants were made. This designation gave Elizabeth Warren an extraordinary standing in the colony.[80]

Richard Warren was a passenger on the *Mayflower;* Elizabeth arrived later in 1623, sailing on the *Anne,* with five daughters, Mary, Anna, Sarah, Elizabeth, and Abigail. The couple would produce two more children, both boys—Nathaniel and Joseph—while in Plymouth.[81,82]

Richard was awarded two lots in the 1623 Division of Land, lying "on the north side of the town." Five more lots near the Eel River were awarded for "those who came over in the ship called the *Anne,*" which included Richard Warren's wife and daughters. In the 1627 Division of Cattle, nine shares were awarded to him, his wife, and their seven children, in the form of five heifers and two she-goats. Only one year later Richard Warren died. Elizabeth never remarried, and in fact outlived her husband by forty-five years. She took up the responsibilities of repaying her family's portion of the debt to the investors and was regarded and respected as an independent agent and head of one of the wealthiest families in the colony.[83,84]

She paid her taxes under her own name, one of the few women to be found on the tax list. On March 25, 1633, she was rated at twelve shillings, slightly above the minimum rate of nine shillings. Her name comes up several times in court records regarding business and property dealings. For example, she was given mowing rights to public property, just as the male colonists were. On July 1, 1633, she and Robert Bartlett were permitted to "mow where they did last year, and the marsh adjoining, as high as Slowly House." On October 28, that same year, her fencing rights were defended in court.[85]

Part of the responsibilities of property holdings and management was dealing with servants. As already discussed, Elizabeth brought her servant, Thomas Williams, into court for "profane and blasphemous speeches against the majesty of God." He was released with a warning.[86]

The widow Warren was most likely regarded as a woman of means, and as such she became the focus of lawsuits against her. On January 5, 1636, Thomas Clarke charged her "for taking a boat of his, which was lost in the Eel River, where she left it." A storm had come up and the boat was lost, and Clarke wanted fifteen pounds damage. The court, however, acquitted the defendant, "finding the boat to be borrowed, and laid in an ordinary place of safety." For "other considerations," however, they awarded Clarke 30 shillings.[87]

Elizabeth assumed many of the roles that would have been filled by her husband, had he lived. When her daughters married, she dutifully gave each couple parcels of land. When her daughter Sarah married John Cooke, Jr., on March 27, 1634, Elizabeth gave them an eighteen-acre parcel near the Eel River. This land was adjacent to another parcel she had given to Robert Bartlett when he married Mary in 1637, "another of the said Mistress Warren's daughters." (On November 11, 1637, Bartlett and Cooke traded their lands.) Abigail Warren married Anthony Snow, on November 8, 1639, and the following January Elizabeth gave to Anthony "her house situated near the place called Wellingsly [also known as] Hobs Hole with the eight acres of land and thereunto adjoining." Elizabeth and her family were granted enlargements of their holdings on May 5, 1640, "from the heads of their lots to the foot of the Pine Hills." They were reminded to "leave a way betwixt them and the Pine Hills, for the cattle and carts to pass by."[88,89]

As the only woman designated as an original purchaser of Plymouth Colony, Elizabeth Warren received many land grants, but her right to those grants was questioned on at least one occasion. Her son-in-law Robert Bartlett came before the court on October 5, 1652, complaining that "sundry speeches have passed from some who present themselves to be the sole and right heirs unto the lands on which the said Robert Bartlett now liveth, at the Eel River." The complainers are not named, but Robert argued that this land was "bestowed on him; by his mother in law, Mistress Elizabeth Warren, in marriage with her daughter." This gossip, he testified, questioning his rightful ownership of the land, had left him "disheartened" and unsure about proceeding with improvements.[90]

The court took the issue "into serious consideration," searched back records and the memories of "those that then were chief and had special hand in carrying on and managing the former affairs of the country." The courts found that "Mistress Elizabeth Warren, who gave the said lands unto the said Robert and others in like condition, had power so to do," citing the court order of March 7, 1637, naming her as a purchaser. That court decided to "further ratify and confirm the aforesaid acts of court whereby the said Elizabeth Warren is declared to have right to dispose of the aforesaid lands, approving and allowing of the above said gift of land unto the said Robert Bartlett and others in like condition...."[91]

Sadly, the complainers were later revealed to be Nathaniel Warren, Elizabeth's son, and Jane Collier, Nathaniel's grandmother-in-law. Perhaps Nathaniel believed or was encouraged by Jane Collier to believe, that as the eldest son of Richard Warren he was entitled to all the grants and holdings.[92]

Elizabeth and Nathaniel agreed to have an arbitration panel settle the disagreement. Each chose two members; Elizabeth chose William Bradford and Thomas Willet, Nathaniel chose Thomas Prence and Myles Standish. The decision was swift and unanimous; Elizabeth's authority over her lands was confirmed. The arbitrators found that she "shall enjoy all the rest of her lands and all of them to whom she hath already at any time heretofore disposed any part thereof by gift, sale or otherwise, or shall hereafter do the same, to them and their heirs for ever without any trouble or molestation." Nathaniel was ordered to cease all claims, "or any molestations or disturbance at any time hereafter concerning the premises, but that his said mother and all her children, or any other to whom she has any way disposed any lands or shall hereafter do the same, but that they may quietly and peaceably possess and enjoy the same."[93]

Perhaps fences were mended among family members because over the years Elizabeth's children and grandchildren worked together and became successful farmers who participated in community affairs. They had large herds of cattle and horses, their animals marked in 1661 "with two slits in the near ear and so the bit cut out, which mark is on the outside of the said ear and also the said mare is branded with a P on the top of the buttock." Joseph marked his own stock in 1669 with "a piece cut out behind the top of the near ear like unto an arrow head: or link unto a V." Elizabeth's grandsons registered their own marks about 1683, attesting to successful breeding of the family stock.[94]

Elizabeth Warren died in October 1673 and was buried on October 24. The court record states that the 90-year-old widow, "having lived a godly life, came to her grave as a shoke [shock or sheave] of corn fully ripe." She had fifty-seven grandchildren at the time of her death. Her daughter, Mary Warren Bartlett, had eight children, Anna Warren Little had nine, Sarah Warren Cooke had five, Elizabeth Warren Church had eleven, Abigail Warren Snow had six, Nathaniel Warren and his wife Sarah Walker had twelve, and Joseph Warren and his wife Priscilla Faunce had six.[95,96]

No will or estate inventory has ever been found for Elizabeth Warren. After her daughter, Mary Bartlett, testified in court that she and her sisters "hath received full satisfaction for whatsoever [they] claim as due from the estate of Mistress Elizabeth Warren, deceased," the remainder of the estate was settled on Elizabeth's son, Joseph. Her son, Nathaniel, died before her, in 1667.[97,98,99]

The following year, her namesake granddaughter was charged with fornication, an action that would no doubt have distressed her grandmother greatly. On October 27, 1674, Joseph Doten (Doty) was accused by Elizabeth Warren, Nathaniel's daughter, "to have committed fornication with her, whereby she is with child." (As discussed above, two years earlier Joseph's brother, Thomas, was similarly charged by Mary Churchill.) Joseph Doten was ordered to appear in court the following March, "to make further answer respecting the said fact, and not depart the said court without license." No further record has been found, but the child born that same year was named Elizabeth.[100,101]

Chapter Fourteen

Plymouth Colony Becomes Plymouth County

In 1691 Plymouth Colony was folded into the larger and more successful Massachusetts Colony. The Charter of Massachusetts Bay, issued that same year by William III and Mary II, consolidated the colonies of Massachusetts Bay, Plymouth, Martha's Vineyard, Nantucket, Maine, and parts of Nova Scotia, into the Province of Massachusetts. This new charter established English rule overall. Plymouth would no longer govern itself. Boston was established as the new government center, with a royally-appointed governor rather than a democratically elected one.[1]

Plymouth was in no position to put up much of a fight. As early as 1665, Governor Thomas Prence confessed that among the other settlements, the original Pilgrim colony was "the meanest [poorest] and weakest, least able to stand of ourselves, and little able to contribute any helpfulness to others and we know it, though none should tell us of it." The destruction wrecked on the colony from King Philip's War between the years 1675 to 1678 did not help things. A subsequent drought in 1690 was devastating to the colony. Governor Thomas Hinkley wrote that "our crops generally failing by the sore drought this last year hath reduced us to great straits." The colony's residents, seven hundred seventy-five in 1690, were living in deep poverty. On March 3, 1691, the Plymouth court admitted that they were "labor[ing] under many inconveniences, being small in number, low in estate, and [with] great public charges."[2,3,4,5]

Furthermore, the colony seemed to be suffering from malaise. At the court meeting of June 24, 1690, the record noted that there was a possibility that Plymouth was "like[ly] to be annexed to Boston," but, "if we speedily address to their majesties [and] employ a suitable person to manage and raise sufficient monies to carry the same an end, [we] might attain a charter for ourselves." Two years earlier, Duxbury minister Ichabod Wisewall has been sent to England to petition the king to grant Plymouth its own patent. In England Henry Ashurst, a baronet, was working on the colony's behalf in the same effort. A new urgency in 1690 moved the court to spread the news of the possible annexation throughout the colony. Constables were charged to meet with residents and ask them, "whether it be their minds we should sit still and fall into the hands of those that might catch us, without using means to procure that which may be for our good, or prevent that which may be our inconvenience, or if they will act." Action required funding, and colonists were asked "what money they can raise." Procuring a patent for Plymouth was estimated by the court to cost five hundred pounds sterling.[6]

At the March, 1691, court, it was ordered that one-hundred pounds sterling, "be sent to Sir Henry Ashurst towards the charge of procuring a charter."[7] Wisewall had to admit that this last desperate effort was too little, too late. The colony could only blame itself, he wrote in a letter: "There is a time to speak, and a time to keep silence. We might have been happy, or, at least, not so miserable, had some been able or willing to be taught their proper seasons." The new Province of Massachusetts, he added, will put us "under such restrictions as I believe will not be very acceptable to those inhabitants who must lose their ancient names [identity]." But the inhabitants, it seems, could not be rallied. They were, as one historian put it, "caught in an economic vise of subsistence farming and local fishing and without capital or a developed industry or commerce, were concerned for their immediate needs. The newer generations had lost the zeal of the original mission into the wilderness."[8,9,10]

On July 7, 1691, the Plymouth Colony General Court held its final meeting; the Court of Assistants met for the last time on April 5, 1692. The persistent Elizabeth Williams was the last woman mentioned in the Plymouth Colony court records at the meeting held on June 2, 1691. Back in 1665, Elizabeth had been awarded a yearly maintenance from her husband, John Williams, in a lengthy and complicated case of separation, already addressed above. Apparently, John had once again

The Plymouth Wilderness.

fallen behind in his spousal support and Elizabeth and her brother, Barnabas Lothrop, were suing. Her case was referred: "… the trial of that case doth now properly belong to a county court." Changes in the court system were a part of the Massachusetts colonial consolidation.[11,12]

The new Plymouth County encompassed seven towns, with the town of Plymouth as county seat. All counties answered to the governor in Boston, appointed by the king and queen, and assisted by a council of twenty-eight men. Justice was administered through a tiered court system. Actually the county system dated back to 1686, during the short-lived authority of the Dominion of New England under Governor Andros. The highest court was the General Court, which "appointed officers, passed laws and orders, organized all courts, established fines and punishments, and levied taxes, all with the consent of the governor." On the county level were the Court of Common Pleas which handled all local civil litigation and the

Court of General Sessions addressed minor criminal cases and many administrative matters. There were still town courts, which handled the distribution of town funds, decided on the routing of roads, the construction of dams, mills, distilleries, and other local issues.[13]

The Charter of Massachusetts Bay made it clear that the governor in Boston and his assistants had "full power and authority from time to time to make, ordain, and establish all manner of wholesome and reasonable orders, laws, statutes and ordinances, directions and instructions either with penalties or without," for the province, just as long as those actions "be not repugnant or contrary to the laws of this our realm of England."[14]

But what was not clear, especially during the transition period, was *which* laws would be in effect in each county—the original Plymouth Colony laws, or the new Province of Massachusetts laws. What was also unclear is *when* the newer laws were to be implemented. This was important because the laws of each colony varied quite a bit. For example, in the *Book of General Laws and Liberties Concerning the Inhabitants of the Massachusetts*, established in 1648, under the heading of Capital Laws, it is stated that "If any person commit adultery with a married, or espoused wife; the Adulterer & Adulteress shall surely be put to death." The 1658 law against adultery in Plymouth Colony stated that "That whosoever shall commit adultery shall be severely punished by whipping two …times; namely once while the court." Which law was in effect in 1692?[15,16]

Massachusetts law scholar, Michael Hindus, wrote that "although it may appear that by the end of the seventeenth century, Massachusetts had constructed a rational system of courts of progressively greater jurisdiction, in fact this system was the height of inefficiency." It was a very confusing time. Even the church became concerned. In April 1692 the Plymouth church sent a letter to other churches in the colony lamenting the "unsettled and doubtful state of the whole country." "We in this colony are brought exceedingly low as to our civil government," the letter read, with "many openly casting off the yoke of subjection to our civil rules, and there being no strong rod for a scepter to rule, whereby we are in great danger of being given into the hands of strangers to manage us at their pleasure, and so of losing the liberty of those most precious enjoyments for the sake of which our blessed fathers followed God into this wilderness." The transition period was an exceedingly difficult and uncertain time.[17,18]

Changes for Women

What did the changes that accompanied the dissolution of Plymouth Colony mean for the women and children who lived there? In some ways, not very much. While the name of the court might be different, the types of offenses and crimes remained similar. Not only that, but the authorities in these different courts were often the same men. For example, on September 14, 1687, the County Court of General Sessions and Common Pleas were presided over by Judge Nathaniel Thomas, and Justices of the Peace Peregrine White, John Cushing and Ephraim Morton. On the first Tuesday of April 1692, Plymouth Colony's Court of Assistants was presided over by "William Bradford, Governor, and his Assistants, Deputy Governor John Walley, Daniel Smith, John Cushing, and John Thatcher." The next meeting of the County Court of General Sessions was held on the last Tuesday in July 1692, "before Justices William Bradford, John Cushing, and Ephraim Norton." (This William Bradford was the son of Governor William Bradford).[19]

Furthermore, it took time for the new charter to be put into effect. In general, things did not move quickly in the seventeenth century, and it may be that for some time Plymouth County functioned under the same laws it had when it was an independent colony.

The few records that do exist from the transition period are frustratingly incomplete. "Like any records," writes David Thomas Konig, who transcribed the Massachusetts court records from the transition period, "they are only as reliable as the persons keeping them." The clerks appear to have been distracted. In some cases, they recorded the actions of the court afterward and left out the names of those involved. There are blank pages in the record books with lapses in time indicating that some cases were never recorded. For example, there is a gap in the records Konig transcribed between December 1692 and June 1698.[20] Other records are simply missing, lost over time.

From the existent records it is also difficult to determine the exact date an action occurred. Courts met over several days. For instance, in December 1701, the session began on December 16, but it lasted for three days, and there is no indication on which day each case was heard.[21]

What is more frustrating to historians is that many details surrounding each case are missing, either never recorded by the court clerk, or overlooked in the 1978 transcription. Without knowing the particulars of each case, it is impossible to determine which factors influenced the court in their decisions.

Crimes of a Sexual Nature

We do know that crimes of a sexual nature were still prosecuted, and that Plymouth's inhabitants were still counting the days between a couple's marriage and the birth of their first child, but it appears that fines had been reduced. Under colony laws, the fines for fornication were ten pounds or a whipping, and might even include jail time. In September 1692, at the newer county court, Sarah Howland was fined only fifty shillings for fornication, plus court costs. In June 1698, Richard Everson and his wife were fined four pounds for fornication before marriage. In September 1698, Samuel and Eunice Wetherell were fined forty shillings each "for carnal copulation with each other before marriage." In December 1699, Israel and Elizabeth Hatch were charged with fornication "with each other while single persons." The couple was fined four pounds. In September 1700, John Bayley, Jr. and his wife Abigail, of Scituate, were fined four pounds, "for committing fornication while single persons." Not only were fines less, but no physical punishment was ordered in these cases as it had previously been under colony law.[22,23]

Two cases, however, did involve whipping. Hester Andrew was presented in March 1699, for "having a bastard child by fornication." Hester argued that she was married when the child was conceived. She was ordered to "make proof of her said marriage" by the next Quarter Sessions in June, "or else that she forthwith pay a fine of fifty shillings or be publicly whipped four stripes." At the September 1698 session of the court, Sarah Curtis stood before the court charged with fornication with "Joe a Negro servant to William Holbrooke of Scituate." She had the choice of either being fined fifty shillings or being whipped ten stripes. Joe paid Sarah's fifty shillings, apparently to cover her fines so she could escape the whipping, but he was publicly whipped ten stripes.[24]

Why were the fines so much lower than earlier in the colony's history? Was fornication considered a lesser crime than before? No explanation has been found, but perhaps the inhabitants simply could not afford larger fines. As has been shown, Plymouth was very poor by the end of the seventeenth century, and perhaps imposing larger fines would have been unduly harsh, even futile.

The courts were still interested in punishing fathers who failed to support illegitimate children. In June 1700, Deborah Fox was fined forty shillings, "for having a bastard child born of her body." Deborah named Joseph Rogers, Jr. as the father, and a warrant was issued for his arrest. Not only was Joseph in trouble, but so was his father. Joseph Rogers, Sr., was charged with hiding his son, "counselling and concealing his son Joseph Rogers who stands accused and charged by Deborah Fox to be the father of the Bastard child lately borne of her body." With his father's help, young Joseph "hath made his escape and is fled from Justice." Rogers, Sr., was ordered to pay Deborah fifty shillings, or "twelve pence by [the] week for the space of one whole year to come from the date." Furthermore, he was ordered to make quarterly payments "in equal proportion," apparently to the government, until "he shall [sur]render his said son to one of the justices of this county" for questioning.[25]

The General Sessions of the court held in June 1700 were busy ones, with even more charges of fornication and more judgments for child support. Three women from Scituate were charged and fined four pounds each for "having a bastard child lately begotten and borne... out of wedlock." Martha Wright named Ebenezer Pincin (Pinson) as the father of her child; Rebecca Nichols specified William Wetherell, and Abigail Standlake identified Jabez Rose. The fathers were ordered to pay maintenance of two shillings each week until the child became two years old. Between the ages of two and eight years old, they were ordered to pay one shilling, six pence. Odd by today's standards, as a baby grew older, the child support became less. Perhaps the court believed that older children would be more productive by performing household chores and thereby contributing to their own maintenance. The arrangement was to be monitored by the "overseers of the poor of Scituate."[26]

In September 1700, Hannah Delano fought a charge of fornication and won. The wife of Thomas Delano, Jr., she "was presented for fornication." Hannah asked for a jury trial and defended herself. She must have been convincing, for the jury found her innocent. Perhaps she had evidence that the child was premature and had been conceived after marriage, but the record does not include details.[27]

Widows and Women in Need of Care

Before Plymouth Colony became Plymouth County, when a woman was in need the courts often ordered family members to intervene. For example, at a Plymouth Town meeting held September 27, 1686, "the town voted and ordered the removal of Sarah Downham's house and to be set up at the house of Giles Rickards senior." Giles Rickard was married to Hannah Dunham at the time and Sarah may have been a relative. That practice did not change after the new charter. The town of Plymouth still maintained a commitment to aid the poor, and on June 29, 1696, the needs of two women were addressed. The town voted that "five pounds should be allowed towards the payment for the care of Mr. Hunter's wife, now under doctor's hands." Likewise, John Nelson was allowed five pounds "to keep Nan Ramsden [for] one year...and to furnish her at the expiration of said year with clothing as good as now she hath."[28,29]

To prevent the town from having to provide public relief, orders were issued to family members to contribute to the care of relatives in need. In June 1698, Jonathan and Anthony Eames, both of Marshfield, were ordered to appear at the next court of Quarter Sessions "in order to the maintenance of Sarah their sister." In September 1700, the court appointed Jonathan Eames of Marshfield as guardian to his sister, Sarah Eames, who "by reason of weakness of understanding is incapable to take care of and provide for her own support and livelihood."[30]

In March 1699, Plymouth Town decided that all the children of Mary Child should contribute equally towards her care. Her son Joseph brought the case to court, asking the justices to "direct and order in what manner his mother who is aged and weak of understanding may be supported and relieved by her children in quality according to their several abilities and that the burden may not wholly be on himself or the Town charged." With four children capable of contributing to Mary Child's care, the town was not about to support her with public funds. The court ordered that Mary's children—Joseph Child, Jane Coleman, Elinor Pierce, and Benjamin Child—each pay twenty-five shillings "annually during her natural life or until the court shall other ways order."[31]

The church stepped in as well to aid a widow. In 1691, "a liberal contribution was made ...for the Elder's widow [Elder Thomas Cushman] as our acknowledgment of his great services to the church whilst living."[32]

Land grants were still being made to widows. On August 31, 1702, widow Patience Holmes, widow of John Holmes, was granted "half an acre of land near to Deacon Woods' land on the westerly side of the road or an acre on the west side of the road to Lakenham near where Jonathan Pratt formerly lived."[33]

Women as Innkeepers

One avenue to a woman's independence was closed when they were no longer issued licenses to run inns and ordinaries after Plymouth became a county. The last woman licensed as an innholder was Hannah Pontus Rickard of Plymouth, widow of Giles Rickard, who died in 1684. At the Plymouth town meeting held on September 27, 1688, John Rickard and "the Widow Rickard," among others, "had each of them the town's approbation to keep ordinaries for this present year." After Hannah's death in 1690, the license was issued only to her son, John Rickard.[34,35]

There is no way of determining whether the male innkeepers were aided by their wives or daughters in the running of the ordinaries. Was Susanna Cole, wife of John Cole, a licensed innkeeper, working in the ordinary when she sold to "an Indian woman named Hope… three half-pints of rum"? For this violation, in December 1701 Susanna was fined three pounds, plus court costs, or spend two months in prison.[36]

There is also no way of knowing if women were distilling liquor on their own. Was Mary Howard selling her own product when, at the county court held in June 1698, she was fined two pounds for "selling cider to an Indian?" In September, that same year, John Turner's wife, Abigail, was convicted for selling rum to a Native American, and was fined twenty shillings. The source of the rum was not recorded.[37]

Women's Other Crimes

Records of women committing crimes are sparse for this time period. We do know that in September 1700, "Rebecca the wife of Robert Stanford [was] convict[ed] for receiving stolen goods [from an Indian] named Job Mark to the value of twenty-five shillings." Rebecca, about thirty-six years old at the time, was ordered to return the goods to the victim of the theft and to pay him or her twenty-five shillings. She was further sentenced to "pay cost and charges of prosecution."[38]

At that same court, a case of slander and defamation was heard. Alexander Standish and his wife Desire sued John Partridge, a husbandman. Both plaintiffs had impressive Pilgrim pedigrees. Both of their fathers were *Mayflower* passengers: Alexander was the son of Myles Standish and Desire the daughter of Edward Doty. The court considered the case, but instead of passing judgement themselves, referred it to "arbitration," after which Alexander and Desire withdrew their action. Arbitration was not new in Plymouth. The case of Elizabeth Warren and her son Nathaniel, recounted above, was settled by arbitration. In the Standish vs. Partridge case, we have no further details; cases handled by arbitration were not usually recorded.[39]

Women as Members of the Plymouth Church

On March 10, 1703, the Plymouth Church recorded a "catalogue of the names and number of communicants or members of this church at this time." Male members numbered "in all thirty-six men." Female members numbered "in all sixty-seven women." The records note that "the whole number of communicants just a hundred and three." Later an additional eighteen more women were added to the roster. In a congregation of one hundred and twenty-one members, it appears that eighty-five members were women, or about seventy percent.[40]

Why were women so drawn to the Plymouth Church? This was a society still dominated by men, and women were still assuming subservient roles. Perhaps they were seeking spiritual comfort, or possibly they were looking for the fellowship of other women. As noted, women were very dependent on each other, and their church relationships would only strengthen these bonds. Or perhaps they were simply seeking something interesting to do outside the home, and interesting things did happen during church meetings.

Church courts addressed many cases that had already appeared in secular courts, such as drunkenness, fornications, breach of sabbath, and similar occurrences. After someone had been punished and fined in the municipal court, the church would mete out their own punishments, such as public censure and admonition, public confession, repentance and restitution, and in very serious situations, excommunication. On July 25, 1686, the church considered whether offenses should be dealt with in public meeting or in private. They decided that "if the sin were public, they would continue their former practice in public dealing for it." [41,42]

While the censure was held in public, in their records the church did not cite the names of those involved. On July 13, 1681, the elders met after lecture to discuss "a sister having sundry ill reports concerning her...giving...offense to another sister of the church." On July 27, "many of the church came together at the Pastor's house" prayed over the matter and heard the testimony of the offended person. The "offending sister" was convinced to admit "sorrow for what was amiss," not only at that semi-private meeting, but also on the following Sabbath in front of the entire congregation. "The whole matter was satisfyingly issued," the record simply states.[43]

On July 3, 1687, a female member of the church had "given offense to another of the church in words and actions." She was called to appear before the congregation, and the "matter of fact was made evident." This unnamed woman, however, "carr[ied] herself offensively" when her transgression was made public, so the church admonished her that "they expected she should give satisfaction by repentance." She was ordered "to withdraw." It was not until 1690 when she finally "manifested her repentance before the church for her irregular [actions]" and the church forgave her.[44]

Changes for Children

In Plymouth, children had always been trained within their families to take on their eventual adult roles. Boys learned to work with tools as they helped their fathers at various farming tasks. Girls helped their mothers and learned how to be homemakers. They were also taught the religious precepts of Separatism in the home and at church meetings. Parents who were literate no doubt taught their children to read, to "cypher" (solve simple mathematic problems), and to write, but efforts to establish public schools were rather hit and miss.

There is tantalizing evidence in the court records about children attending school, but apparently these were informal arrangements. Recall the case of the servant Benjamin Eaton. When he went into service with Bridget Fuller in 1641, she was required "to keep him at school for two years." Was she teaching him herself or sending him off to someone else to teach him? See also the inquest into the death of little Elizabeth Walker, recounted above, who was drowned in 1665, "while walking to school." Was this a proper school or a case of one neighbor doing a favor for another?[45,46]

The town records note that in December 1670, John Morton "proffered to teach the children and youth of the town to read and write and cast accounts on reasonable consideration." Morton wanted to be paid for his work by the community, which indicates that his school was to be a public one. (It is interesting to note that at the same town meeting, Morton was granted four acres of land, "to set a house." Was this to be the eventual schoolhouse? The record does not say).[47]

At the May 20, 1672, town meeting the court ordered that "their lands at Sippican, Agawam, and places adjacent," be "improved and employed," with the profits going "towards the maintenance of the free school now begun and erected at Plymouth." The colony courts also established a tax on fishing in 1673 to support a school in Plymouth. Profits "as should or might annually accrue or grow due to this colony from time to time for fishing with nets or seines at Cape Cod for mackerel, bass, or herrings," would be "employed and improved for and towards a free school in some town of this jurisdiction for the training up of youth in literature for the good and benefit of posterity."[48,49]

The court acknowledged that "several of the town of Plymouth, out of their good affections, have freely given out of their own estates for the erecting or procuring a convenient school house, not only for the better accommodating of the scholars, but also for the schoolmaster to live and reside in." It was hoped, the court continued that "God may please so to smile upon this our day of small things as to make it a blessing to the rising generation." Thomas Hinckley was named to manage the school and the funds that would support it.[50]

It was never stated in the record, so it is unclear if both boys and girls were welcome at the Plymouth free school. The word "scholars" is not gender specific, but the court record of Elizabeth Walker's death "while walking to school" is evidence that girls were sometimes educated alongside boys.

After the colony became a county, a town meeting on February 12, 1693, addressed the state of the local school. "The inhabitants of said town [Plymouth]," the record states, "voted that the selectmen… should endeavor to get a schoolmaster to teach children to read and write and the inhabitants will take care to defray the charge thereof." Again, the non-gender term "children" indicates that both boys and girls were attending school.[51]

At a town meeting held on July 29, 1696, "…it was ordered by the town that the Upper Society [Plympton] should have the school master the next quarter and the third quarter to remove to the Eel

River and the fourth quarter to remove no further northward in said town for settlement to keep school." John Gray was the schoolmaster, and apparently he was moved to different villages within the township throughout the year. It is unclear if the children in each of the villages listed received schooling for only a quarter of the year or were expected to walk from their homes to neighboring communities.[52]

The location of the schoolmaster, and presumably the school itself, came up again on July 31, 1699 in the town court. It was ordered that, "the select men should take care to provide a school master for the town with all convenient speed and should settle him as near the center of the town." This school, however, was no longer a public school. Every "scholar" who wanted to learn to read would pay, "by their masters or parents," three half pence per week. If they also wanted to learn mathematics and Latin, the tuition would be three full pence each week. If those fees did not cover the cost of the school and the teacher, then the town would charge the shortfall to all the "inhabitants in the just and equal proportion." In other words, those who could afford the tuition could have their children educated. If there were not enough students paying for schooling, the entire community would make up the difference. In effect, those who could not afford the tuition would be required to subsidize the education of those who could.[53]

It is interesting to note that Latin was offered in this school. Was this perhaps to prepare boys to apply for admission to Harvard College in Cambridge? If so, this new aspiration marks yet another significant change from the goals of the original Pilgrims. John Robinson, the Pilgrim's pastor in Leiden, cautioned parents to discourage aspiration in their children. Children should be accustomed to simple things, he wrote, and brought up to "some course in life...[at] the same, rather under that above, their estate." Apparently, ambition to achieve a higher station in life was now commended.[54]

Perhaps Plymouth's colonists were apathetic about losing their status as an independent colony because they were simply exhausted— and more worried about feeding their families. Besides the political wrangling over combining New England's several colonies, two other events battered the colonists at the same time. As noted above, a severe drought occurred in 1690. On April 19, Governor Hinckley wrote that, "our crops [are] generally failing by the sore drought that last year has reduced us to great straits." "Great straits" doesn't fully describe what was nearly a famine. Furthermore, that same year, Plymouth sent a unit of two hundred men to fight against the French in King William's War. The goal was to capture Quebec for the English, but they failed spectacularly. Not only was a great financial debt incurred by the colony as a result, but twenty-two men died.[55]

These events would have directly affected individual families, probably even more than the threat of the colony losing its independence. Hunger, rising taxes, and the loss of twenty-two men would have had an immediate impact on the lives of women and children.

Epilogue

Through the Plymouth Colony Court Records and other primary documents, we have learned what was expected of women and children in the Pilgrim colony and have also gleaned some knowledge of their daily lives. On occasion, we have heard them speak in their defense, albeit recorded and probably edited by men.

Even more rarely, we have heard women speaking of their feelings, sharing their own emotions and opinions. Recall the case of Elizabeth Williams, who demanded that the courts formally restore her good reputation after being vilified by her husband. Then there was Jane Powell, who traded her chastity for the hope that David OKillia would marry her and rescue her from a life of miserable service. And the unforgettable Mercy Tubbs, who swore she would not return to her husband, William, while her eyes "were still open."

What the court records do not reveal are the little details of the daily lives of those who quietly and steadfastly did their jobs, loved their families, and supported their neighbors, which was probably what most of the female Pilgrims did. They got up early every morning, stirred the fire to life, prepared breakfast for the family, and set a stew to simmer for the large noon meal. They washed and repaired clothes. They planted seeds, weeded, and harvested vegetables and herbs from their kitchen gardens. They prepared herbal "physics" to support their family's health and healing. They also got pregnant on a regular schedule, and nursed newborns between pregnancies. They fed and clothed, tended and taught their children. They comforted the dying, mourned the dead, and prepared bodies for burial. They attended church meetings on Sabbath and helped their neighbors during childbirth.

Whether this life of repetition was pleasant, boring, or simply bearable to these women, we do not know. We have seen evidence that some of the women of Plymouth chafed against the constraints; their discontent and subsequent actions lead to appearances before the courts, where they were chastised. More likely most of them quietly accepted their roles as wives and mothers and, whether they were happy or not, hopefully they derived some comfort and a sense of achievement from within their families.

All of them would have been judged against the Pilgrim's *ideal* of womanhood. That ideal woman should be quietly and pleasantly subservient to her husband, fertile and readily available for his attention, devoted to her family and their care, spiritually devout, tirelessly productive, active in her community, and more—and all the while, remain uncomplaining. Those who achieved the ideal were celebrated, usually on the occasion of their deaths. An excellent example is Anne Bradstreet's epitaph of her mother, Dorothy Dudley, written in 1643:

> "Here lies,
> A worthy matron of unspotted life,
> A loving mother and obedient wife,
> A friendly neighbor, pitiful to poor,
> Whom oft she fed and clothed with her store;
> To servants wisely awful, but yet kind,
> And as they did, so they reward did find.
> A true instructor of her family,
> The which she ordered with dexterity.
> The public meetings ever did frequent,
> And in her closet constant hours she spent;
> Religious in all her words and ways,
> Preparing still for death, till end of days:
> Of all her children, children lived to see,
> Then dying, left a blessed memory."[1]

Anne Bradstreet's mother was a remarkable woman, and no doubt, worthy of such an epitaph. We have seen many women who rebelled against those expectations and ended up in court to answer for their impudence. What we don't know is if there were any women who performed as they were expected to, but silently resented the pressure for perfection. If they complained to their husbands or fussed with their children is unknown. Those thoughts and feelings are nowhere recorded, but that does not mean they did not exist.

Acknowledgments

I became interested in the Pilgrims when I discovered an ancestor who lived in Plymouth Colony. My ninth-great-grandmother was Alice Bishop, the woman who murdered her child and was hanged for the crime in 1648. After writing *Diverse Gashes: Governor William Bradford, Alice Bishop, and the Murder of Martha Clarke,* I knew I had more to share about the women and children of Plymouth.

This new book was compiled almost completely from primary documents, and I once again express my appreciation to the historians and scholars who copied the handwritten seventh-century documents, especially Nathaniel B. Shurtleff, who transcribed the Plymouth Court Records in 1855. David Thomas Konig worked with the Court Records of 1686-1859 in 1978, making them accessible to modern researchers. Jeremy Dupertuis Bangs took on the seventeenth century Dutch records in 2009, revealing usable data that had been hidden for centuries.

While all conclusions are my own, I am indebted to those who auzhored the many secondary sources I consulted. Their insights and interpretations were helpful to my understanding of events. I have made good use of those internet sites that make obscure books available online. It is still amazing to me that a simple Google search brings the holdings of a distant library right to my desktop.

I have further frequently visited websites devoted to the Pilgrims. As with my first book, two were especially useful to me. Patricia Scott Deetz, Christopher Fennell, and J. Eric Deetz manage the award winning "Plymouth Colony Archive Project" (http://www.histarch. illinois.edu/plymouth/). This comprehensive resource is an essential site for anyone interested in the Plymouth Pilgrims. I also used author and historian Caleb Johnson's excellent "Mayflower History" (http://www. mayflowerhistory.com). This site provides not only biographies and related material, but also doorways to other online sources for primary documents.

How fortunate for me that genealogists—professional and amateur—have gone before me and ferreted out the families and relationships of those women and children I have studied. I am grateful to those descendants of the Pilgrims who have shared the results of DNA testing. These results have often updated long-accepted assumptions about our ancestors, and have helped me answer the constant question of what happened to these people after their appearances in the courts. I am grateful to the librarians at the University of California at Irvine and California State University Fullerton for their assistance in finding the books I needed, and for providing access to online databases.

I have received so much encouragement from many individuals who patiently listened to me rattle on about Plymouth Colony. David Lupher, Ph.D., Professor Emeritus of Classics, University of Puget Sound, and author of *Greeks, Romans, and Pilgrims: Classical Receptions in Early New England,* remains a tireless source of support, helping me understand what I've unearthed. He always challenges me to aim higher and this book is better for his involvement and his edit. Jeremy Dupertuis Bangs, Plymouth historian extraordinaire, generously offered his time and expertise to read and edit this book. His notes challenged me to dig deeper into the research and update more than one careless assumption. I am honored and grateful to have his participation in this project.

I would not be the author of not only one book, but two, were it not for the enthusiasm and encouragement of Francis Ferguson and David Kane at American History Press. They took a chance on a newbie and gently guided me through the process of writing coherent and accessible prose. The editing has been excellent and patiently administered. I am so grateful.

How patient my family have been, listening to me relate the latest Pilgrim story I have discovered, never complaining that I've told that story before. Thank you to my boys, David Watkins and Brian Clark, for your unwavering encouragement and professional advice. Thank you to the Korchas, Karen (Watkins), Michael, and Anica for believing in me. And thank you to my brother, Bill Jennings, for always offering a brotherly boost.

Special appreciation to my husband, Dennis Watkins, who not only lovingly and patiently supported this project, but also participated by proofreading the manuscript many times over and digitizing the illustrations.

Endnotes

Abbreviations Used

CCL   *The Compact with the Charter and Laws of the Colony of New Plymouth.*

CHR   *Plymouth Church Records*

ODM *Observations Divine and Moral* in *Works of John Robinson,* by John Robinson.

OPP   *Of Plymouth Plantation* by William Bradford, edited by Samuel Eliot Morison.

PCR   *Plymouth Colony Records*

RTP   *Records of the Town of Plymouth.*

PCHP *Plymouth Colony, Its History and People,* by Eugene Stratton.

Prologue [pages 1-8]

1. Wayne Franklin, *Discoverers, Explorers, Settlers: the Diligent Writers of Early America* (Chicago, The University of Chicago Press, 1979) 180.
2. William Bradford, *Of Plymouth Plantation, 1620-1647.* Edited by Samuel Eliot Morison. (New York: Alfred A. Knopf, 2004, first published in 1952), Book 1, Ch. 2, 9.
3. Bradford, *Of Plymouth Plantation, 1620-1647.* Book 1, Ch. 3, 17.
4. Bradford, *Of Plymouth Plantation,* Book 1, Ch. 6, 44.
5. Bradford, *Of Plymouth Plantation,* Book 1, Ch. 10, 64.
6. Edward Winslow, William Bradford, and others, *Mourt's relation; or, Journal of the plantation at Plymouth.* (Massachusetts: Applewood Book, 1963) 19.
7. John Smith, "New England," map dated 1616, Wikimedia, https://commons. wikimedia.org/wiki/File:John_Smith_1616_New_England_map.PNG (accessed on 12/3/2018).
8. Bradford, *Of Plymouth Plantation,* Book 1, Ch. 4, 27.
9. Bradford, *Of Plymouth Plantation,* Book 1, Ch. 2, 14.
10. John Winthrop, *History of New England from 1630-1649,* commonly known as

Winthrop's Journal, Vol. 1, Edited by James Savage, (Boston: Little, Brown and Company, 1853) 91.

Chapter One [pages 9-23]

1. John Josselyn, *An Account of Two Voyages to New England: Made During the Years, 1638, 1663*. (Boston: William Weazie, 1865), Originally published in 1674, 9.
2. *OPP*, Book 1, Ch. 9, 59.
3. Eugene Aubrey Stratton, *Plymouth Colony, Its History & People, 1620-1691*, (Salt Lake City, Utah: Ancestry Publishing, 1986), 257.
4. "The Parish Registers of Austerfield 1559-1812 & Cowthorpe 1568-1812," (Austerfield and Cowthorpe, West Yorkshire, Parish Registers Originally Published in 1910), np.
5. *Registers of Worksop, County Nottingham, 1558-1771*, Edited by George W. Marshall. (Guildford: Billing and Sons, 1894), 5.
6. *OPP*, Book 2, Ch. 24, 1633, 260.
7. Jeremy Dupertuis Bangs, *Strangers and Pilgrims, Travellers and Sojourners: Leiden and the Foundations of Plymouth Plantation* (Plymouth, MA: General Society of *Mayflower* Descendants, 2009), 706.
8. Kristi S. Thomas, "Medieval and Renaissance Marriage: Theory and Customs," http://celyn.drizzlehosting.com/mrwp/mrwed.html (accessed on January 20, 2017).
9. David Lindsay, *Mayflower Bastard: A Stranger Among the Pilgrims* (New York: Thomas Dunne Books, 2002), 14
10. Ibid., 17.
11. Ibid., 19.
12. Ibid., 25.
13. Ibid., 25, 29.
14. *OPP*, 444.
15. *OPP*, Book 2, Ch. 11, 1620, 77.
16. *Records of the Colony of New Plymouth in New England*. Edited by Nathaniel B. Shurtleff. 12 vols. (Boston: William White, 1855), 12:10.
17. *PCR*, 1:45.
18. Robert Charles Anderson, *The Pilgrim Migration: Immigrants to Plymouth Colony, 1620-1633* (Boston: New England Historic Genealogical Society, 2004), 330-335.
19. *PCR*, 12:22.
20. Lindsay, 102.
21. Ibid., 166,189.
22. *The Records of the First Church in Salem, Massachusetts 1629-1736*, p. 166, cited in Stratton, *Plymouth Colony, Its History and People, 1620-1691*, 329.
23. *The Records of the First Church in Salem ...*, cited in *PCHP*, 329.
24. *PCHP*, 328.
25. *OPP*, 441.
26. *PCHP*, 333.
27. Edward Winslow, William Bradford, and others. A *Relation or Journall of the beginning and proceedings of the English Plantation settled at Plimoth in New*

England by certaine English Adventurers both Merchants and others. (*"Mourt's Relation"*) 1622. Ed. Dwight B. Health. (Bedford, Massachusetts: Applewood Books, 1963), 41. Hereafter referred to as *Mourt's Relation*.

28. *Mourt's Relation*, 41.

29. *PCHP*, 333.

30. *OPP*, Book 2, Ch. 22, 1631, 239.

31. "Remember Allerton. Caleb Johnson's *Mayflower* History. http://mayflowerhistory.com/allerton-remember (accessed on August 30, 2017).

32. Besides Bartholomew Allerton, *Mayflower* passengers Desire Minter and Gilbert Winslow returned to England. Desire "returned to her friends, and proved not very well;" she died in England. *OPP*, 443. Gilbert Winslow, "after divers years' abode here, returned into England and died there. *OPP*, 447.

33. *PCHP*, 233.

34. "Moses Maverick." Marblehead Magazine. http://www.legendinc.com/Pages/ MarbleheadNet/MM/PeoplePlacesThings/MosesMaverick.html (accessed on August 30, 2017).

35. "Remember Allerton." Caleb Johnson's *Mayflower* History. http:// mayflowerhistory.com/allerton-remember (accessed on August 30, 2017).

36. *PCHP*, 276.

37. Ibid.

38. Bangs, *Strangers and Pilgrims,* 376.

39. Bradford Smith, *Bradford of Plymouth*. (Philadelphia: J.B. Lippincott Co., 1951), 81.

40. Smith, 81, 87.

41. Other sources list John May as Dorothy's father. See *PCHP*, 325.

42. *OPP*, Book 1, Ch. 2, 14.

43. *OPP*, 444.

44. Cotton Mather, *Magnalia Christi Americana; or the Ecclesiastical History of New England.* Originally published in 1702. (Hartford: Silas Andrus and Son, 1855), Book II, Ch. 1, 111.

45. Jane G. Austin, *David Alden's Daughter and Other Stories of Colonial Times* (Boston: Houghton, Mifflin and Co., 1893), 109.

46. Austin, *David Alden's Daughter,* 109.

47. George Ernest Bowman, "Governor William Bradford's First Wife, Dorothy (May) Bradford, Did Not Commit Suicide." *The Mayflower Descendant*, Vol. 29, No. 3 (July 1931): 97-102.

48. Bowman, 101, 102.

49. Ernest Gebler, *The Plymouth Adventure: a Chronicle Novel of the Voyage of the Mayflower,* (New York: Doubleday & Company, Inc., 1950.

50. Bosley Crowther, "The Screen in Review: 'Plymouth Adventure,' a Vivid Portrayal of Pilgrim Voyage, Opens at the Music Hall." New York Times, Nov. 14, 1952.

51. Nickerson, 88-98.

52. Ibid., 92.

53. David Lupher, *Greeks, Romans, and Pilgrims: Classical Receptions in Early New England,* (Leiden: Brill, 2017), 283, fn. 33.

54. George F. Willison, *Saints and Strangers* (New York: Reynal & Hitchcock, 1945), 156-7.

55. Smith, 144-145.

56. Samuel Eliot Morison, *The Story of the "Old Colony" of New Plymouth; 1620-1692* (New York: Alfred A. Knopf, 1956), 56.

57. R.G. Kainer, "Do Not Go Gently: The Quiet Death of Dorothy (May) Bradford, *New England Ancestors,* (Fall 2001): 24-26.

Chapter Two [pages 24-39]

1. James Deetz and Patricia Scott Deetz, *The Times of Their Lives: Life, Love and Death in Plymouth Colony* (New York: W.H. Freeman and Co., 2000), 110.

2. *PCHP,* p. 155.

3. John Robinson, *The Works of John Robinson, Pastor of the Pilgrim Fathers, With a Memoir and Annotations by Robert Ashton, 3 Vols.* (London: John Snow, 1851), *Observations Divine and Moral,* Ch. 8, "Of the Holy Scriptures," 43, 46-47, 51.

4. *The Compact with the Charter and Laws of the Colony of New Plymouth: Together with the Charter of the Council at Plymouth and an Appendix Containing the Articles of Confederation of the United Colonies of New England and Other Valuable Documents* (Boston: Dutton and Wentworth, 1836), 99.

5. *ODM,* Ch. 8, "Of the Holy Scriptures," 50.

6. Edward Winslow, *New England's Salamander Discovered* (London: Printed by Ric. Cotes, for John Bellamy. 1647). See Item 2 under "An Answer to the Postscript."

7. *OPP,* Book 1, Ch. 5, 33.

8. *OPP,* Book 2, Ch. 32, 1624, 317.

9. *ODM,* Ch. 37, "Of Society and Friendship. 158-159.

10. John Demos, *A Little Commonwealth: Family Life in Plymouth Colony.* Second edition. (Oxford University Press, 2000), 30-31.

11. *ODM,* Ch. 37, "Of Society and Friendship," 157.

12. John Crowley, *The Invention of Comfort* (Baltimore: Johns Hopkins University Press, 2003), 67.

13. *PCR,* 1:54.

14. *CCL,* 1641, 70.

15. *CCL,* 1671, 256.

16. *PCR,* 4:141.

17. Plymouth Colony used the British system of currency - pounds, shillings, and pence. There were twelve pence in a shilling, twenty shillings in a pound.

18. *CCL,* 1643, 74.

19. *CCL,* 1636, 41.

20. *CCL,* 1637, 61.

21. *ODM,* Ch. 53, "Of Rewards and Punishments by Men," 215.

22. Martha L. Finch, *Dissenting Bodies: Corporealities in Early New England* (Columbia University Press, 2009), 133.

23. *PCR,* 2:174.

24. *PCR,* 1:35.

25. *PCR,* 1:9.

26. "Prices of Grain and other Commodities, for the Payment of Taxes in Plymouth Colony." In *Collections of the American Statistical Association* (Boston: T.R. Marvin, 1847), Vol. 1, 289.

27. Darrett B. Rutman, *Husbandmen of Plymouth: Farms and Villages in the Old Colony, 1620-1692* (Boston: Beacon Press, 1967), 43.

28. *PCR*, 1:12.
29. *PCR*, 12:213.
30. *PCR*, 1:61.
31. *PCR*, 3:212.
32. Amos Otis, *Genealogical Notes of Barnstable Families*, Vol. 1, (Barnstable, MA: FB and FP Goss, 1888), 260.
33. *PCR*, 1:127.
34. John Josselyn, *New England's Rarities Discovered* (London: G. Widdowes, 1672), 35.
35. *PCR*, 6:113-114.
36. Ibid.
37. Ibid.
38. Finch, 126.
39 *PCR*, 1:132.
40. *PCR*, 3:111-112.
41. *PCR*, 3:111-113.
42. *PCR*, 1:96-97.
43. *CCL*, 1636, 42.
44. *OPP*, Book 2, Ch. 21, 1630, 234.
45. *PCR*, 2:44.
46. *PCR*, 5:167-168.
47. *PCR, Judicial Acts*, 305-307.
48. *PCR*, 6:153-154.
49. *PCR*, 2:132-133.
50. Ibid.
51. *PCR*, 2:132.
52. *PCR*, 2:133.
53. *PCR*, 2:134.
54. *PCR*, 11:32.
55. *PCR*, 2:134.
56. See Donna Watkins, *Diverse Gashes: Governor William Bradford, AliceBishop, and the Murder of Martha Clarke, Plymouth Colony, 1648* (Virginia: American History Press, 2019), for a full discussion of this incident.

Chapter Three [pages 40-53]

1. *CCL*, 44.
2. *PCR*, 3:5.
3. *PCR, Judicial Acts*, 101
4. *Ibid.*, 218.
5. *PCR*, Miscellaneous Records, 52.
6. *PCR, Judicial Acts*, 218.
7. *CCL*, 61.
8. Ibid., 44.
9. *PCR*, 2:112.
10. "Ann Crooker of Sinclair," *The American Monthly Magazine*, Vol. 27, No. 4, October 1905, 689.
11. *PCR*, 2:110.
12. *PCR*, 5:137-138.

13. Ibid., 123.
14. *PCR*, 4:140.
15. Ibid.
16. *PCR*, 4:158-159.
17. Cited in Isaac Backus, *A History of New England with Particular Reference to the Denomination of Christians Called Baptists.* (Boston: Edward Draper, 1777), 428.
18. *PCHP*, 94.
19. Howland, Arthur and Elizabeth Howland. "The Sufferings of Arthur Howland," in Bangs, Jeremy Dupertuis. *The Town Records of Marshfield during the time of Plymouth Colony, 1620-1692.* (Leiden, The Netherlands: Leiden American Pilgrim Museum, 2015), 16-18.
20. Ashley, Linda Ramsey. *In the Pilgrim Way: The First Congregational Church, Marshfield, Massachusetts 1640-2000.* (Plymouth, MA: Powderhorn Press, 2001), 19-20.
21. Ashley, 19-20,
22. *CCL,* 43, 79, 80.
23. *PCR,* 1:12.
24. Lisa M. Lauria, "Sexual Misconduct in Plymouth Colony," the Plymouth Colony Archive Project, http://www.histarch.illinois.edu/plymouth/Lauria1.html (accessed on August 1, 2020).February 21, 2018).
25. Finer, Laurence, "Trends in Premarital Sex in the United States, 1954-2003," Public Health Report, 2007 Jan-Feb: 122(1): 73-78.
26. Lauria.
27. *CCL,* 79,80.
28. *PCR,* 3:6.
29. *PCR,* 5:32.
30. David Thomas Konig and William E. Nelson, *Plymouth Court Records, 1686-1859,* Vol. 1 (Wilmington, Delaware: Michael Glazier Inc., 1978), 194.
31. *CCL,* 246.
32. *PCR,* 3:91.
33. *PCR,* 3:82,91.
34. *PCR, Misc. Rec.*, 186.
35. R. Dudley Kelley, "David Okillea of Yarmouth, Massachusetts and Some of His Descendants," *New England Historical and Genealogical Register,* Vol. 151, 1997, 131-152.
36. John D. Crimmins, *Irish-American Historical Miscellany,* (New York City: Published by the Author), 1905, 21.
37. *PCR, Judicial Acts,* 111
38. *PCR,* 4:34.
39. *PCR, Judicial Acts,* 111.
40. *PCR,* 4:162.
41. Caleb H. Johnson, *The Mayflower and Her Passengers,* (Xlibris Corp.), 2006, 208.
42. Johnson, *The Mayflower and Her Passengers,* 208.
43. *PCR,* 5:51.
44. Ibid.
45. Ibid.
46. *PCR,* 1:103.

47. *PCR*, 3:206, 220.
48. *PCR*, 3:209.
49. *PCR*, 3:220.
50. *PCR*, 4:9.
51. *PCR*, 6:20.
52. *PCR* 7:173-174.
53. Ibid.
54. *PCHP*, 285.
55. *PCR*, 1:93.
56. *PCR*, 1:61.
57. *PCR*, 1:94.
58. *PCR*, 2:72..
59. *PCR*, 2:124.
60. Anderson, 60-61.
61. *PCR*, 6:176,177.
62. *PCR*, 4:106.
63. *PCR*, 5:16, 31, 87, 117-118.
64. *PCR*, 5:260-261.

Chapter Four [pages 54-66]

1. Caleb Johnson, "Women of Early Plymouth," Caleb Johnson's Mayflower History, http://mayflowerhistory.com/women/ (accessed on February 21, 2018).
2. *OPP*, Book 2, Ch. 12, 86.
3. Johnson, *The Mayflower and her Passengers* (Xlibris: 2006), 252.
4. *PCHP*, p. 371.
5. Johnson, *The Mayflower and her Passengers*, 247.
6. *PCHP*, 371.
7. *OPP*, Book 2, Ch. 12, 86.
8. "Edward Winslow." Caleb Johnson's Mayflower History.com, http://mayflowerhistory.com/winslow-edwar/ (accessed on January 24, 2017).
9. Demos, 92-95.
10. *CCL*, 86.
11. *PCR*, 6: 6.
12. Willystine Goodsell, *A History of the Family as a Social and Educational Institution* (New York: McMillan Company, 1920), 249.
13. *PCR*, 6:125.
14. *PCR*, 5: 28.
15. *PCR*, 3:63.
16. *PCR*, 3:64.
17. *PCR, Misc. Rec.*,181.
18. *PCR*, 4:50.
19. William Richard Cutter, *Genealogical and Family History of Western New York* ..., Vol. 1, (New York: Lewis Historical Publishing Company), 1912, 195.
20. *PCR*, 5:32.
21. Ibid.,118.
22. *PCR, Misc. Rec.*, 157.
23. Cutter, *Genealogical and Family History of Western New York*, 195.
24. *PCR*, 2:149.
25. Ibid.

26. *PCR*, 3:174.
27. Gary Boyd Roberts, "The English Origins of John Spring of Watertown," *The American Genealogist,* Vol. 55, no. 2 (April 1979): 70-71.
28. *PCR*, 5:10.
29. Ibid., 23.
30. Nahum Mitchell, *History of the Early Settlement of Bridgewater, in Plymouth County, Massachusetts …* (Boston: Kidder & Wright, 1840), 175.
31. *PCR*, 5:23.
32. Mitchell, 176.
33. *PCR*, 5:50.
34. Ibid.
35. There were at least two John Williams in Plymouth Colony. This John Williams, born about 1624, lived in Scituate.
36. *PCHP*, 164.
37. Shirley Segerstrom Bailey, "John Bailey (Bayley) of Scituate," *The Mayflower Quarterly* March 2004, 48.
38. Bangs, *The Seventeenth Century Town Records of Scituate, Massachusetts.* (NEHGS, 2001), 112-113.
39. *PCR, Judicial Acts*, 110, 113-114.
40. *PCR*, 4:50.
41. Ibid., 93.
42. Ibid.
43. Samuel Deane, *A History of Scituate, Massachusetts, From Its First Settlement to 1831.* (Boston: James Loring, 1831), 229.
44. *PCR*, 4:107.
45. Ibid.
46. Ibid,107-8.
47. *PCR, Judicial Acts*, 125.
48. *PCR*, 4:121
49. *PCR*, 4:125.
50. Ibid.
51. *PCR*, 4:125-126.
52. *PCR*, 4:126.
53. *PCR, Judicial Acts*, 138.
54. *PCR, Judicial Acts*, 138-139.
55. *PCR, Judicial Acts*, 139-140.
56. *PCR, Judicial Acts*, 140-141.
57. *PCR, Judicial Acts*, 141-142.
58. *PCR, Judicial Acts*, 142.
59. "Will of John Williams of Scituate, dated October 15, 1691," "Abstracts from the First Book of Plymouth County Probate Records," *The Genealogical Advertiser,* Vol. 4, No. 1, (March 1901): 25-27.
60. *PCR*, 4:107.

Chapter Five [pages 67-79]

1. Deetz, 144.
2. *ODM*, "Of Marriage," 241, 242.
3. *PCR*, 6:191.

4. *PCHP*, 297.

5. *PCR*, 6:191.

6. *PCR*, 6:192, 204.

7. Francis Baylies, *An Historical Memoir of the Colony of New Plymouth …*, Vol. 2 (Boston: Wiggin & Lunt, 1866), 48.

8. Deane, 104-105.

9. *PCR*, 6:207-208.

10. "Plymouth Church Records," Vol. 1, Part 5, in *Publications of the Colonial Society of Massachusetts*, Vol 12 (Boston: Published by the Society, 1920), 266, 267.

11. William W. Johnson, *Clarke-Clark Genealogy. Records of the Descendants of Thomas Clarke, Plymouth, 1623-1697.* (Milwaukee, Wisconsin: Riverside Printing Co., 1884), 18.

12. Fred W. Scott, *Clifford William Scott and Mildred Evelyn Bradford Scott of Ashfield, Massachusetts: Ancestors, Descendants and New England Heritage* (New York: iUniverse, Inc., 2004), 119.

13. *PCR*, 6:44.

14. *PCR*, 6:45.

15. *PCR*, 4:156.

16. *PCR, Misc. Rec.*, 54.

17. *PCR*, 4:156.

18. *PCR*, 4: 151.

19. Estate of William Hacke, "Plymouth Colony Wills and Inventories," *The Mayflower Descendant*, Vol. 17, No. 1, (January 1915): 22.

20. *PCR*, 4:155.

21. *PCR*, 5:33.

22. Ibid.

23. George H. Banks, *The History of Martha's Vineyard*, Vol. 2 (Boston: George H. Dean, 1911), 72-73.

24. *PCR*, 11:95.

25. *PCR*, 3:221.

26. *PCR, Misc. Rec.*, 6.

27. *PCR*, 3:221.

28. Elizabeth Burgess, *Burgess Genealogy: Memorial of the Family of Thomas and Dorothy Burgess* (Boston: T.R. Marvin & Son. 1865), 12.

29. *PCR*, 5:29.

30. Ibid.

31. *PCR*, 5: 31.

32. *PCR*, 5: 31,32.

33. *PCR*, 5:41-42.

34. *PCR*, 4:187.

35. *PCR, Misc. Rec.*, 65.

36. *PCR*, 5: 51.

37. *PCR*, 5: 81, 82.

38. *PCR*, 5: 82.

39. *PCR*, 5:159.

40. Deane, 295.

41. Anna Glover, *Glover Memorials and Genealogies. An Account of John Glover of Dorchester and His Descendants, with a Brief Sketch of Some of the Glovers*

who First Settled in New Jersey, Virginia, and Other Places, (Boston: David Clapp & Son, 1867), 205-206.

42. *PCR,* 6:190.
43. Ibid.
44. Glover, 205-206.
45. *PCR,* 4:187
46. *PCR,* 1:68.
47. Louis MacCartney, *The Descendants of William Tubbs of Duxbury* (Boston: LM MacCartney, 1959?), page numbers not available.
48. *PCR,* 3:5.
49. *PCR, Judicial Acts,* 107-108.
50. *PCR,* 4:42.
51. Ibid.
52. *PCR, Judicial Acts,* 112.
53. *PCR,* 4:46-47.
54. *Register of the National Society of Colonial Dames in the State of New York, 1893 to 1913,* (New York: Published by the Authority of Managers, 1913), 361.
55. *PCR,* 4:66
56. *PCR,* 4:104.
57. *PCR,* 4:187.
58. *PCR,* 4:192.
59. Ibid.
60. MacCartney.
61. *PCR, Judicial Acts,* 188-189.
62. Barbara Newhall, *The Barker Family of Plymouth Colony and County* (Cleveland: Press of F.W. Roberts, 1900), 12-15.
63. Will of William Tubbs, "Abstracts from the First Book of Plymouth County Probate Records. *The Genealogical Advertiser,* Vol. 1, No. 1 (March 1898): 19.

Chapter Six [pages 80-97]

1. Demos, p. 92-95.
2. *PCR,* 11:18
3. "The Massachusetts Body of Liberties", Item 80, p. 271. https://history.hanover.edu/texts/masslib.html. (accessed on September 26, 2018).
4. *PCR,* 4:47.
5. *PCR,* 4:103-104.
6. *PCR,* 5:16.
7. *PCR,* 4:51,55.
8. *PCR,* 6:7-8.
9. *PCR,* 5:61.
10. *PCR,* 2:94.
11. *PCR, Misc. Rec.,* 7.
12. *PCR,* 3:102.
13. Lucy Kellogg, Ed., *Mayflower Families Through Five Generations: Descendants of the Pilgrims Who Landed at Plymouth, Mass. December 1620, Vol. 1.* (General Society of Mayflower Descendants, 1975).
14. *PCR,* 3:75
15. Robert Charles Anderson, Melinde Lutz Sanborn, and George F. Sanborn,

Jr., *The Great Migration, Vol. I, A-B: Immigrants to New England, 1634-1635,* "Anthony Bessey," (Boston: New England Historic Genealogical Society, 1999), 268.

16. *PCR,* 4:7.
17. *PCR,* 4:10.
18. Anderson, "Anthony Bessey," in The Great Migration, Vol.1, 368.
19. *PCR,* 4:10.
20. George Bishop, *New England Judged by the Spirit of the Lord,* (London: T. Sowle, 1703), 144.
21. Amos Otis, *Genealogical Notes of Barnstable Families,* Vol. 1 (Barnstable, Mass.: FB & FP Goss Publishers, 1888), 249, 258.
22. Henry C. Kittredge, *Cape Cod Its People and Their History,* (Boston: Houghton Mifflin Co., 1930), 270.
23. *PCR,* 3:141,167.
24. Otis, 260.
25. James Bowden, *History of the Society of Friends in American,* Vol. 1 (London: Charles Gilpin, 1850), 116.
26. *PCR,* 3:158.
27. *PCR,* 3:206.
28. *PCR,* 4:88.
29. *PCR,* 4:117.
30. Otis, 144.
31. Otis, 266.
32. Charles Henry Pope, *The Plymouth Colony Scrapbook* (Boston: C.E. Goodspeed, 1918), 51-52.
33. "Will of George Barlow," Massachusetts, Plymouth County, Probate Records, 1633-1967. FamilySearch (https://familysearch.org/ark:/61903/3:1:3QS7-897D-VSYF?cc=2018320&wc=M6BX-F29%3A338083801 : 20 May 2014), Wills 1633-1686 vol 1-4>image 578 of 616; State Archives, Boston, (accessed on January 22, 2019).
34. Anderson, "Anthony Bessey," in *The Great Migration,* Vol.1, 368.
35. *PCR,* 5:16.
36. Mrs. John E. Barclay, "Mary Bartlett (Foster) Morey, Her Husbands and Children." *The American Genealogist* (Vol. 32, No. 4, October,1956): 193.
37. *PCR,* 6:152.
38. *PCR, Misc. Rec.,* 13,14.
39. Barclay, 193.
40. *PCR, Misc. Rec.,* 22.
41. Barclay, 194.
42. *PCR,* 6:152.
43. *PCR,* 6:201.
44. *PCR,* 5:16.
45. Paul W. Prindle, F.A.S.G., "A Bartlett-Foster-Morey Epilogue." *The American Genealogist* (Vol. 53, No., 3, January 1977): 155.
46. *PCR,* 5:16.
47. Barclay, 194.
48. Prindle, 155.
49. *PCR,* 3:197,198.
50. *PCR,* 3:199.

51. *PCHP*, 199.
52. *PCR*, 5:245.
53. *PCR*, 5:13.
54. Ibid.
55. Ibid.
56. Ibid.
57. *PCR*, 5:21.
58. *PCR*, 5:23.
59. *Massachusetts, Town and Vital Records, 1620-1988*, online database ancestry. com (accessed on November 10, 2016).
60. Cynthia Hagar Krusell, *Plymouth Colony to Plymouth County*. Lulu, 2010, 44.
61. "Inventory of Christopher Winter," http://www.histarch.illinois.edu/plymouth/ P417.htm (accessed on October 2, 2018).
62. James Savage, *A Genealogical Dictionary of the First Settlers of New England ...*, Vol. 1, (Boston: Little, Brown, and Company, 1860), 139.
63. *PCR*, 5:253.
64. *PCR*, 5:260.
65. *PCR*, 5:253.
66. *PCR*, 5:261.
67. *PCR*, 5:260, 261.
68. *PCR*, 5:262.
69. *PCR*, 5:8.
70. Ibid.
71. *PCR*, 4:51.
72. *PCR*, 4:136, 137.
73. *PCR*, 3:74.
74. Quoted in *So Dreadfull a Judgment: Puritan Responses to King Philip's War, 1676–1677*, edited by Richard Slotkin, James K. Folsom, (University Press of New England: Wesleyan University, 1978), 112.
75. Craig S. Chartier, "Clarke Garrison House Murders," Plymouth Archaeological Rediscovery Project (PARP), http://plymoutharch.tripod.com/id16.html (accessed on October 2, 2018).
76. *PCR*, 5: 204-206.
77. Ibid.
78. Ibid.
79. Ibid.
80. Ibid.
81. Ibid.
82. *PCR*, 5: 209.
83. *PCR*, 5: 204-206.
84. *PCR*, 5: 209.

Chapter Seven [pages 98-124]

1. *PCR*, 2:105.
2. *PCR*, 2:73.
3. *PCR*, 2:81.
4. *PCR*, 3:160.
5. *PCR*, 3:171-172.

6. *PCR*, 4:22

7. "Thomas Bird's Will," Plymouth Colony Wills and Inventories, *The Mayflower Descendant*, Vol. 16, 1914, 123-124.

8. *PCR*, 1:48-49.

9. *PCR*, 1:118, 131.

10. *ODM*, Ch. 60, "Of Children and Their Education," 249.

11. *PCR*, 2:112-113.

12. *PCR*, 2:82.

13. Ruth Story Devereaux Eddy, *The Eddy Family in America* (Boston: T.O. Metcalf Co., 1930), 25.

14. "Capt. Joshua Eddy. *New England Historical and Genealogical Register*, (Vol. 8. No. 3, July 1854): 201-203.

15. Bradford. *Of Plymouth Plantation*, 234.

16. *PCHP*, 245.

17. *PCR*, 1:31.

18. *OPP*, 447.

19. Susan E. Roser, *Mayflower Increasings* (Genealogical Publishing: 1995), 16.

20. *PCR*, 1:36-37,43.

21. *RTP*, 86.

22. *PCR*, 2:38.

23. *RTP*, 12.

24. Ibid.

25. Ibid.

26. Roser, 17.

27. *PCR*, 2:58-59

28. Ruth C. McGuyre, Robert S. Wakefield, Harriet W. Hodge, General Society of Mayflower Descendants, M*ayflower Families Through Five Generations. Volume 5, Families Edward Winslow, John Billington: Descendants of the Pilgrims Who Landed at Plymouth, Mass., December 1620.* 2nd Ed., (Plymouth MA: General Society of Mayflower Descendants, 1997), 31-47.

29. *PCR*, 5:94.

30. *PCR, Misc. Rec.*, 137.

31. Susan E. Roser, George Ernest Bowman: Massachusetts Society of Mayflower Descendants, *Mayflower Deeds and Probates: From the Files of George Ernest Bowman at the Massachusetts Society of Mayflower Descendants* (Baltimore: Genealogical Pub. Co., 1994), 57.

32. *RTP*, 83.

33. Roser, *Mayflower Increasings,* 17.

34. McGuyre, 44-46.

35. Roser, *Mayflower Deeds*, 57.

36. "Francis Billington to Isaac Billington. May 11, 1665." "Plymouth Colony Deeds." *The Mayflower Descendant* (Vol. 35, no. 1, January 1985): 32.

37. Roser, *Mayflower Deeds*, 57.

38. Ibid.

39. Harriet Woodbury Hodge, "Desire Billington and Her Grandfather Francis Billington's Estate," *The Mayflower Quarterly* (Vol. 52, No. 3, 1986): 137-144.

40. Hodge, 137-144.

41. *PCR*, 3:201.

42. Mary Elizabeth Sinnott, *Annals of the Sinnott, Rogers, Corlies, Reeves, Bodine,*

and Allied Families (Philadelphia: Lippincott, 1905), 215.

43. "Thomas Lumbert's Will. *The Mayflower Descendant*, (Vol. 16, 1914): 124-6.
44. Mary Blauss Edwards, "Descendants of John Everson of Plymouth, Massachusetts." *New England Historical and Genealogical Register* (No.169, Winter 2015) p. 37.
45. *Records of the Town of Plymouth: Published by Order of the Town, Vol. 1.* (Boston: W.B. Clarke and Co., 1889), 106. Hereinafter referred to as *RTP.*
46. *RTP*, 105,112.
47. Edwards, p. 37.
48. Edwards, p. 37, 39-40, 44-46, *PCR* 49-50.
49. Edwards, p. 43.
50. "Kingston, Massachusetts," www.kingstonmass.org (accessed on December 3, 2016).
51. *PCR*, 6:54.
52. *PCR*, 6:54,56.
53. *PCR*, 6:66.
54. "Indenture of Benjamin Savory." Plymouth Colony Deeds, Vol. 4: 86, *The Mayflower Descendant*, Vol. 5, 1903: 90-91.
55. "Indenture of Benjamin Savory." 90-91.
56. A. W. Savary, *A Genealogical and Biographical Record of the Savery Families ...* (Boston: The Collins Press, 1893), 20.
57. *PCR, Judicial Acts*, 213.
58. *PCR*, 12:181-182.
59. Ibid.
60. *PCR*, 1:103, 127.
61. "Plymouth Colony Vital Records," *The Mayflower Descendant*, Vol.17, 1915, 185.
62. *PCR*, 5:10-11, 8:25.
63. Thomas P. Adams, "The Harlowe Family," *New England Historical and Genealogical Record*, Vol. 14:227, 1860.
64. *PCHP*, 298.
65. *PCR*, 5:10-11
66. Lee D Van Antwerp, Ruth Ann Wilder Sherman, *Vital Records of Plymouth, Massachusetts to the Year 1850,* (Camden, Maine: Picton Press, 1993), 86.
67. Nathaniel Morton's Will, Massachusetts, Plymouth County, Probate Records, 1633-1967, Probate records 1717-1724 and 1854-1862 vol 4-4Q > image 191 of 485; State Archives, Boston.
68. W. J. Litchfield, *Litchfield Family in America*, Vol. 1, *Lawrence Litchfield and His Descendants*, Part 1, No. 1 (October 1901), 38.
69. Litchfield, 38.
70. Litchfield, 39.
71. *PCR*, 4:39.
72. Litchfield, 51, 55-56, 97-98
73. Judith Litchfield, the younger, married Joseph Briggs, and had a daughter in 1725, whom they named Judith. Judith Briggs married William Collier, and had a daughter in 1754 also named Judith. Judith Collier married John Briggs and named their daughter, born in 1788, Judith, who married Joseph Gannett. She did not have children of her own, but helped raise several step-children. See Family Search, "Josias Litchfielf," https://ancestors.familysearch.org/en/LZDZ-

2N4/josiah-litchfield-1647-1708 (Accessed on 2/25/2021).

74. *PCR*, 6:20.

75. Michael L. Godfrey, *Footprints in the Sand: The Godfrey Story*, (Lulu.com, 2012), 13.

76. *PCR*, 6:201.

77. Godfrey, 13.

78. *PCHP*, 366.

79. *PCR*, 3:126.

80. *PCR*, 3:219.

81. Anderson, *Pilgrim Migration*, 35.

82. *PCR*, 3:22-23.

83. *PCR*, 5:88.

84. Anderson, *The Pilgrim Migration*, 263.

85. *PCR*, 1:167-168.

86. *PCR*, 2:29, 31, 35.

87. *PCR*, 3:6

88. *PCR*, 3:126.

89. Ibid.

90. *PCHP*, 366.

91. *PCR*, 5:207.

92. Ibid.

93. *PCR*, 5:223.

94. *PCR*, 11:255.

95. Baylies, 190-191, fn.

96. Ibid.

97. Ibid.

98. Ibid.

99. The Pilgrims referred to him as Massasoit, which was his title and means Great Sachem. Actually, his name was Ousamequin.

100. Deetz. *Times of Their Lives*. 156.

101. *PCR*, 1:141-142.

102. *PCR*, 3:63-4

103. *PCR*, 3:83.

104. *PCR*, 3:46,119.

105. *PCR*, 3:51.

106. *PCR*, 3:71.

107. Hermon Alfred Kelley, *A Genealogical History of the Kelley Family...*, (Privately Printed at Cleveland, Ohio, 1897), 86.

108. Johnson, Caleb. "William Latham." Caleb Johnson's Mayflower History. http://mayflowerhistory.com/latham/ (accessed on October 6, 2016).

109. *PCR*, 3:71.

110. Ibid.

111. Ibid.

112. *PCR*, 3:71-73.

113. *PCR*, 3:73.

114. *PCR*, *Judicial Acts*, 75.

115. Ibid.

116. *PCR*, 3:143.

117. Ibid.

118. *PCR*, 5:23.
119. *PCR*, 4: 155, 192-193, 5:37.
120. *PCR*, 5:91
121. *PCR, Misc. Rec.*, 153.

Chapter Eight [pages 125-144]

1. Winslow, *New England's Salamander Discovered*. See Item 2 under "An Answer to the Postscript."
2. *ODM*, Ch. 29, "Of Riches and Poverty," 124.
3. Caleb Johnson, *The Mayflower and Her Passengers*, 110.
4. Ruth A. McIntyre, *Debts Hopeful and Desperate*. (Plimoth Plantation,1963) 20.
5. Caleb Johnson, "Mrs. Mary Brewster." Caleb Johnson's Mayflower History. http://mayflowerhistory.com/brewster-mary/ (accessed on September 22, 2017).
6. *OPP*, Book 1, Ch. 2, 12-13.
7. *OPP*, Book 1, Ch. 2, 13.
8. *OPP*, Book 1, Ch. 2, 14.
9. *OPP*, Book 1, Ch. 2, 14,15n.
10. *PCHP*, p. 18.
11. Bangs, *Strangers and Pilgrims*, 563-568.
12. Jeremy Dupertuis Bangs, Ed., *Intellectual Baggage: The Pilgrims and Plymouth Colony Ideas of Influence, a catalogue of an imagined exhibition, 2020.* (Leiden, The Netherlands: Leiden American Pilgrim Museum, 2020), 46.
13. *OPP*, 376.
14. Caleb Johnson, "Mrs. Mary Brewster."
15. Caleb Johnson, "William Brewster. Caleb Johnson's Mayflower History." http://mayflowerhistory.com/brewster-william/ (accessed on September 22, 2017).
16. The Mary Brewster mentioned in the PCR, 12:10, is most likely the daughter of Jonathan Brewster, and the elder Mary's granddaughter.
17. *OPP*, 324-328.
18. *OPP*, Book One, Ch. 6, 42, fn.
19. *PCHP*, 18.
20. *OPP*, App. 4, 367.
21. Caleb Johnson, *The Mayflower and Her Passengers,* 107-114.
22. *OPP*, App. 13, 441.
23. *OPP*, Book One, Ch. 11, 76.
24. *Mourt's Relation*, 55-57.
25. *OPP*, Book Two, Ch. 12, 86.
26. Ibid.
27. Nathaniel Morton, *New England's Memorial, 1669.* Edited by Howard J. Hall. Facsimile of the first edition. (New York: Scholars Facsimiles & Reprints, 1937), 30.
28. *OPP*, Book 2, Ch. 12, 86.
29. Nathaniel Morton, 31.
30. *OPP*, 443-444.
31. *OPP*, Book Two, Ch. 14, 130.
32. Ibid.
33. Bangs, *Strangers and Pilgrims*, 283. See pp. 410-422 for a full explanation of the textile production industry.

34. Anderson, *The Pilgrim Migration,* 439, 443.

35. Caleb Johnson, "Passenger Lists" Caleb Johnson's Mayflower History. http://mayflowerhistory.com/anne/ (accessed on October 22, 2017).

36. *PCHP,* p. 258.

37. *PCHP,* p. 355.

38. Pory, John, Emmanuel Altham, and Isaack De Rasieres. *Three Visitors to Early Plymouth: Letters About the Pilgrim Settlement in New England During Its First Seven Years.* (Massachusetts: Applewood Books. 1997), 29-30.

39. Pory, 30.

40. Anderson, *The Pilgrim Migration,* 437, 440.

41. Willison, *Saints and Strangers,* 452.

42. *PCR,* 3: 120, 8:94, 101, 102, 105, 128, 130.

43. It is not clear from the records if the Bradfords were reimbursed for their hospitality before Bradford's death.

44. Anderson, *The Pilgrim Migration,* 65.

45. *PCR, Misc. Rec.,* 33.

46. "Will of Alice Bradford," Pilgrim Hall Museum, http://www.pilgrimhallmuseum.org/pdf/Alice_Carpenter_Southworth_Bradford_Will_Inventory.pdf (accessed on October 13, 2018).

47. Samuel G. Webber, *A Genealogy of the Southworths (Southards) Descendants of Constant Southworth, With a Sketch of the Family in England,* (Boston: The Fort Hill Press, 1905), 10-11.

48. Willison, *Saints and Strangers,* 430.

49. Peggy M. Baker, "The Godmother of Thanksgiving: the Story of Sarah Josepha Hale," 2007, Pilgrim Hall Museum, http://www.pilgrimhallmuseum.org/pdf/Godmother_of_Thanksgiving.pdf (accessed on October 23, 2018).

50. John Seelye, *Memory's Nation: The Place of Plymouth Rock.* (Chapel Hill: University of Northern Carolina Press, 1998), 384.

51. William S. Russell, *Pilgrim Memorials, and Guide to Plymouth.* (Boston: Crosby, Nichols, Lee and Co., 1860), 23

52. It wasn't long before the descendants of John Alden claimed that their ancestor was the first to step on Plymouth Rock. See Seelye.

53. *PCHP,* p. 262.

54. Anderson, *The Pilgrim Migration,* 104.

55. *PCR,* 12:4.

56. *PCR,* 12:11.

57. *OPP,* 538.

58. "John Winslow," Pilgrim Hall Museum, http://www.pilgrimhallmuseum.org/john_winslow.htm (accessed on October 23, 2018).

59. Anderson, *The Pilgrim Migration,* 513.

60. "John Winslow's Will" Pilgrim Hall Museum. http://www.pilgrimhallmuseum.org/pdf/John_Winslows_Will_Inventory.pdf (accessed on September 21, 2017).

61. "Last Will & Testament of Mary (Chilton) Winslow, 1676." The Plymouth Colony Archive Project. http://www.histarch.illinois.edu/plymouth/winslowwill.html (accessed on September 21, 2017).

62. *OPP,* 442,445.

63. Seelye, 379.

64. Henry Wadsworth Longfellow, *The Courtship of Miles Standish [and] Elizabeth,* (Boston: Houghton, Mifflin and Company, 1858), 15, 18, 26, 28, 47, 49.

65. Longfellow, 59.
66. Longfellow, 62, 65, 66.
67. Longfellow, 69, 70.
68. "Henry Wadsworth Longfellow," Poetry Foundation, https://www. poetryfoundation.org/poets/henry-wadsworth-longfellow (accessed on October 22, 2018).
69. *PCR*, 3:195.
70. Anderson, *The Pilgrim Migration*, 4.
71. *PCR*, 12:10.
72. Bowman, George Ernest. "Broadsides on the Death of John Alden." *The Mayflower Descendant*. Vol. 34, no. 2 (1937): 49-53.
73. "John Alden Senior," Find a Grave, https://www.findagrave.com/memorial/15/john-alden (accessed on October 23, 2018).
74. "Priscilla Mullins Alden," Find a Grave, https://www.findagrave.com/memorial/749/priscilla-alden (accessed on October 23, 2018).
75. Anderson, *The Pilgrim Migration*, 7-8.
76. John Winthrop, *History of New England from 1630-1649*, commonly known as *Winthrop's Journal*, Vol. 1, Edited by James Savage, (Boston: Little, Brown and Company, 1853), 259.
77. Samuel Hopkins Emery, *History of Taunton, Massachusetts, From Its Settlement to the Present Time*, (Syracuse, NY: D. Mason & Co., 1893), 68.
78. *PCHP*, 67.
79. *PCR*, 1:53.
80. James Edward Seaver, "The First Settlement of Ancient Taunton," in *Quarter Millennial Celebration of the City of Taunton, Massachusetts, Tuesday and Wednesday, June 4 and 5, 1889*,114.
81. *PCHP*, 67.
82. Seaver, 114.
83. *PCR*, 1:142-143.
84. *Quarter Millennial Celebration of the City of Taunton, Massachusetts, Tuesday and Wednesday, June 4 and 5, 1889.* (Taunton, Massachusetts: Published by the City Government, 1889), 252.
85. *PCR*, 1:143.
86. J.W.D. Hall, "Ancient Iron Works in Taunton," *New England Historical and Genealogical Register*, Vol. 38, July 1884, 266.
87. "The Will of Elizabeth Poole," *Mayflower Descendant*, Vol. 14, 1912, 24-26.
88. Ibid.
89. Emery, 131.
90. *PCR*, 5:12.
91. *PCR*, 5:28-29, 159.
92. Emery, 131.
93. *Quarter Millennial Celebration of the City of Taunton, Massachusetts, Tuesday and Wednesday, June 4 and 5, 1889.* (Taunton, Massachusetts: Published by the City Government, 1889) 240.
94. Seaver, 116.
95. *Quarter Millennial Celebration of the City of Taunton ...*, 288.
96. Seaver, 126.
97. "Elizabeth Poole," *Wikivisually*, https://wikivisually.com/wiki/Elizabeth_Poole (accessed on November 17, 2018).

98. "Elizabeth Pole [sic]" *Find-a-grave*, https://www.findagrave.com/memorial/22055303/elizabeth-pole (accessed on November 16, 2018).

99. "Taunton, Massachusetts" https://en.wikipedia.org/wiki/Taunton,_Massachusetts (accessed on November 16, 2018).

100. Seaver, 130.

Chapter Nine [pages 145-165]

1. Gouge, *Of Domesticall Duties, Eight Treatises*, The Third Treatise: Of Wives Particular Duties, Ch. 13, "Of a Wife's Reverend Speech to Her Husband," 281.

2. *ODM*, Ch. 22, "Of Speech and Silence," 103-104.

3. *CCL*, 48.

4. *PCR*, 11:57-58

5. *PCR*, 11:57-58, 137, 214. 224-225.

6. *PCR*, 2:173.

7. John Saffin, "John Saffin Diary. Rhode Island Historical Society, Manuscripts Division. http://www.rihs.org/mssinv/MSS696.htm (accessed on May 5, 2018).

8. *PCR*, 3:186.

9. *PCR, Judicial Acts*, 112.

10. *PCR*, 5:253-254.

11. *PCR*, 11:57.

12. *PCR*, 2:172-174.

13. James Boswell, *The Life of Samuel Johnson* Vol. 1 (New York: Alexander V. Blake, 1844), 205-206.

14. *PCR*, 3:111, 112.

15. *PCR*, 2:68, 83, 94.

16. *PCR*, 3:96.

17. *PCR*, 3:200.

18. *PCR*, 4:61.

19. Edwin Salter, *A History of Monmouth and Ocean Counties ...* (Bayonne, N.J.: F. Gardner & Son, 1890), ii (444).

20. *CCL*, 162.

21. *PCR, Judicial Acts*, 96.

22. *PCR*, 3:210.

23. *PCR*, 4:50.

24. *PCR*, 4:111-112.

25. *PCR*, 5:87.

26. Ibid.

27. *OPP*, Book 2, Ch. 21, 234.

28. *PCR*, 1:40.

29. *PCR*, 1:41, 42.

30. *PCR*, 12:28-30.

31. *PCR*, 12:33-34.

32. Ibid.

33. *Society of Mayflower Descendants in the State of New York*, Fifth Record Book, (New York, The Society, 1922), 226.

34. Demos, 49-50.

35. *PCR, Judicial Acts*, 107.

36. Ibid., 111.

37. Ibid., 152.
38. Ibid., 114.
39. Ibid.
40. Ibid., 145.
41. Ibid., 151.
42. Ibid., 157.
43. Ibid.
44. *PCR*, 5:32.
45. *PCR, Judicial Acts*, 158.
46. *PCR*, 5:42.
47. *PCR*, 5:127.
48. *PCR*, 3:159.
49. *PCR, Judicial Acts*, 148.
50. Ibid.
51. *PCR*, 3:170-180.
52. *PCR*, 4:11.
53. *PCR, Judicial Acts*, 143.
54. *PCR, Judicial Acts*, 63, 143, 174.
55. Ibid.
56. *CCL*, 43.
57. Stacy Schiff, *The Witches, Salem, 1692* (New York: Little and Brown, 2015), 65.
58. *PCR*, 3:205, 207.
59. *PCHP*, 307.
60. *Vital Records of Weymouth Massachusetts to the year 1850*, Vol. 1., (Boston: New England Historical Genealogical Society, 1910), 275.
61. *PCR*, 3:207.
62. *PCR*, 3:211.
63. Ibid.
64. Ibid.
65. *PCR, Judicial Acts*, 101, 115.
66. Albert Henry Silvester, "Richard Silvester and His Descendants," *New England Historical and Genealogical Register*, 1931, 85:252.
67. *PCR, Judicial Acts*, 134.
68. *PCR*, 4:162.
69. *PCR*, 5:22.
70. *PCR*, 5:223-224.
71. William Atwater Woodworth, *Descendants of Walter Woodworth of Scituate, Mass.* (White Plains, NY, January 1898), 7.
72. Deane, 291.
73. *PCR*, 5:223-224.
74. Addis, Cameron, Ph.D. "6 New England, 1620-1692." History Hub, http://sites.austincc.edu/caddis/new-england-1620-1692/ , accessed on October 19, 2019.

Chapter Ten [pages 166-179]

1. Lisa M. Lauria, "Sexual Misconduct in Plymouth Colony," the Plymouth Colony Archive Project, http://www.histarch.illinois.edu/plymouth/Lauria1.html (accessed on February 21, 2018).

2. *OPP*, Book 2, Ch. 32, 317.
3. Deetz, 144.
4. Deetz, 144.
5. *PCR*, 6:71.
6. *PCR*, 2:170.
7. *PCR*, 2:172.
8. It is impossible to know the marital status of Martha Haward. She was the daughter of Thomas and Susanna Haward and married her cousin, John Haward, keeping the same last name. See George Washington Hayward's *Centennial Gathering of the Hayward Family with Address, Easton, August 14, 1878* (Taunton, MA: John S. Sampson, 1879), 5.
9. *PCR*, 2:172.
10. *PCR*, 3:6, 37.
11. Anderson, *The Pilgrim Migration*, 263-265.
12. L. P. Allen, *The Genealogy and History of the Shreve Family from 1641*, (Greenfield, Illinois: Privately Printed, 1901), 16, 17, 18.
13. *PCR*, 4:162.
14. *Genealogical Notes of Barnstable Families* ... Vol. 2 (Barnstable, MA: F.B. & F.P. Goss, 1890), 236-237.
15. *PCR*, 5:48.
16. *PCR, Misc. Rec.*, 158.
17. *PCR*, 4:77, 84.
18. M. Lutz Sanborn, *Third supplement to Torrey's New England marriages prior to 1700.* (Baltimore: Genealogical Pub. Co., 2003), 161.
19. *PCR*, 5:27.
20. *PCR*, 4:77, 84, 99, 101, 5:27, 8:112, 114.
21. H. Roger King, *Cape Cod and Plymouth Colony in the Seventeenth Century* (Maryland: University Press of America, 1994), 141, fn 23.
22. Sanborn, 161.
23. *PCR*, 6:20.
24. Katharine Elizabeth Chapin Higgins, *Richard Higgins: a Resident and Pioneer Settler at Plymouth and Eastham,* (Worcester, MA: privately printed, 1918), 41-42.
25. *PCR*, 6:20.
26. *PCR*, 3:11.
27. Deetz, 133.
28. *ODM*, Ch. 61, "Of Youth and Old Age," 252.
29. *PCR*, 2:97-98.
30. Ibid.
31. Ibid.
32. Dorothy A. Mays, *Women in Early America: Struggle, Survival, and Freedom in a New World,* (Santa Barbara, California: ABC-CLIO, 2004), 47, 48.
33. Lisa M. Lauria, "Sexual Misconduct in Plymouth Colony," http://www.histarch.illinois.edu/plymouth/lauria1.html#XI (accessed on May 25, 2018).
34. *PCR*, 5:94, 99-100.
35. *PCR*, 6:63-64.
36. *PCR, Misc. Rec.*, 77.
37. *PCR*, 5:161, 173.
38. *PCR*, 1:111.

39. *PCR*, 1:112.
40. *PCR*, 1:113.
41. *PCR*, 1:127.
42. *PCR*, 6:190.
43. Mays, 171.
44. *PCR*, 2:44.
45. *OPP*, Book 2, Ch. 32, 320-321.
46. Ibid.
47. Ibid.
48. Ibid.
49. *PCR*, 2:50-51.
50. *PCR*, 11:12.
51. *PCR*, 2:137.
52. *PCR*, 2:163.
53. *PCR, Misc. Rec.*, 7.
54. J.R. Roberts, "Leude Behavior Each with Other Upon a Bed: The Case of Sarah Norman and Mary Hammond," *Sinister Wisdom 14, a Journal of Words and Pictures for the Lesbian Imagination in All Women*, Iowa City Women's Press, 1980, , 7-62.
55. Philip Battell, "Descendants of Benjamin Hammond," *New England Historical and Genealogical Register*, Vol. 30, 30.
56. *PCR*, 3:8, 5:18, 5:165
57. *PCR*, 1:134.
58. "A Writing Appointed to be Recorded 1654" (Regarding Hugh Norman) "Plymouth Colony Deeds. *The Mayflower Descendant* Vol. 6, No. 2 (April 1904), 102-103.
59. Ibid.
60. Ibid.
61. *PCR*, 1:132.
62. *PCR*, 2:28.
63. *PCR*, 2:27.
64. Charles P. Noyes, Noyes-Gilman Ancestry, (New York: Gilliss Press, 1907).
65. *PCR*, 2:36-37.

Chapter Eleven [pages 180-193]

1. John J. Navin, "Decrepit in Their Early Youth," *Children in Colonial America* (New York: New York University Press, 2007), 127.
2. *OPP*, Book 1, Ch. 2, 14.
3. Patricia Scott Deetz and James F. Deetz, "Passengers on the Mayflower: Ages & Occupations, Origins & Connections," The Plymouth Colony Archive Project, http://www.histarch.illinois.edu/plymouth/Maysource.html (accessed on November 2, 2018).
4. *OPP*, Book 1, Ch. 9, 59.
5. Caleb Johnson, "Girls on the Mayflower," *Caleb Johnson's Mayflower History. Com* http://mayflowerhistory.com/girls/ (accessed on June 20, 2018).
6. Navin, 133.
7. *OPP*, Book 1, Ch. 6, 43-44.
8. Navin, 131.

9. *OPP,* Book 2, Ch. 14, 120.

10. Demos, 68, 194.

11. *CCL,* 86-87.

12. *Mourt's Relation,* 41.

13. *PCR, Misc. Rec.,* 6, 11.

14. *PCR, Misc. Rec.,* 3, 4-5, 10.

15. Demos, 131-132.

16. *PCR, Misc. Rec.,* 3-14, 24.

17. *PCR, Misc. Rec.,* 8.

18. John K. Allen, *George Morton of Plymouth Colony and Some of His Descendants* (Chicago: "Printed for Private Circulation by John K. Allen, 1908), 12.

19. "John Morton of Plymouth/Middlebury, 1616-ca 1673," The Plymouth Colony Archive Project, http://histarch.illinois.edu/plymouth/MORTON1.HTM (accessed on June 20, 2018).

20. *PCR, Misc. Rec.,* 15.

21. William Richard Cutter, *Genealogical and Personal Memoirs Relating to the Families of Boston and Eastern Massachusetts* Vol. 2 (New York: Lewis Historical Publishing Co., 1908), 1076.

22. Cutter, *Genealogical and Personal Memoirs,* Vol. 4, 2240.

23. *PCR, Misc. Rec.,* 83, 86.

24. Cutter, *Genealogical and Personal Memoirs,* Vol. 4, 2240.

25. Cutter names Susanna as a later wife. See Cutter, Vol. 4, 2040.

26. Demos, 131.

27. *PCR, Misc. Rec.,* 81.

28. *PCR, Misc. Rec.,* 28, 4-89.

29. Tyler Seymour Morris, *The Tucker Genealogy, a Record of Gilbert Ruggles and Evelina Christina (Snyder) Tucker, their Ancestors and Descendants* (Chicago: np, 1901),130.

30. *PCR, Misc. Rec.,* 15,57,82.

31. "Family/Spouse: Francis Curtis / Hannah Smith (F5521)," Western Michigan Genealogical Society, http://trees.wmgs.org/familygroup.php?familyID=F5521 &tree=Schirado (accessed on November 2, 2018).

32. *PCR, Misc. Rec.,* 4, 5, 8.

33. "George Watson," *The Illustrated Pilgrim Memorial* (Boston: Office of the National Monument to the Forefathers, 1866), 24.

34. *PCR, Misc. Rec.,* 13.

35. *OPP,* Book 2, Ch. 24, 260.

36. *OPP,* Book 2, Ch. 25, 270.

37. *OPP,* Book 2, Ch. 25, 270-271.

38. *OPP,* Book 2, Ch. 25, 271.

39. "Days of Humiliation. June 10, 1641. "Scituate and Barnstable Church Records," *The New England Historical and Genealogical Register.* Vol. 10, no. 1 (January 1856): 38.

40. Ibid.

41. Dr. Ernest Caulfield, "Some Common Diseases of Colonial Children," *The Colonial Society of Massachusetts,* Vol. 35, April 1942: 47.

42. Caulfield, 65.

43. Ibid.

44. George Sheldon, *Half Century at the Bay, 1636-1686, Heredity and Early Environment of John Williams, "The Redeemed Captive."* (Boston: George W.B. Clarke Co., 1905), 32.
45. *PCR,* 3:92.
46. *PCR,* 4:169.
47. *PCR,* 4:83-84.
48. *PCR,* 5:209.
49. *PCR,* 5:94, 101, 130-131.
50. *PCR,* 5:208.
51. *PCR,* 2:175-176.
52. *PCR, Misc. Rec.,* 7.
53. *PCR,* 2:174-175.
54. Ibid.
55. *PCR,* 2:175.
56. *PCR,* 3:223.
57. *PCR,* 4:85.
58. *PCR,* 4:170.
59. *PCR,* 6:45.
60. *Winthrop's Journal,* Vol. 2, 72.
61. *PCHP,* 352.
62. *PCR,* 3:213.
63. *PCR,* 5:75.
64. *PCR,* 6:113.
65. Ibid.
66. Ibid.
67. Ibid.
68. *PCR,* 6:153.
69. *PCR,* 6:154.

Chapter Twelve [pages 194-214]

1. Josselyn, *An Account of Two Voyages,* 22
2. Zachary McLeod Hutchins, "Rattlesnakes in the Garden, the Fascinating Serpents of the Early, Edenic Republic," *Early American Studies,* Fall 2011, 690.
3. *OPP,* Book 1, Chap. 12, 96.
4. *CCL,* 33.
5. *PCR,* 3:50.
6. *PCR,* 11:38, 214.
7. *PCR,* 4:130.
8. *PCR,* 4:83.
9. Rufus N. Meriam, "John and Thomas Totman," *Proceedings of the Worcester Society of Antiquity for the Year 1891,* (Worcester, MA: Published by the Society, 1892), 45-46.
10. *PCR,* 5:262.
11. Meriam, 46.
12. *Mourt's Relation,* 47.
13. *OPP,* Book 1, Chap. 14, 136-137.

14. Josselyn, *An Account of Two Voyages*, 188.
15. *CCL*, 43, 56.
16. *PCR, Judicial Acts*, 41.
17. Mays, 256.
18. *PCR, Judicial Acts*, 84.
19. *PCR*, 3:172.
20. *PCR*, 5:154, 157.
21. *PCR*, 5:272.
22. *PCR*, 6:176.
23. *PCR*, 3:149
24. *PCR*, 3:158.
25. William Tubbs was on the 1643 Able to Bear Arms list for the town of Duxbury.
26. *PCR*, 3:158, 168-169.
27. *PCR*, 3:174, 197.
28. *PCR*, 2:80.
29. Anderson, Robert C. "The Wives of Michael Barstow and Richard Carver of Watertown, Massachusetts, and The Identity of the Wives of William Randall of Scituate and William Perry of Marshfield," in *The New England Historical and Genealogical Register*, Vol. 146, NEHGS, Boston, Massachusetts, 1992, 230-4
30. Alice H. Dreger, "William Perry of Scituate and Marshfield, Massachusetts" in *The American Genealogist*, Volume 70, New Haven, Connecticut, 42-48 (Online database. AmericanAncestors.org. New England Historic Genealogical Society, 2009 - .)
31. Dreger, 42-48.
32. *PCR*, 3:28, 36.
33. *PCR*, 3:75, 82.
34. *PCHP*, 164.
35. Clarence Almon Torrey, *New England Marriages Prior to 1700*, (Boston: Genealogical Publishing Co., 1985), 66.
36. LaVerne W. Noyes, *Descendants of Reverend William Noyes ...* (Chicago, Illinois: Published by LaVerne W. Noyes, 1900), 62.
37. *PCR*, 3:37.
38. *PCR*, 2:146-147.
39. *PCR*, 3:74.
40. *PCR, Judicial Acts*, 90, 92, 94-95.
41. *PCR*, 3:176-177.
42. Simeon Deyo, Ed., *History of Barnstable County, Massachusetts*, (New York: Blake, 1890), 459.
43. Charles F. Swift, *History of Old Yarmouth ...* (Yarmouth Port: published by the author, 1884), 66.
44. "Berry-Crisp. An Agreement to be Recorded, January 19, 1660," "Plymouth Colony Deeds. *Mayflower Descendant*, Vol. 15, No. 1, January 1913, 34.
45. Josiah Paine, "Early Settlers of Eastham: Containing Sketches of All Early Settlers of Eastham," *Library of Cape Cod History and Genealogy*, Vol. 32, (Yarmouth Port, MA: C. W. Swift, 1916): 18.
46. Paine, 18.
47. *PCR*, 4:47, 183.
48. *PCR*, 5:16.
49. *PCR*, 5:169.

50. Ruth Ann Wilder Sherman, *Plymouth Colony Probate Guide*, (Plymouth Colony Research Group, No. 2, 1983), 8.
51. *PCR*, 6:101.
52. W. P. Davis, "The Berry Family of Yarmouth," *Library of Cape Cod History and Genealogy*, No. 80, (Yarmouth Port, MA: C.W. Swift, 1912): 1.
53. *PCR*, 5:40.
54. *PCR*, 2:172.
55. *PCR*, 5:39.
56. *PCR*, 4:101.
57. *PCR, Misc. Rec.*, 116, 120.
58. *PCR*, 3:4-5.
59. *PCR, Judicial Acts*, 58.
60. *PCR*, 1:65.
61. *CCL*, 162.
62. *PCR*, 5:33.
63. *PCR*, 2:35-36.
64. Ibid.
65. *PCR*, 3:97.
66. *PCR*, 2:112.
67. *PCR*, 3:75.
68. *PCR*, 5:43-44.
69. *PCR*, 5:53.
70. *PCR, Judicial Acts*, 126.
71. *PCR*, 3:97.
72. *PCR*, 3:180.
73. *PCR*, 5:107.
74. *PCR*, 4:101.
75. *PCR*, 2:165.
76. *PCR*, 3:36, 41.
77. *PCR*, 5:112.
78. Deetz, 134.
79. *CCL*, 43, 162.
80. *PCR*, 6:98.
81. Paige, Lucius. *History of Hardwick, Massachusetts*. (Boston: Houghton, Mifflin and Co., 1883), 379.
82. *PCR*, 6:97, 98.
83. Paige, 379.
84. "Sandwich, Mass., Records" *The Genealogical Advertiser.* Vol. 4, No. 4, December 1901, 101.
85. "Falmouth, Mass., Records" *The Genealogical Advertiser.* Vol. 4, No. 4, December 1901, 116.
86. *PCR*, 4:83.
87. *Records of the Governor and Company of the Massachusetts Bay in New England, 1628-1686,* Edited by Nathaniel B. Shurtleff. (Boston: William White, 1853), Vol. 1: 202-3, 255.
88. Anderson, *The Great Migration*, "Edward Sale," Vol. 6:141,143.
89. *Winthrop's Journal*, Vol. 2, 427.
90. Anderson, *The Great Migration*, "Edward Sale." 143.
91. *PCR*, 5:249-250.

92. Caroline Lewis Kardell and Russell A. Lovell, *Vital Records of the Towns of Barnstable and Sandwich*, (Boston: New England Historical and Genealogical Society, 1996), 121.

93. Charles Banks, "The Claghorn Family." *The History of Martha's Vineyard*, Vol. 3: 80-87.

94. *PCR, Misc. Rec.*, 42.

95. *PCR*, 3:75.

96. *PCR, Misc. Rec.*, 42.

97. "James Claghorn," *Barnstable Town Records, 1643-1714*, Vol. 1, 2003 Transcription by Eben Lennard Johnson. (Barnstable: Town of Barnstable, 2007), 210.

98. Samuel Green, *Diary Kept by Capt. Lawrence Hammond, of Charlestown, Mass, 1677-1694.* (Cambridge: John Wilson and Son, 1892), 28.

Chapter Thirteen [pages 215-236]

1. Demos, 192, 193.

2. *ODM*, Ch. 61, "Of Youth and Old Age," 251.

3. Deetz, 110.

4. Mays, 417-418.

5. *CCL*, 32.

6. Demos, 85.

7. *CCL*, 43, 300.

8. *PCR*, 4:36.

9. *PCR*, 1:151.

10. *PCR*, 5:28.

11. *PCR*, 5:272.

12. *PCR*, 5:246.

13. *PCR*, 3:207-208.

14. *PCR*, 4:105.

15. *PCR*, 4:164, 167.

16. Roser, *Mayflower Increasings,* 16.

17. Susan Roser, *Mayflower Births and Deaths,* Vol. 1 (Baltimore, MD: Genealogical Publishing Co., 1992), 106.

18. *PCR*, 5:50.

19. *CCL*, 299-300

20. Demos, 194.

21. Demos, 66-67.

22. "Will of Richard Sylvester," *Mayflower Descendant* Vol. 15, 60-62.

23. *PCR*, 4:46.

24. Gervase Markham, Edited by Michael R. Best, *The English Housewife, Containing the Inward and Outward Virtues Which Ought to be in a Complete Woman ...* (London: John Beale, 1615), Ch. 1, 8.

25. Finch, 41.

26. Bangs, *Plymouth Colony's Private Libraries,* 30.

27. *OPP*, 360-361, 442.

28. Edward Arber, *The Story of the Pilgrim Fathers, 1606-1623 A.D.; as Told by Themselves, their Friends, and their Enemies.* (London: Ward and Downey Limited, 1897), 122-124.

29. *PCHP*, 295.

30. *PCR*, 12:5-6.

31. William Bradford, *Governor William Bradford's Letter Book*. Reprinted from *The Mayflower Descendant*. (Boston: Massachusetts Society of Mayflower Descendants, 1906), 23-24.

32. *Mourt's Relation*, 297.

33. *OPP*, Bk. 2, Ch. 24, 260.

34. *OPP*, Bk. 2, Ch. 20, 223.

35. "Plymouth Colony Wills and Inventories," *Mayflower Descendant*, Vol. 1, 79-82, 83-86,154-157, 158-160, 197-200.

36. Roser, *Mayflower Increasings*, 60.

37. *OPP*, Bk. 2, Ch. 24, 260.

38. *CHR*, Part 1, 83.

39. "Will of Samuel Fuller," The Plymouth Colony Archive Project, http://www.histarch.illinois.edu/plymouth/fullerwill.html (accessed on November 25, 2018).

40. Ibid.

41. *PCR:* 12:5-6.

42. *RTP,* 1.

43. *PCR*, 1:40, 50, 84, 95.

44. *PCR*, 2:26.

45. *PCR*, 2:13.

46. *PCR*, 1:36-37.

47. *PCR*, 1:143.

48. *PCR, Judicial Acts,* 16.

49. *PCR*, 2:50.

50. *PCR*, 12:64.

51. Leonard Bliss, *The History of Rehoboth, Bristol County, Massachusetts,* (Boston: Otis, Broaders, and Company, 1836), 53.

52. John G. Erhardt, *Rehoboth Plymouth Colony, 1645-1692*, Vol. 2, (Seekonk, MA: The Author, 1983), 141.

53. James Thacher, *History of the Town of Plymouth, From Its First Settlement in 1620, to the Present Time,* (Boston: Marsh, Capen & Lyon, 1835), 279.

54. "The Samuel and Bridget Fuller Society," Pilgrim Hall Museum, http://www.pilgrimhallmuseum.org/pdf/Samuel_Bridget_Fuller_Society.pdf (accessed on November 25, 2018).

55. *OPP,*445.

56. Roser, *Mayflower Increasings,* 54, 60.

57. *PCR*, 4:54.

58. Krusell, 40.

59. *PCR*, 6:141.

60. *CCL*, 84.

61. *CCL*, 62, 83.

62. *CCL*, 140, 164.

63. *CCL*, 286-288.

64. *CCL*, 171, 198-199.

65. *PCR*, 5:139, 271-272.

66. *PCR*, 1:153, 156.

67. *PCR*, 3:166.

68. *PCR*, 3:207.

69. *PCR*,4:107.
70. *PCR*, 5:15.
71. Deetz, *The Times of Their Lives*, 203.
72. *PCR*, 6:187.
73. *PCR*, 4:44.
74. *CCL*, 148, 287.
75. Markham, 8.
76. *OPP*, Book 2, Ch. 23, 334.
77. *CCL*, 72-73.
78. *RTP*, 3.
79. *PCR*, 2:103.
80. *PCHP*, 419.
81. Peggy Baker, "A Woman of Valor: Elizabeth Warren of Plymouth Colony," Pilgrim Hall Museum, http://www.pilgrimhall.org/richard_elizabeth_warren. htm (accessed on January 22, 2019).
82. *PCHP*, 367.
83. *PCR*, 12:3-4, 5-6, 12.
84. *PCHP*, 367.
85. *PCR*, 1:10, 15, 18.
86. *PCR*, 1:35.
87. *PCR*, 1:36.
88. *PCR*, 12:27, 28, 53-54.
89. *PCR*, 1:29, 134, 152
90. *PCR*, 3:19.
91. Ibid.
92. Peggy M. Baker, "A Woman of Valor: Elizabeth Warren of Plymouth Colony," *Pilgrim Hall Museum*, http://www.pilgrimhallmuseum.org/pdf/Elizabeth_ Warren_Essay.pdf (accessed on November 29, 2018).
93. Ibid.
94. *RTP*, 211-212, 213, 214.
95. *PCR*, *Misc. Rec.*, 35.
96. Roser, *Mayflower Increasings*, 111-117.
97. George Ernest Bowman, "Richard Warren and His Descendants," *Mayflower Descendant*, Vol. 3, no. 1 (January 1901): 50.
98. *PCR*, 5:139-140.
99. Roser, *Mayflower Increasings*, 115.
100. *PCR*, 5:156.
101. Roser, *Mayflower Increasings*, 49.

Chapter Fourteen [pages 237-251]

1. "Historical Sketch – Colonial Period (1692-1774)," *Massachusetts Archive Collection*, https://www.sec.state.ma.us/arc/arccol/colmac.htm (accessed on December 17, 2018).
2. Baylies, 278.
3. *PCHP*, 135.
4. David Thomas Konig and William E. Nelson, *Plymouth Court Records, 1686-1859*, Vol. 1 (Wilmington, Delaware: Michael Glazier Inc., 1978), 5.
5. *PCR*, 6:260.

6. *PCR,* 6:259, 260.

7. Ibid.

8. Ibid.

9. The Hinckley Papers, Ichabod Wisewall to Thomas Hinckley," *Collections of the Massachusetts Historical Society,* Vol. 5, (Boston: Printed for the Society, 1861): 299.

10. Harry Ward, *Statism in Plymouth Colony* (Port Washington, NY: Kennikat Press, 1973), 156-8.

11. *PCR,* 6:267, 268.

12. *PCR, Judicial Acts,* 311.

13. "Historical Sketch – Provincial Period (1692-1774)," *Massachusetts Archive Collection,* https://www.sec.state.ma.us/arc/arccol/colmac.htm (accessed on December 17, 2018).

14. "The Charter of Massachusetts," *The Avalon Project,* Yale Law School, http://avalon.law.yale.edu/17th_century/mass07.asp (accessed on December 24, 2018).

15. *The Book of the General Lawes and Libertyes Concerning the Inhabitants of the Massachusetts* (1648; facsimile edition, Cambridge: Harvard University Press, 1929).

16. *PCR,* 11:95.

17. *Records of the Church of Plymouth,* Vol. 1 (Cambridge: University Press, 1920), 167. Hereinafter referred to as *CHR.*

18. Michael S. Hindus, "A Guide to the Court Records of Early Massachusetts," *Colonial Society of Massachusetts,* https://www.colonialsociety.org/node/930 (accessed on December 29, 2018).

19. Konig, 192, 218.

20. Konig, 143, 144, 223-224.

21. Konig, 259-260.

22. Konig, 221, 224, 226, 233, 235, 240.

23. *CCL,* 79.

24. Konig, 226, 229.

25. Konig, 231.

26. Konig, 236.

27. Konig, 240.

28. "A Genealogical Profile of John Dunham," *Plymouth Ancestor,* https://www.plimoth.org/sites/default/files/media/pdf/dunham_john.pdf (accessed on December 28, 2018).

29. *RTP,* 188, 245.

30. Konig, 224, 240.

31. Konig, 230.

32. *CHR,* 166.

33. *RTP,* 302.

34. *RTP,* 188.

35. Konig, 206.

36. Konig, 258.

37. Konig, 224, 227.

38. Konig, 240.

39. Konig, 241.

40. *CHR,* 190-195.

41. For a full discussion of courts that ruled in Plymouth, see William E. Nelson,

"Introductory Essay: The Larger Context of Litigation in Plymouth County, 1725-1825," in Konig, 1-41.

42. *CHR*,159.

43. *CHR*, 156.

44. *CHR*, 164, 165.

45. *PCR*, 4:83-84.

46. *PCR*, 1:36-37.

47. *RTP*, 115.

48. *RTP*, 124.

49. *PCR*, 5:107-108.

50. Ibid.

51. *RTP*, 224.

52. *RTP*, 245.

53. *RTP*, 270.

54. *ODM*, Ch. 60, "Of Children and their Education," 248.

55. Stratton, 133-135.

Epilogue [pages 252-254]

1. Anne Bradstreet, *The Works of Anne Bradstreet*, (Cambridge, Massachusetts: The Belknap Press of Harvard University Press, 1967), 204.

Bibliography

Primary Sources

Bangs, Jeremy Dupertuis, *The Seventeenth Century Town Records of Scituate, Massachusetts*. (NEHGS, 2001), 112-113.

———. *The Town Records of Marshfield during the time of Plymouth Colony, 1620-1692*. Leiden, The Netherlands: Leiden American Pilgrim Museum, 2015,

"Berry-Crisp. An Agreement to be Recorded." January 19, 1660. "Plymouth Colony Deeds. *The Mayflower Descendant*. Vol. 15, No. 1 (January 1913): 34.

Bishop, George. *New England Judged by the Spirit of the Lord*. London: T. Sowle, 1703.

The Book of the General Lawes and Libertyes Concerning the Inhabitants of the Massachusetts, 1648; facsimile edition, Cambridge: Harvard University Press, 1929.

Bowman, George Ernest. "Broadsides on the Death of John Alden." *The Mayflower Descendant*. Vol. 34, no. 2 (1937): 49-53.

Bradford, William. *Governor William Bradford's Letter Book*. Reprinted from *The Mayflower Descendant*. Boston: Massachusetts Society of Mayflower Descendants, 1906.

Bradford, William. *Of Plymouth Plantation*. Edited by Samuel Eliot Morison. New York: Alfred A. Knopf, 1952.

Bradstreet, Anne. *The Works of Anne Bradstreet*. Cambridge, Massachusetts: The Belknap Press of Harvard University Press, 1967.

"The Charter of Massachusetts." *The Avalon Project, Yale Law School*, http://avalon. law.yale.edu/17th_century/mass07.asp (accessed on December 24, 2019).

The Compact with the Charter and Laws of the Colony of New Plymouth: Together with the Charter of the Council at Plymouth and an Appendix Containing the Articles of Confederation of the United Colonies of New England and Other Valuable Documents. Boston: Dutton and Wentworth, 1836.

"Days of Humiliation. June 10, 1641." "Scituate and Barnstable Church Records," *The New England Historical and Genealogical Register*. Vol. 10, no. 1 (January 1856):38.

"Estate of William Hacke." "Plymouth Colony Wills and Inventories." *The Mayflower Descendant*. Vol. 17, no. 1 (January 1915): 22.

"Falmouth, Mass., Records." *The Genealogical Advertiser*. Vol. 4, no. 4 (December 1901): 116.

"Francis Billington to Isaac Billington. May 11, 1665." "Plymouth Colony Deeds. *The Mayflower Descendant*. Vol. 35, no. 1 (January 1985): 32.

Gouge, William. *Of Domestical Duties: Eight Treatises*. London: John Haviland for William Bladen, 1622.

"The Hinckley Papers, Ichabod Wisewall to Thomas Hinckley." *Collections of the Massachusetts Historical Society*, Vol. 5, (Boston: Printed for the Society, 1861) 299.

Howland, Arthur and Elizabeth Howland. "The Sufferings of Arthur Howland," in Bangs, Jeremy Dupertuis, *The Town Records of Marshfield during the time of Plymouth Colony, 1620-1692*. Leiden, The Netherlands: Leiden American Pilgrim Museum,2015.

"Indenture of Benjamin Savory." *The Mayflower Descendant*. Vol. 5 (1903): 90-91.

"James Claghorn." *Barnstable Town Records, 1643-1714*. Vol. 1. (2003) Transcription by Eben Lennard Johnson. Barnstable: Town of Barnstable, 2007.

Josselyn, John. *An Account of Two Voyages to New England: Made During the Years 1638, 1663*. Boston: William Weazie, 1865, (Originally published in 1674.)

Josselyn, John. *New England Rarities Discovered*. London: G. Widdowes, 1672.

Konig, David Thomas and William E. Nelson, *Plymouth Court Records, 1686-1859*, Vol. 1. Wilmington, Delaware: Michael Glazier Inc., 1978.

"Last Will & Testament of Alice Bradford." *Pilgrim Hall Museum*. http://www.pilgrimhallmuseum.org/pdf/Alice_Carpenter_Southworth_Bradford_Will_Inventory.pdf (accessed on October 13, 2018).

"Last Will & Testament of George Barlow." *Massachusetts, Plymouth County, Probate Records, 1633-1967*. Wills 1633-1686 vol 1-4>image 578 of 616; State Archives, Boston.

"Last Will & Testament of Elizabeth Poole." *Mayflower Descendant*. Vol. 14 (1912): 24-26.

"Last Will & Testament of John Williams." dated Oct. 15, 1691. "Abstracts from the First Book of Plymouth County Probate Records," *The Genealogical Advertiser* Vol. 4, no. 1 (March 1901): 25-27.

"Last Will & Testament of John Winslow." *Pilgrim Hall Museum*. http://www.pilgrimhallmuseum.org/pdf/John_Winslows_Will_Inventory.pdf (accessed on September 21, 2017).

"Last Will & Testament of Mary (Chilton) Winslow." 1676. *The Plymouth Colony Archive Project*. http://www.histarch.illinois.edu/plymouth/winslowwill.html (accessed on September 21, 2017).

"Last Will & Testament of Nathaniel Morton." *Massachusetts, Plymouth County, Probate Records, 1633-1967*. Probate records 1717-1724 and 1854-1862 vol 4-4Q > image 191 of 485; State Archives, Boston.

"Last Will &Testament of Richard Sylvester." *Mayflower Descendant*. Vol. 15 (1913):60-62.

"Last Will & Testament of Samuel Fuller." *The Plymouth Colony Archive Project*. http://www.histarch.illinois.edu/plymouth/fullerwill.html (accessed November 25, 2018).

"Last Will & Testament of Thomas Lumbert." *The Mayflower Descendant*. Vol. 16 (1914): 124-126.

"Last Will & Testament of William Tubbs." dated Feb. 20, 1677. "Abstracts from the First Book of Plymouth County Probate Records. *The Genealogical Advertiser*, Vol. 1, no. 1 (March 1898):19.

Lincoln, Abraham. "Proclamation of Thanksgiving." *Abraham Lincoln Online*, http://www.abrahamlincolnonline.org/lincoln/speeches/thanks.htm (accessed on December 22, 2018).

Markham, Gervase. *The English Housewife: Containing the Inward and Outward Virtues Which Ought to be in a Complete Woman*. 1615. Montreal & Kingston: Mc Gill-Queen's University Press, 1986. Originally published in 1615.

"The Massachusetts Body of Liberties." Item 80, p. 271. *Hanover College Historical Texts Project.* https://history.hanover.edu/texts/masslib.html (accessed on November 30, 2018).

Massachusetts, Town and Vital Records, 1620-1988. ancestry.com, (accessed on November 10, 2016).

Mather, Cotton. *Magnalia Christi Americana; or the Ecclesiastical History of New England.* Hartford: Silas Andrus and Son, 1855. Originally published in 1702.

Morton, Nathaniel. *New England's Memorial, 1669.* Edited by Howard J. Hall. Facsimile of the first edition. New York: Scholars Facsimiles & Reprints, 1937.

Mourt's Relation – see Winslow.

"The Parish Registers of Austerfield 1559-1812 & Cowthorpe 1568-1812." Austerfield and Cowthorpe, West Yorkshire, Parish Registers Originally Published in 1910. Np.

Plymouth Church Records, 1620-1859. Vol. 1, Part 1. Boston: Colonial Society of Massachusetts, 1920.

Plymouth Church Records. Vol. 1, Part 5, in *Publications of the Colonial Society of Massachusetts*, Vol 12. Boston: Published by the Society, 1920.

"Plymouth Colony Division of Land." *The Plymouth Colony Archive Project.* http://www.histarch.illinois.edu/plymouth/landdiv.html (accessed on November 30, 2018).

Pope, Charles Henry, ed. *The Plymouth Scrap Book: The Oldest Original Documents Extant in Plymouth Archives.* Boston, MA: C.E. Goodspeed & Co., 1918.

Pory, John, Emmanuel Altham, and Isaack De Rasieres. *Three Visitors to Early Plymouth: Letters About the Pilgrim Settlement in New England During Its First Seven Years.* Massachusetts: Applewood Books, 1997.

Records of the Colony of New Plymouth in New England. (Commonly referred to as PCR.) Edited by Nathaniel B. Shurtleff. 12 vols. Boston: William White, 1855.

The Records of the First Church in Salem, Massachusetts 1629-1736. Edited by Richard D. Pierce. Salem: Massachusetts: Essex Institute, 1974.

Records of the Governor and Company of the Massachusetts Bay in New England, 1628-1686. Edited by Nathaniel B. Shurtleff. Boston: William White, 1853.

Records of the Town of Plymouth: Published by Order of the Town. Vol. 1. Boston: W.B. Clarke and Co., 1889.

Registers of Worksop, County Nottingham, 1558-1771. Edited by George W. Marshall. Guildford: Billing and Sons, 1894.

Robinson, John. *The Works of John Robinson, Pastor of the Pilgrim Fathers, with a Memoir and Annotations by Robert Ashton.* 3 Vols. London: John Snow, 1851.

Saffin, John. "John Saffin's Diary." Rhode Island Historical Society, Manuscripts Division. http://www.rihs.org/mssinv/MSS696.htm (accessed on May 5, 2018).

"Sandwich, Mass., Records." *The Genealogical Advertiser.* Vol. 4, no. 4 (December 1901): 101.

Sewell, Samuel. "The Diary of Samuel Sewall." *Collections of the Massachusetts Historical Society.* Vol. 5. Boston: Published by the Society, 1878.

Smith, John. "New England" Map. 1616. *Wikimedia.* https://commons.wikimedia.org/wiki/File:John_Smith_1616_New_England_map.PNG (accessed on December 3, 2018).

Vital Records of Weymouth Massachusetts to the Year 1850. Vol. 1. Boston: New England Historical Genealogical Society, 1910.

Winslow, Edward. *Hypocrisie Unmasked, a True Relation of the Proceedings of the Governor and Company of the Massachusetts Against Samuel Gorton of Rhode Island*. Providence, Rhode Island: The Club for Colonial Reprints, 1916. Originally published in 1646.

Winslow, Edward. *New England's Salamander Discovered*. London: Printed by Ric. Cotes, for John Bellamy, 1647.

Winslow, Edward, William Bradford, and others. A *Relation or Journall of the beginning and proceedings of the English Plantation settled at Plimoth in New England by certaine English Adventurers both Merchants and others*. ("*Mourt's Relation*") *1622*. Edited by Dwight B. Health. Bedford, Massachusetts: Applewood Books, 1963.

Winthrop, John. *History of New England from 1630-1649*. (Commonly known as *Winthrop's Journal*) Vol. 2. Edited by James Savage. Boston: Little, Brown & Company, 1853.

"A Writing Appointed to be Recorded 1654" (Regarding Hugh Norman). "Plymouth Colony Deeds. *The Mayflower Descendant* Vol. 6, No. 2 (April 1904):102-103.

Secondary Sources

Adams, Thomas P. "The Harlowe Family." *New England Historical and Genealogical Record*, Vol. 14 (1860):227.

Addis, Cameron, Ph.D. "6 New England, 1620-1692." History Hub, http://sites. austincc.edu/caddis/new-england-1620-1692/ , accessed on October 19, 2019.

Allen, John K. *George Morton of Plymouth Colony and Some of His Descendants*. Chicago: "Printed for Private Circulation by John K. Allen," 1908.

Anderson, Robert Charles, Melinde Lutz Sanborn, George F. Sanborn, Jr. *The Great Migration*, Vol. I, A-B, *Immigrants to New England, 1634-1635*. Boston: New England Historic Genealogical Society, 1999.

Anderson, Robert Charles. *The Pilgrim Migration: Immigrants to Plymouth Colony, 1620-1633*. Boston: New England Historic Genealogical Society, 2004.

Anderson, Robert C. "The Wives of Michael Barstow and Richard Carver of Watertown, Massachusetts, and The Identity of the Wives of William Randall of Scituate and William Perry of Marshfield." *The New England Historical and Genealogical Register*, Vol. 146 (1992): 230-234.

Arber, Edward. *The Story of the Pilgrim Fathers, 1606-1623 A.D.; as Told by Themselves, their Friends, and their Enemies*. London: Ward and Downey Limited, 1897.

Ashley, Linda Ramsey. *In the Pilgrim Way: The First Congregational Church, Marshfield, Massachusetts 1640-2000*. Plymouth, MA: Powderhorn Press, 2001.

Ashton, Robert. "Memoir of Rev. John Robinson." In *The Works of John Robinson*, Vol. 1. London: John Snow, 1851. 14-76.

Austin, Jane G. *David Alden's Daughter and Other Stories of Colonial Times*. Boston: Houghton, Mifflin and Co., 1893.

Backus, Isaac. *A History of New England, with Particular Reference to the Denomination of Christians Called Baptists*. Boston: Edward Draper, 1777.

Bailey, Shirley Segerstrom. "John Bailey (Bayley) of Scituate," *The Mayflower Quarterly* (March 2004): 48.

Baker, Peggy M. "The Godmother of Thanksgiving: the Story of Sarah Josepha Hale." 2007, *Pilgrim Hall Museum*, http://www.pilgrimhallmuseum.org/pdf/ Godmother_of_Thanksgiving.pdf (accessed on October 23, 2018).

Baker, Peggy. "A Woman of Valor: Elizabeth Warren of Plymouth Colony." *Pilgrim Hall Museum*. http://www.pilgrimhall.org/richard_elizabeth_warren.htm (accessed on November 30, 2018).

Bangs, Jeremy Dupertuis, Ed., *Intellectual Baggage: The Pilgrims and Plymouth Colony Ideas of Influence, a catalogue of an imagined exhibition, 2020*. Leiden, The Netherlands: Leiden American Pilgrim Museum, 2020.

Bangs, Jeremy Dupertuis. *Strangers and Pilgrims, Travellers and Sojourners: Leiden and the Foundations of Plymouth Plantation*. Plymouth, MA: General Society of Mayflower Descendants, 2009.

Banks, Charles. "The Claghorn Family." *The History of Martha's Vineyard*. Vol. 3. Edgartown, Massachusetts: Dukes County Historical Society, 1925. 80-87.

Barclay, Mrs. John E. "Mary Bartlett (Foster) Morey, Her Husbands and Children." *The American Genealogist* Vol. 32, no. 4 (October 1956): 193.

Battell, Philip. "Descendants of Benjamin Hammond." *New England Historical and Genealogical Register* Vol. 30, (January 1876): 30.

Baylies, Francis. *An Historical Memoir of the Colony of New Plymouth*. Vol. 2, *From the Flight of the Pilgrims into Holland in the Year 1608, to the Union of That Colony with Massachusetts in 1692*. Boston: Wiggin & Lunt, 1866.

Bliss, Leonard. *The History of Rehoboth, Bristol County, Massachusetts*. Boston: Otis, Broaders, and Co., 1836.

Book of the First Church of Christ in Middleborough, Plymouth County. Boston: C.P. Moody, 1852.

Boswell, James. *The Life of Samuel Johnson*. Vol. 1. New York: Alexander V. Blake, 1844.

Bowden, James. *History of the Society of Friends in America*. Vol. 1, London: Charles Gilpin, 1850.

Bowman, George Ernest. "Governor William Bradford's First Wife, Dorothy (May) Bradford, Did Not Commit Suicide." *The Mayflower Descendant*, Vol. 29, No. 3 (July 1931): 97-102.

Bowman, George Ernest. "Richard Warren and His Descendants." *The Mayflower Descendant*, Vol. 3, no. 1 (January 1901): 50.

Burgess, Elizabeth. *Burgess Genealogy: Memorial of the Family of Thomas and Dorothy Burgess*. Boston: T.R. Marvin & Son, 1865.

"Butten Meadow, Austerfield." Mayflower 400. http://www.mayflower400uk.org/explore/austerfield-doncaster/austerfield-attractions/butten-meadow-austerfield/ (accessed on August 30, 2017).

Carpenter, Delores Bird. "William Bradford's First Wife: A Suicide." *Early Encounters – Native Americans and Europeans in New England: from the papers of W. Sears Nickerson*. East Lansing: Michigan State University Press, 1994. 88-98.

"Capt. Joshua Eddy." *New England Historical and Genealogical Register*, Vol. 8. no. 3 (July 1854): 201-203.

Caulfield, Dr. Ernest. "Some Common Diseases of Colonial Children." *The Colonial Society of Massachusetts*, Vol. 35 (April 1942): 4-65.

Chartier, Craig S. "Clarke Garrison House Murders." *Plymouth Archaeological Rediscovery Project (PARP)*, http://plymoutharch.tripod.com/id16.html (accessed on October 2, 2018).

Crimmins, John D. *Irish-American Historical Miscellany*. New York City: Published by the Author, 1905.

Crowley, John. *The Invention of Comfort.* Johns Hopkins University Press, 2003.

Crowther, Bosley. "The Screen in Review: 'Plymouth Adventure,' a Vivid Portrayal of Pilgrim Voyage, Opens at the Music Hall." *New York Times*, Nov. 14, 1952.

Cutter, William Richard. *Genealogical and Family History of Western New York ...,* Vol. 1. New York: Lewis Historical Publishing Co., 1912.

Cutter, William Richard. *Genealogical and Personal Memoirs Relating to the Families of Boston and Eastern Massachusetts.* Vol. 2. New York: Lewis Historical Publishing Co., 1908.

Davis, W. P. "The Berry Family of Yarmouth." *Library of Cape Cod History and Genealogy.* No. 80. Yarmouth Port, MA: C.W. Swift. 1912.

Deane, Samuel. *A History of Scituate, Massachusetts, From its First Settlement to 1831.* Boston: James Loring, 1831.

Deetz, Patricia Scott and James F. Deetz, "Passengers on the Mayflower: Ages & Occupations, Origins & Connections." *The Plymouth Colony Archive Project,* http://www.histarch.illinois.edu/plymouth/Maysource.html (accessed on November 11, 2018).

Deetz, James, and Patricia Scott Deetz. *The Times of Their Lives: Life, Love and Death in Plymouth Colony.* New York: W.H. Freeman and Co., 2000.

Demos, John. *A Little Commonwealth: Family Life in Plymouth Colony.* Second edition. Oxford University Press, 2000.

Deyo, Simeon. *History of Barnstable County, Massachusetts.* New York: Blake, 1890.

Dreger, Alice H. "William Perry of Scituate and Marshfield, Massachusetts." *The American Genealogist*, Vol. 70 (January 1995): 42-48.

Eddy, Ruth Story Devereaux. *The Eddy Family in America.* Boston: T.O. Metcalf Co., 1930.

Edwards, Mary Blauss. "Descendants of John Everson of Plymouth." Massachusetts. *New England Historical and Genealogical Register* Vol. 169 (Winter 2015):35-50.

Emery, Samuel Hopkins. *History of Taunton, Massachusetts, From Its Settlement to the Present Time.* Syracuse, New York: D. Mason & Co., 1893.

Erhardt, John G. *Rehoboth Plymouth Colony, 1645-1692.* Vol. 2. Seekonk, MA: The Author, 1983.

Finch, Martha L. *Dissenting Bodies: Corporealities in Early New England.* Columbia University Press, 2009.

Finer, Laurence, "Trends in Premarital Sex in the United States, 1954-2003," Public Health Report, 2007 Jan-Feb: 122(1): 73-78.

Fisher, Linford D. "Dangerous Designes: The 1676 Barbados Act to Prohibit New England Indian Slave Importation." *William and Mary Quarterly*, 3rd Series, Vol. 71, no.1 (January 2014).

Gebler, Ernest. *The Plymouth Adventure: a Chronicle Novel of the Voyage of the Mayflower.* New York: Doubleday & Company, Inc., 1950.

"A Genealogical Profile of John Dunham." *Plymouth Ancestor*, https://www.plimoth. org/sites/default/files/media/pdf/dunham_john.pdf (accessed on December 28, 2018).

"George Watson." *The Illustrated Pilgrim Memorial.* Boston: Office of the National Monument to the Forefathers, 1866.

Glover, Anna. *Glover Memorials and Genealogies. An Account of John Glover of Dorchester and His Descendants, with a Brief Sketch of Some of the Glovers Who First Settled in New Jersey, Virginia, and Other Places.* Boston: David Clapp & Son, 1867.

Godfrey, Michael L. *Footprints in the Sand: The Godfrey Story.* Lulu.com, 2012.

Goodsell, Willystine. *A History of the Family as a Social and Educational Institution.* New York: McMillan Company, 1920.

Gould, James Warren. "A New Account of the History of the Society of Friends on Cape Cod." *Sandwich Monthly Meeting.* http://www.capecodquakers.org/smm_history.html (accessed on October 17, 2017).

Green, Samuel. *Diary Kept by Capt. Lawrence Hammond, of Charlestown, Mass, 1677-1694.* Cambridge: John Wilson and Son, 1892.

Hayward, George Washington. *Centennial Gathering of the Hayward Family with Address, Easton, August 14, 1878.* Taunton, MA: John S. Sampson, 1879.

Higgins, Katharine Chapin. *Richard Higgins, a Resident and Pioneer Settler at Plymouth and Eastham, Massachusetts, and at Piscataway, New Jersey, and His Descendants.* Worcester, MA: printed for the author, 1918.

Hindus, Michael S. "A Guide to the Court Records of Early Massachusetts." *Colonial Society of Massachusetts,* https://www.colonialsociety.org/node/930 (accessed on December 29, 2018).

"Historical Sketch – Provincial Period (1692-1774)." *Massachusetts Archive Collection,* https://www.sec.state.ma.us/arc/arccol/colmac.htm (accessed on December 17, 2018).

Hodge, Harriet Woodbury. "Desire Billington and Her Grandfather Francis Billington's Estate." *The Mayflower Quarterly* Vol. 52, no. 3, (1986): 137-144.

Hutchins, Zachary McLeod. "Rattlesnakes in the Garden, the Fascinating Serpents of the Early, Edenic Republic." *Early American Studies* Vol. 9, no. 3 (Fall 2011):677-715.

"John Morton of Plymouth/Middlebury, 1616-ca 1673." *The Plymouth Colony Archive Project,* http://histarch.illinois.edu/plymouth/MORTON1.HTM (accessed on June 20, 2018).

Johnson, Caleb. "Edward Winslow," *Caleb Johnson's Mayflower History.* http://mayflowerhistory.com/women/ (accessed on February 21, 2018).

Johnson, Caleb. "Girls on the Mayflower." *Caleb Johnson's Mayflower History.com* http://mayflowerhistory.com/girls/ (accessed on June 20, 2018).

Johnson, Caleb. *The Mayflower and Her Passengers.* Xlibris: 2006.

Johnson, Caleb. "Mrs. Mary Brewster." *Caleb Johnson's Mayflower History.* http://mayflowerhistory.com/brewster-mary/ (accessed on September 22, 2017).

Johnson, Caleb. "Passenger Lists." *Caleb Johnson's Mayflower History.* http://mayflowerhistory.com/anne/ (accessed on October 22, 2017).

Johnson, Caleb. "Remember Allerton." *Caleb Johnson's Mayflower History.* http://mayflowerhistory.com/allerton-remember (accessed on August 30, 2017).

Johnson, Caleb. "Women of Early Plymouth." *Caleb Johnson's Mayflower History.* http://mayflowerhistory.com/women/ (accessed on February 21, 2018).

Johnson, William W. *Clarke-Clark Genealogy. Records of the Descendants of Thomas Clarke, Plymouth, 1623-1697.* Milwaukee, Wisconsin: Riverside Printing Co., 1884.

Kainer, R.G. "Do Not Go Gently: The Quiet Death of Dorothy (May) Bradford." *New England Ancestors* Fall (2001): 24-26.

Kardell, Caroline Lewis, Russell A. Lovell. *Vital Records of the Towns of Barnstable and Sandwich.* Boston: New England Historical and Genealogical Society, 1996.

Kelley, Hermon Alfred. *A Genealogical History of the Kelley Family* … Privately Printed at Cleveland, Ohio, 1897.

Kelley, R. Dudley, "David Okillea of Yarmouth, Massachusetts and Some of His Descendants." *New England Historical and Genealogical Register*, Vol. 151 (April 1997): 131-152.

Kellogg, Lucy, Ed. *Mayflower Families Through Five Generations: Descendants of the Pilgrims Who Landed at Plymouth, Mass. December 1620*, Vol. 1. General Society of Mayflower Descendants, 1975.

King, H. Roger. *Cape Cod and Plymouth Colony in the Seventeenth Century*. Maryland: University Press of America, 1994.

"Kingston, Massachusetts." https://www.kingstonmass.org/ (accessed on October 5, 2018).

Kittredge, Henry C. *Cape Cod, Its People and Their History*. Boston: Houghton Mifflin Co., 1930.

Krusell, Cynthia Hagar. *Plymouth Colony to Plymouth County*. Lulu, 2010.

Lauria, Lisa M. "Sexual Misconduct in Plymouth Colony." *Plymouth Colony Archive Project*, http://www.histarch.illinois.edu/plymouth/Lauria1.html (accessed on February 21, 2018).

Lindsay, David. *Mayflower Bastard: A Stranger Among the Pilgrims*. New York: Thomas Dunne Books, an imprint of St. Martin's Press, 2002.

Litchfield, W. J. *The Litchfield Family in America*. Vol. 1. *Lawrence Litchfield and His Descendants*, Part I, No. 1, (October 1901)

Longfellow, Henry Wadsworth. *The Courtship of Miles Standish [and] Elizabeth*. Boston: Houghton, Mifflin and Company, 1858.

Lupher, David. *Greeks, Romans, and Pilgrims: Classical Receptions in Early New England*, Leiden: Brill, 2017.

MacCartney, Louis. *The Descendants of William Tubbs of Duxbury*. Boston: LM MacCartney, 1959.

Mays, Dorothy A. *Women in Early America: Struggle, Survival, and Freedom in a New World*. Santa Barbara, California: ABC-CLIO, 2004.

McGuyre, Ruth C., Robert S. Wakefield, Harriet W. Hodge, General Society of Mayflower Descendants. *Mayflower Families Through Five Generations. Volume Five, Families Edward Winslow, John Billington: Descendants of the Pilgrims Who Landed in Plymouth, Mass. December 1620*. Plymouth, MA: General Society of Mayflower Descendants, 1997.

McIntyre, Ruth. *Debts Hopeful and Desperate: Financing the Plymouth Colony*. Plimoth Plantation, 1963.

Meriam, Rufus N. "John and Thomas Totman." *Proceedings of the Worcester Society of Antiquity for the Year 1891*, Worcester, MA: Published by the Society, 1892: 45-46.

Mitchell, Nahum. *History of the Early Settlement of Bridgewater, in Plymouth County, Massachusetts, Including an Extensive Family Register*. Boston: Kidder & Wright, 1840.

Morison, Samuel Eliot. *The Story of the "Old Colony" of New Plymouth; 1620-1692*. New York: Alfred A. Knopf, 1956.

Morris, Tyler Seymour. *The Tucker Genealogy, a Record of Gilbert Ruggles and Evelina Christina (Snyder) Tucker, their Ancestors and Descendants*. Chicago: NP, 1901.

"Moses Maverick." *Marblehead Magazine*. http://www.legendinc.com/Pages/MarbleheadNet/MM/PeoplePlacesThings/MosesMaverick.html (accessed on August 30, 2017)

Navin, John J. "Decrepit in Their Early Youth." *Children in Colonial America*. New York: New York University Press, 2007.

Neuzil, Anna. "Women in Plymouth Colony, 1633-1668." Section VII. *The Plymouth Colony Archive Project*. http://www.histarch.illinois.edu/plymouth/PCR.htm (accessed on November 13, 2018).

Newhall, Barbara. *The Barker Family of Plymouth Colony and County*. Cleveland: Press of F.W. Roberts, 1900.

Noyes, LaVerne W. *Descendants of Reverend William Noyes, born, England, 1568, in direct line to LaVerne W. Noyes and Frances Adelia Noyes-Giffen*. Chicago, Illinois: Published by LaVerne W. Noyes, 1900.

Otis, Amos. *Genealogical Notes of Barnstable Families, Being a Reprint of the Amos Otis Papers*. Vol. 1, 2. Barnstable, Mass.: FB and FP Goss, 1888 and 1890.

Paige, Lucius. *History of Hardwick, Massachusetts*. Boston: Houghton, Mifflin and Co., 1883.

Paine, Josiah. "Founders' Day Edition, August 26, 1916, of the Early Settlers of Eastham, Containing Sketches of All Early Settlers of Eastham." *Facsimile Edition of 108 Pamphlets Published in the Early 20th Century, Baltimore*: Genealogical Publishing Co., Inc., 1992: 457-488.

Pope, Charles Henry. *The Plymouth Colony Scrapbook*. Boston: C.E. Goodspeed, 1918.

"Presidential Thanksgiving Proclamations." *Pilgrim Hall Museum*. http://www.pilgrimhallmuseum.org/pdf/TG_Presidential_Thanksgiving_Proclamations_1862_1869.pdf (accessed on October 13, 2018).

"Prices of Grain and other Commodities, for the Payment of Taxes in Plymouth Colony." In *Collections of the American Statistical Association*. Vol. 1, 289. Boston: T.R. Marvin, 1847.

Prindle, Paul W. "A Bartlett-Foster-Morey Epilogue." *The American Genealogist* Vol. 53, no. 3 (January 1977): 155.

Register of the National Society of Colonial Dames in the State of New York, 1893 to 1913. New York: Published by the Authority of Managers, 1913.

Roberts, Gary Boyd. "The English Origins of John Spring of Watertown." *The American Genealogist*, Vol. 55, no. 2 (April 1979): 70-71.

Roberts, J.R. "Leude Behavior Each with Other Upon a Bed: The Case of Sarah Norman and Mary Hammond." *Sinister Wisdom 14, a Journal of Words and Pictures for the Lesbian Imagination in All Women*. Iowa City Women's Press. (1980): 57-62.

Roser, Susan E., George Ernest Bowman: Massachusetts Society of Mayflower Descendants, *Mayflower Births and Deaths*. Vol. 1 Baltimore, MD: Genealogical Publishing Co., 1992.

Roser, Susan E., George Ernest Bowman: Massachusetts Society of Mayflower Descendants, *Mayflower Deeds and Probates: From the Files of George Ernest Bowman at the Massachusetts Society of Mayflower Descendants*. Baltimore: Genealogical Pub. Co., 1994.

Roser, Susan E. *Mayflower Increasings*. Second edition. Baltimore, MD: Genealogical Publishing Co., Inc., 1996.

Russell, William S. *Pilgrim Memorials, and Guide to Plymouth*. Boston: Crosby, Nichols, Lee and Co., 1860.

Rutman, Darrett B. *Husbandmen of Plymouth: Farms and Villages in the Old Colony, 1620-1692*. Boston: Beacon Press, 1967.

Salter, Edwin. *A History of Monmouth and Ocean Counties Embracing a*

Genealogical Record of Earliest Settlers ... Bayonne, N.J.: F. Gardner & Son, 1890.

"The Samuel and Bridget Fuller Society." *Pilgrim Hall Museum.* http://www.pilgrimhallmuseum.org/pdf/Samuel_Bridget_Fuller_Society.pdf (accessed on November 25, 2018).

Sanborn, M. Lutz. *Third Supplement to Torrey's New England Marriages Prior to 1700.* Baltimore: Genealogical Publishing Co., 2003.

Savage, James. *A Genealogical Dictionary of the First Settlers of New England.* Vol. 1, Baltimore: Genealogical Publishing Co., 1969.

Savary, A. W. *A Genealogical and Biographical Record of the Severy Families ...* Boston: The Collins Press, 1893.

Schiff, Stacy. *The Witches, Salem, 1692.* New York: Little and Brown, 2015.

Scott, Fred W. *Clifford William Scott and Mildred Evelyn Bradford Scott of Ashfield, Massachusetts: Ancestors, Descendants and New England Heritage.* New York: iUniverse, Inc., 2004.

Seelye, John. *Memory's Nation: The Place of Plymouth Rock.* Chapel Hill: University of Northern Carolina Press, 1998.

Sheldon, George. *Half Century at the Bay, 1636-1686, Heredity and Early Environment of John Williams, the Redeemed Captive.* Boston: George W.B. Clarke Co., 1905.

Sherman, Ruth Ann Wilder. *Plymouth Colony Probate Guide.* Plymouth Colony Research Group, No. 2, 1983.

Silvester, Albert Henry. "Richard Silvester and His Descendants." *New England Historical and Genealogical Register* Vol. 85 (July 1931): 247-265.

Sinnott, Mary Elizabeth. *Annals of the Sinnott, Rogers, Corlies, Reeves, Bodine, and Allied Families.* Philadelphia: Lippincott, 1905.

Smith, Bradford. *Bradford of Plymouth.* Philadelphia: J.B. Lippincott Co., 1951.

So Dreadfull a Judgment: Puritan Responses to King Philip's War, 1676–1677. Edited by Richard Slotkin, James K. Folsom. University Press of New England: Wesleyan University, 1978.

Society of Mayflower Descendants in the State of New York, Fifth Record Book. New York, The Society, 1922.

Sterns, George Warren. *Two Hundredth Anniversary of the First Congregational Church of Middleboro.* Middleboro: Published by the Church, 1895.

Stratton, Eugene Aubrey. *Plymouth Colony: Its History and People, 1620-1691.* Salt Lake City, Utah: Ancestry Publishing, 1986.

Swift, Charles F. *History of Old Yarmouth Comprising the Present Towns of Yarmouth and Dennis ...* Yarmouth Port: published by the author, 1884.

Thacher, James. *History of the Town of Plymouth, From Its First Settlement in 1620, to the Present Time.* Boston: Marsh, Capen & Lyon, 1835.

Thomas, Kristi S., "Medieval and Renaissance Marriage: Theory and Customs." http://celyn.drizzlehosting.com/mrwp/mrwed.html (accessed January 20, 2017).

Torrey, Clarence Almon, *New England Marriages prior to 1700.* Baltimore: Genealogical Publishing Co., 1985.

Van Antwerp, Lee D, Ruth Ann Wilder Sherman. *Vital Records of Plymouth, Massachusetts to the Year 1850.* Camden, Maine: Picton Press, 1993.

Samuel G. Webber, *A Genealogy of the Southworths (Southards) Descendants of Constant Southworth, With a Sketch of the Family in England.* Boston: The Fort Hill Press, 1905.

Ward, Harry. *Statism in Plymouth Colony.* Port Washington, NY: Kennikat Press, 1973.

Willison, George F. *Saints and Strangers.* New York: Reynal & Hitchcock, 1945.

Woodworth, William Atwater. *Descendants of Walter Woodworth of Scituate, Mass.* White Plains, NY, 1898.

Illustration Credits

Front cover: Detail from "Pilgrims Going to Church," 1867,wood print by George Henry Boughton. http://colonialdays.pbworks.com/w/page/16140810/Clothing

Page 2. Lewis, H. Elvet. Homes and Haunts of the Pilgrim Fathers. Illustrations by Charles Whymper. London: The Religious Tract Society, 1920.

Page 5. Bryant, William Cullen, Gay, Sydney Howard. A Popular History of the United States from the First Discovery of the Western Hemisphere by the Northmen, to the End of the First Century of the Union of the United States. Boston: Scribner, Armstrong, and Co. 1876.

Page 10. "Mayflower at Sea," illustration by John Clark Ridpath, 1840-1900. Wikimedia. https://commons.wikimedia.org/wiki/File:The_Mayflower_at_sea.jpg (accessed on December 3, 2018).

Page 18. Otis, James. Mary of Plymouth: A Story of the Pilgrim Settlement. New York: American Book Co., 1910.

Page 28. Illustration by Mary Carter based on a drawing by Henry Glassie and used with his kind permission.

Page 33. Drake, Samuel Adams. A Book of New England Legends and Folk Lore in Prose and Poetry. Illustrated by F. T. Merrill. Boston: Little and Brown, 1884.

Page 42. Cyr, Ellen M. The Children's Third Reader. Boston: Ginn & Co., 1901.

Page 52. Markham, Richard. Colonial Days, Being Stories and Ballads for Young Patriots. New York: Dodd, Mead, & Co., 1879.

Page 56. Otis, James. Mary of Plymouth: A Story of the Pilgrim Settlement. New York: American Book Co., 1910.

Page 74. Crafts, William A. Pioneers in the Settlement of America. Vol. 1. Boston: Samuel Walker & Co., 1876.

Page 76. Otis, James. Mary of Plymouth: A Story of the Pilgrim Settlement. New York: American Book Co., 1910.

Page 93. Coffin, Charles Carleton. Old Times in the Colonies. New York: Harper & Brothers, 1881.

Page 95. Blaisdell, Albert F. The Story of American History for Elementary Schools. Boston: Ginn & Company, 1902.

Page 99. Otis, James. Mary of Plymouth: A Story of the Pilgrim Settlement. New York: American Book Co., 1910.

Page 104. Pratt, Mara L. Stories of Colonial Children. Boston: Educational Publishing Co., 1925.

Page 127. Bryant, William Cullen Bryant, Sydney Howard Gay. A Popular History of the United States from the First Discovery of the Western Hemisphere by the Northmen, to the end of the First Century of the Union of the United States. Boston: Scribner, Armstrong, and Co., 1876.

Page 136. Bryant, William Cullen Bryant, Sydney Howard Gay. A Popular History of the United States from the First Discovery of the Western Hemisphere by the Northmen, to the end of the First Century of the Union of the United States. Boston: Scribner, Armstrong, and Co., 1876.

Page 139. Drake, Samuel Adams. A Book of New England Legends and Folk Lore in Prose and Poetry. Illustrated by F. T. Merrill. Boston: Little and Brown, 1884.

Page 147. Pratt, Mara L. Stories of Colonial Children. Boston: Educational Publishing Co., 1925.

Page 150. Credit Line: "The Quakers Meeting," by Carel Allard after Egbert van Heemskerck, etching 1678-79. Accessed at Http://www.britishmuseum.org/research/collection_online/collection_object_details.aspx?objectId=1659703&partId=1&searchText=1847,0713.51&page=1 on 10/28/18.

Page 170. "The Pilgrims underestimated how much food ..." Image ID BDTF06. Ivy Close Images/Alamy Stock Photo

Page 183. "Pilgrims: Public Worship at Plymouth," accessed at http://ushistoryimages.com/images/pilgrims/fullsize/pilgrims-6.jpg on 1/9/2020.

Page 188. Otis, James. Mary of Plymouth: A Story of the Pilgrim Settlement. New York:American Book Co., 1910.

Page 196. Otis, James. Mary of Plymouth: A Story of the Pilgrim Settlement. New York:American Book Co., 1910.

Page 210. 1600s Portrait ... by Boughton. ID: M66PDG. ClassicStock/Alamay Stock Photo.

Page 227. The Miriam and Ira D. Wallach Division of Art, Prints and Photographs: PrintCollection, The New York Public Library. "Old Blue-Bell Tavern, Kingsbridge Road" New York Public Library Digital Collections. http://digitalcollections.nypl/" http://digitalcollections.nypl. org/items/510d47da-262c-a3d9-e040-e00a18064a99 (accessed on December 4, 2018).

Page 231. Otis, James. Mary of Plymouth: A Story of the Pilgrim Settlement. New York:American Book Co., 1910.

Page 239. Coffin, Charles Carleton. Old Times in the Colonies. New York: Harper & Brothers,1881.

Index

abandonment, 75, 78
  of family, 58-60
Adams, John, 120
Adkinson, Marmaduke, 48
Adkinson, Mary, 48
adultery, 35-36, 62, 64, 67, 72-76,
  174, 178, 212, 240
  as capital crime, 53, 72
  confession of, 12-13
  punishments for, 13, 15, 53, 72-73,
  75, 77, 100, 178-179
Agawam, Plymouth Colony, 249
Aines, Alexander, 35
Aines, K atherine, 35
alcohol
  laws pertaining to, 58, 147, 218,
  229, 246
  sales of, 229
Alcott, Louisa May, 19
Alden Kindred of America, 140
Alden, John, 59, 137, 138-140, 200
  death of, 140
Alden, Priscilla Mullins, 137-140
Ale, Robert, 49
Allen, Ann, 112
Allen, Benjamin, 85
Allen, George, 149-150
Allen, Hannah, 149
Allen, John, 112-113
Allen, Matthew, 150
Allen, Ralph, 149
Allen, Robert, 212
Allen, Samuel, 156
Allen, Sarah Kerby, 149-150
Allen, Susanna, 149
Allen, William, 149

Allerton, Bartholomew, 14, 16
  returns to England aboard
  Mayflower (ship), 17
Allerton, Fear Brewster, 16
Allerton, Isaac, 16
  marries, 2nd time, 16
Allerton, Mary (daughter of IA), 14,
  16
  death of, 17
  marries Thomas Cushman, 17
Allerton, Mary Norris (wife of IA),
  16-17
  death of, 16
Allerton, Remember, 14, 16
  marries Moses Maverick, 17
Allerton, Sarah, 181
Allin, John, 218
Allyn, Thomas, 178
*An Account of Two Voyages to New
England*, J. Josselyn, 194
Ancient Brethren in Amsterdam, 17
Anderson, Robert Charles, 15
Andrew, Hester, 242
Andrews, John, 58
Andros, Sir Edmund, 68-69, 239
animals, wild (including boars,
  snakes, wolves), 194-195
Annable, Anna, 217
Annable, Anne, 217-218
Annable, John, 218
Annable, Samuel, Sr., 217-218
Annable, Samuel, Jr. (son of SA),
  217-218
Anne (ship), 129, 131, 133, 222, 224,
  232
Armstrong, Gregory, 154

death of, 154
Arnold, Samuel, 44, 117, 201
Arthur, John, 78
Ashurst, Sir Henry, 238
Atkins, Mary, 88
Atkins, Thomas, 88
Atkinson, Marmaduke, 75
Atkinson, Mary Jenkens, 75
    marries Robert Cooke, 76
Atlantic Ocean, 9
Austerfield, Yorkshire, England, 11
Austin, Jane Goodwin, 19-21
Awashunkes of Saconett , Native
American, 192-193

Babworth, Nottinghamshire,
England, 126
Backe, Isaac, 75
Backe, John, 75
Bacon, Daniel, 163
Bahama Islands, 131
Baker, Francis, 118-119
Bangs, Apphia, 184
Bangs, Edward, 184
Bangs, Jeremy Dupertuis, 61
Bangs, Jonathan, family of, 182
Bangs, Lydia, 184
Bangs, Mary Mayo, 182
Bangs, Mercy, 184
Barbados, 70, 178
Barker, Ann, 197
Barker, Anna, 99
Barker, Deborah, 99-100
Barker, Isaac, 79
Barker, John, 66, 99, 110, 197
Barker, Robert, 200
Barker, William, 65
Barlow, George, 83-86, 150
    death of, 85
Barlow, Jane Bessey, 83
    death of, 86
Barlow, John, 86
Barlow, Sarah, 159
Barnard, Robert, 71
Barnes, Anne Plummer, 114

Barnes, Joan, 114, 161
Barnes, John, 103, 114-115, 156, 161
    death of, 114
Barnes, Joshua, 114
Barnes, Mary Plummer, 114
Barnstable, Massachusetts, 50, 58,
    67, 76, 84-85, 93, 107, 167, 169,
    171, 173, 202, 205-206, 209, 213-
    214
Barrows, Robert, 108
Barstow, Mary, 155
Barstow, William, 155
Bartlett, Mary Warren, 159, 233,
    235
Bartlett, Robert, 233-234
Batson, Anne Winter, 90-91
Batson, Robert, 90-91, 121
Bay Colony See Massachusetts Bay
    Colony
Bayley, Abigail, 242
Bayley, John, 61, 65, 242
Beedle, Joseph, 120, 122
beer, brewing and selling of, 218
Bennett, Richard, 173
Berry, Alice, 201-204
Berry, Elizabeth, 202, 204
Berry, John, 202
Berry, Richard, 201-204
Berry, Samuel, 203
Bessey, Aaron, 86
Bessey, Anna, 83, 86
Bessey, Anthony, 83
Bessey, Dorcas, 83, 86
Bessey, Mary, 83, 86
Bessey, Moses, 86
Bessey, Nathan, 86
bestiality, 174-175
Betty, Native American (daughter of
    Awashunkes), 36, 192-193
bigamy, 12, 67, 69-70
Billington, Christian Penn Eaton,
    102, 104-105, 224
    death of, 105
Billington, Dorcas, 104-105
Billington, Eleanor, 54, 102, 151,

153-154
marries Gregory Armstrong, 154
Billington, Elizabeth, 102
Billington, Francis, 82, 93, 102-107,
     113, 153-154, 224
   death of, 105
Billington, Hannah Glass, 105
Billington, Isaac, 104, 105-106
Billington, John, Jr., 102
Billington, John, Sr., 36, 102
   death of, 102, 153
Billington, Joseph, 103-104
Billington, Martha, 103
Billington, Mary, 103
Billington, Mercy, 104
Billington, Rebecca, 104
Billington, Samuel, 103
Bird, Thomas, 99, 100
birth control, 45, 101, 104, 172, 181
Bishop, Alice, 37-39
Bishop, Richard, 37
Blakeway, Jacob, 12-13
Blush, Abraham, 15
Boardman, Elizabeth Rider Cole, 51
Boardman, Lucy, 50-51
   death of, 51
Boardman, Thomas, 50-51
   marries second time, 51
Bond, John, 190
Bonney, Desire Billington, 105-106
Bonney, James, Jr., 106
Bonney, James, Sr., 106
Bonney, Thomas, 171-172
Bonney, Hannah, 51-52
Book of General Laws and Liberties
   Concerning the Inhabitants of the
   Massachusetts, 1648, J. Winthrop,
   240
Boreman, Thomas, 50
Boston, Massachusetts, 34, 64, 68,
   70-71, 107, 117, 135, 137, 141,
   148, 186, 237, 240
Bourne, Richard, 149
Bower, John, 160-161
Bowman, Gene Ernest, 20

Bradbury, Katherine, 40
Bradford, Alice, 134, 223
Bradford, Alice Carpenter
Southworth, 131-133, 222
   death of, 134
Bradford, Dorothy May (wife of
WB), 17-18, 20, 22-23, 132, 134
   cause of death questioned, 19
   death of, 19
   marries William Bradford, 17
   suspicions about cause of death,
      21-22
Bradford, John, 134
Bradford, John (son of WB), 18, 23
   sails for Plymouth Colony, 23
Bradford, Joseph, 134
Bradford, Mercy, 134
Bradford, William, 10-11, 14, 16-23,
   27, 31, 37-38, 55, 102, 120, 127,
   129-135, 153, 166, 175, 180, 185,
   197, 222-223, 230, 234, 241
   becomes citizen of Leiden, 17
   departs for New World leaving son
      in Holland, 18
   marries, 17
   marries 2nd time, 23
   sells inherited lands in Austerfield,
      17
   settles in Amsterdam, 17
Bradford, William (son of WB), 134
Branch, Mary, 92
Bray, Thomas, 179
   breach of sabbath, 247
Brewster, Fear, 128-129
Brewster, Jonathan, 128-129
Brewster, Love, 13, 129, 175
Brewster, Mary May, 13, 23, 54,
   126-129
   death of, 129
Brewster, Patience, 128-129
Brewster, William, 13-14, 16-17, 26,
   126, 128-129, 176, 206
   death of, 129
Brewster, Wrestling, 13
Bridgewater, Massachusetts, 60, 115,

117, 123-124, 143
Briggs, Hugh, 108
Briggs, Jonathan, 73-74
Briggs, Martha Everson, 108
Briggs, Mary, 158
Briggs, William, 183
Brown, John, 102
Browne, Peter, 222
Bryant, Stephen, Jr., 108
Bryant, Stephen, Sr., 108, 110
Buck, Isaac, 62
Buck, Joseph, 86
buggery *See* homosexuality
Bullocks, Elizabeth Billington, 219
Bullocks, Richard, 219
Bumpass, Hannah, 100
Bundy, John, 206
Burges, Elizabeth Bassett, 73
Burges, Thomas, Jr., 72-73
Burges, Thomas, Sr., 150, 190
Burman, Thomas Jr., 56
Burt, Richard, 189
Butler, Dorothy, 150
Butler, Thomas, 85
Butten, William, 10-11, 180, 222
  burial of, 11
  death of, 10

Cape Cod, 9, 11, 14, 16, 19, 22, 130,
  249
Cape Cod Harbor, 19, 130
Carey, John, 123
Carle, Richard, 59
Carpenter, Delores, 21
Carpenter, Mary, 133-134
Carter, Robert, 137
Carver, John, 13, 120, 125, 129-130,
  197
  death of, 130-131
Carver, Katherine White, 13, 54,
  129-130
  death of, 131
Carver, Margaret, 201
Carver, Richard, 201
Caulfield, Ernest, 186

Chadwell, Richard, 28
Charlestown, Massachusetts, 214
•Chase, Mary, 198
➤Chase, William, Jr., 202-203
Chauncy, Rev. Charles, 43
child support, 50, 52-53, 75, 90,
  173-174, 177, 243-244
Child, Benjamin, 245
Child, Joseph, 245
Child, Mary, 245
childbirth
  assistance during, 159
  twins, 184
children
  adoption of, 108, 110-112
  as indentured servants, 109
  as servants, 103, 107, 113-114
  born out of wedlock, 44, 87, 90,
    105, 160, 172-173, 207, 242-243
  deaths, 180
    accidental, 190-191
    drowning, 187-189
    from exposure, 189
    murder, 88
    suicide, 192
    suspicious, 91, 181, 187
    work related, 187, 190
  discipline of, 87
  education, schools, tuition, 218,
    248-249
  incest, 87-89
  indenture agreements, 98
  infants and newborns, 182, 252
  labor of, 98
  mortality rate, 182
  on *Mayflower* (ship), 180
  orphans, 109
  overindulgence of, 101
  sexual abuse and assault of, 88
Chilton, James, 136
Chilton, Mary, 37, 60, 123
Chilton, Susanna, 60, 136
Chittenden, Elizabeth, 184
Chittenden, Isaac, 158, 184
Chittenden, Israel, 184

Chittenden, Mary Vinall, 184
Chittenden, Rebecca, 184
Chittenden, Sarah, 184
Chittenden, Stephen, 184
church, mandatory attendance, 146
church meetings, behavior during, 147
Church of England, 127
Church of God at Plymouth, 223
Church, Elizabeth Warren, 235
Church, Nathaniel, 48
Churchill, Mary, 50, 236
Claghorn, Abia (Abigail) Lumberd, 212-214
Claghorn, Elizabeth, 212-213
Claghorn, James, 212-213
Claghorn, James (son of JC), 213
Claghorn, Mary, 213
Claghorn, Robert, 212-214
Claghorn, Sarah, 213
Claghorn, Shubael, 214
Clarke, Dorothy Lettice Gray, 68-69
Clarke, James, 159
Clarke, Martha, 37-38
Clarke, Nathaniel, 68-69
Clarke, Sarah, 94-96
Clarke, Susanna Ring, 68
Clarke, Thomas, 57, 68, 233
Clarke, William, 94-97, 105
Clyfton, Rev., 126
Code of Laws 1636, 25, 36, 40, 45, 72, 80, 161
Code of Laws 1658, 25
Code of Laws 1672, 25
Code of Laws 1685, 25
Cohanett *See* Taunton, Massachusetts
Cole, James, Jr., 228
Cole, James, Sr., 228-229
Cole, John, Sr., 229, 246
Cole, Mary, 228-229
Cole, Susanna, 246
Coleman, Jane Child, 245
Collections of the Massachusetts Historical Society, S. Davis, 135

Collier, Jane, 234
Collier, William, 38
Collimore, Peter, 155
Combe, Francis, 226
Combe, John, 217
Combe, Mary, 226
Converse, Sarah, 223
Cooke, John, Jr., 103-104, 233
Cooke, John, Sr., 103-104
Cooke, Robert, 76, 112
Cooke, Roger, 197
Cooke, Sarah Warren, 233, 235
Cooper, Naighbor, 71
Copeland, John, 84
corn as a food crop, 180
Cottle, Edward, 148
Cotton, John, 117
Court, General, 29, 38, 51, 78, 100, 109, 238-239
Court, Selectmen's, 29
Courts of Assistants, 29, 38, 238, 241
courtship
  breach of promise, 41
  civil suits, 41
  laws of, 41-42
  parents permission, 40
Courtship of Miles Standish, HW Longfellow, 135, 138
Covell, Nathaniel, 148
Coventry, Jonathan, 40
Cowin, John, 160
Cowin, Rebecca, 160
Cowles, Elizabeth, 223
Crisp, George, 203
Crocker, John, 118
Crooker, Francis, 43
Cross, Daniel, 36
Crow, William, 105
Crowell, Edward, 92
Cudworth, James, 65
Cudworth, Mary, 49
Curtis, Francis, 184
Curtis, Hannah Smith, 184
Curtis, Sarah, 243
Cushing, John, 241

Cushman, Fear, 17
Cushman, Robert, 13
Cushman, Thomas, 245
    death of, 17
Cutbert, Samuel, 167

Danforth, Rev., family of, 186
Dartmouth, Massachusetts, 150, 209
David Hunter, Native American,
    143
Davis, Hannah, 205
Davis, Nicholas, 46
Davis, Samuel, 135-136
Day of Humiliation, 185-186
Day, William, 192
de la Forrest, John Armand, 36
Dean, Bethiah Edson, 182-183
Dean, Ezra, 183
    family of, 182-183
Dean, Walter, 199
Deane, Samuel, 164
deaths in Plymouth Colony, first
    winter, 14
Deetz, James, 24, 166, 171, 215
Deetz, Patricia, 24, 215
defamation and slander, 159
Delano, Hannah, 244
Delano, Thomas, Jr., 244
Demos, John, 154, 182-183
depression (as illness), 22
desertion See abandonment
Dexter, Thomas Jr., 57, 118
Dillingham, Henry, 150
disease, 185
    at Plymouth, 186
    children's, 186
        diphtheria, 186
        dysentery, 186
        measles, 186
        whooping cough, 185-186
    sexually transmitted (including the
        pox, syphilis), 76, 174
    smallpox, 185-186
disfranchisement, 203
Division of Cattle, 1627, 14, 137,
    140, 232
Division of Land, 1623, 137, 232
divorce, 67, 71, 76-77, 178
    adultery and, 67, 71-74, 76-77
    bigamy and, 68
    impotence and, 68
    request for, 67, 75
Doane, Daniel, 187
Dodson, Anthony, 160
Dogged, John, 156
domestic abuse, violence, 80-82, 84
    children as abusers, 83
    law in Massachusetts, 80
    law in Plymouth, 80
    wives as abusers, 83
Domesticall Duties, W. Gouge, 145
Done, John, 153
Dorchester, Massachusetts, 77
Doty (Doten, Doughtey), Edward,
    225, 246
Doty (Doten, Doughtey), James,
    155
Doty (Doten, Doughtey), Joseph,
    235-236
Doty (Doten, Doughtey), Thomas,
    50, 236
Downham, Sarah, 244
Doxey, Elizabeth, 207-208
drought in Plymouth, 1690, 237, 251
drunkenness, 16, 32, 53, 81-82, 84-
    85, 88, 114, 124, 152, 226, 229,
    247
Dudley, Dorothy, 253
Dunham, John, Jr., 81
Dunham, John, Sr., 81, 204
Dunham, Jonathan, 34
Dunham, Joseph, 151-152
Dunham, Samuel, 184
Duxbury Fair, 38-39
Duxbury, Massachusetts, 14, 32, 59,
    77-79, 109, 114-115, 129, 139-
    140, 167, 172, 175, 178, 200, 238
Dwelly, Richard, 229

Eames, Anthony, 244

Eames, Jonathan, 244-245
Eames, Sarah, 245
Earle, Ralph, 81
Early Encounters: Native Americans and Europeans in New England, from the papers of W. Sears Nickerson, D. Carpenter, 21
Eastham, Massachusetts, 184, 203
Eaton, Benjamin, 102-104, 167, 204-205, 224, 248
Eaton, Francis, 82, 102, 106, 222, 224
Eaton, Martha, 93
Eaton, Rachel, 102
Eaton, Samuel, 93, 102-103, 106
Eaton, Sarah, 204-205
Eddenden, Edward, 176
Eddy, Caleb, 102
Eddy, Elizabeth, 101, 148
Eddy, John, 102
Eddy, Obadiah, 102
Eddy, Samuel, 101-102
Eddy, Zachariah, 102
Edward III, King of England, 121
Eel River, Plymouth Colony, 94, 96-97, 232-234, 249
Ellis, John, 152
Elmes, Waitstill, 190
Emerson, John, 100
England, William, 188-189
English Housewife, G. Markham, 221
Ensign, Elizabeth, 208
Ensign, Sarah, 52
environmental dangers, 194-195
Esau (Old Testament), 69
Everson, Elizabeth, 108-109
Everson, John, 107-108
Everson, Penelope, 108
Everson, Richard, 108, 242
Ewen, John, 169-170

Fallowell, Gabriel, 103
farming, 98, 194, 220, 238, 248
Farniseede, Elizabeth, 171-172

Farniseede, John, 171
fire
    dangers of, 197
    for heat, 196-197
fish and fishing, 50, 180, 238, 249
Fish, Ambrose, 88
Fish, Lydia, 88, 210
Fish, Nathaniel, 57, 88
Fish, Thomas, 190
Ford, William, 163
fornication (sex before marriage), 44-51, 104, 111, 113, 156, 163, 166, 168-172, 174, 192-193, 195, 209, 213, 235-236, 242-243, 244, 247
    as path to marriage, 46-48
    laws and punishments, 45, 47-53, 75, 108, 167-169
Fortune (ship), 123, 129, 132, 137
Foster, Benjamin, 86-87
    death of, 87
Foster, George, 223
Foster, Mary, 86
Foster, Richard, 86
Fowling Pond, Plymouth Colony, 189
Fox, Deborah, 243
Freeman, Edmond, Sr., 28, 149, 211
Freeman, Elizabeth, 149
Freeman, John, 211
Freeman, Margaret Perry, 211
Freeman, Sarah, 210-211
Fuller, Agnes Carpenter, 133
Fuller, Bridget Lee, 102-104, 221-225, 248
    death of, 225
Fuller, Edward, 221-222
Fuller, Matthew, 225
Fuller, Mercy Eaton, 223, 225
Fuller, Samuel, 10-11, 102, 133, 185, 221-225
    death of, 222
Fuller, Samuel, Jr., 223, 225

Gannett, Goodwife, 167

Garrett, Lydia, 229
Gaunt, Lydia, 72, 149
  marries Thomas Burge, Jr., 73
Gaunt, Mary, 43
Gaunt, Peter, 149
Gebler, Ernest, 20
George, Native American, 65
Gifford, William, 56
Gilbert, Ann Blake, 184
Gilbert, Mary, 184
Gilbert, Sarah, 184
Gilbert, Thomas, 119, 184
Glass, Hannah, 181
Glass, James, 181
Glass, Roger, 118
Glover, Elizabeth, 217
Glover, John, 76, 174
  death of, 77
Glover, Mary, 76, 174
Godbertson, Godbert, 222
Godey's Lady's Book (magazine),
  135
Godfrey, Hannah Hackett, 113
Godfrey, Robert, 113
Gorum, Jabez, 213
Gorum, John, 207
gossip, 30, 146, 151, 156, 158-160,
  162, 179, 234
Gouge, William, 145
Goulder, Francis, 102
Goulder, Katherine, 102
Grand Inquest or Grand Jury, 28-29,
  37, 47, 51, 54, 57, 80, 88-89, 151,
  163, 176-177, 193, 206
Granger, Thomas, Sr., 36, 176
Gray, Edward, 68, 105
Gray, John, 250
Gray, Joseph, 119
Great Harry, Native American, 36
  death of, 193
Great River, 188
Griffin, William, 203

Hacke, Mary, 70-71
Hacke, William, Jr., 70

Hacke, William, Sr., 70-71
Hale, Sarah Josepha, 135
Hall, John, 118
Hall, Nathaniel, 204
Hall, Samuel, 118
Hallett, Andrew, 83, 86
Halloway, Easter, 75
Halloway, Grace, 217
Halloway, Jane, 73-75
Halloway, John, 75
Halloway, Nathaniel, 75
Halloway, Samuel, 73-75
Halloway, William, 231
Hammond, Benjamin, 177, 201
Hammond, Capt. (of Charlestown),
  214
Hammond, Mary, 176-177
Hanbury, William, 98
Hanmore, Joseph, 46
Harding, Martha, 169
Harlow, Abigail Buck, 112
Harlow, James, 112
Harlow, Mary, 111
Harlow, Nathaniel, 111-112
Harlow, Rebecca, 111
Harlow, William, 111
Harper, Robert, 150
Harper's New Monthly Magazine,
  19
Harris, Arthur, 60, 155
Harris, Isaac, 59-60, 123
Harris, Mercy Latham, 59-60, 123
Harris, Paul, 13
Harvard University, 43, 250
Harvey, William, Sr., 199
Hatch, Elizabeth, 242
Hatch, Jeremy, 46
Hatch, Jonathan, 206
Hatch, Lydia, 206
Hatch, Sarah, 191
Hatch, Thomas, 59, 190-191
Hathaway, John, 212
Hatherly, Timothy, 158, 176
Haward, Lieut., 123
Haward, Martha, 167

Hawkins, William, 58
Haybell, Elizabeth, 206
Hazard, Thomas, 168
Hedges, Anne, 109
Hedges, Tristram, 109
herbs as medicine, 198, 221, 252
Hewitt, John, 89-90
Hewitt, Martha Winter, 89-90
Hewitt, Solomon, 90
Hewitt, Winter, 90
· Hews, Joan, 45
‚ Hews, John, 45
Hicks, Lydia, 150
Higgins, Elizabeth Rogers, 170
Higgins, Hannah Rogers, 49, 170
Higgins, Jonathan, 49, 50, 170
Hinckley, Gov. Thomas, 84, 211,
    237, 249, 251
Hindus, Michael, 240
History of Scituate, S. Deane, 164
Hobson, Henry, 49
Holbrooke, William, 243
Holder, Christopher, 84
Holman, Amy Glass, 168
Holman, Edward, 114-115, 167-168
Holmes, Elizabeth, 161-162
Holmes, John, 174, 245
Holmes, Patience, 245
Holmes, William, 161-162, 191
home invasions, 92-93
homosexuality, 36, 175-176
Hooke, John, 16
Hooke, Mr., 141
Hope, Native American, 246
Hopkins, Elizabeth, 54
Hopkins, Stephen, 173-174
Hoskins, Anne, 152
Howard, Mary, 246
Howes, Jeremiah, 204
Howes, Thomas, 50
Howland, Arthur Jr., 43-44
Howland, Bethiah, 188
Howland, Elizabeth Tilley, 131
Howland, John, 22, 43, 120, 130-
    131, 140

Howland, Sarah, 242
•Huckens, Thomas, 119
Hudson, Ann, 148, 208
Hudson, John, 148, 208
Hues, Lewis, 168
Hull, Blanch, 207
Hull, Sarah, 181
Hull, Tristram, 181, 205
Humber River, 127
Hunt, Elizabeth, 41
Hunt, Peter, 41, 208

Ingham, Mary, 163-164
Ingham, Thomas, 155, 163-164
inheritance and wills, 217
Irish, John, 34

Jackson, Abraham, 160
Jackson, Thomas, 36
James II, King of England, 68-69
Jane, slave to J. Winslow, 137
Jenkens, Edward, 48, 75, 188
Jenkens, Samuel, 188
Jenney, John, 223
Jennings, John, 170
Job Mark, Native American, 246
Joe, Negro servant, 243
• Johnson, Elkanah, 163
ﬞ Johnson, Samuel, 149
Jones River, Kingston, Plymouth
Colony, 109
Jones, Capt. Christopher, 20
Jones, Mary, 169
Jones, Teague, 202
Jones, Thomas, 209
Jones, William, 78
Joseph, Native American, 143
Josselyn, John, 9, 194
Jury of Inquiry, 211
jury trials, 63, 75, 164, 244

Kainer, R. G., 22
Keeweenam, Native American, 96
Keith, James, 117
Kennebec River, Plymouth Colony, 88

Kerby, Richard, 149
Kerby, Sarah, 150
Kerman, John, 229
King Philip's War, 36, 65, 94, 105, 116-117, 192, 237
King William's War (1690), 251
Kingston, Massachusetts, 109
Knott, Widow, 149
Konig, David Thomas, 241

Lake, Richard, 188
Lakenham, Plymouth Colony (today's North Carver), 224, 245
Lanckford, Richard, 222
land grants, 141, 143, 153, 232, 234, 245
Larden Hall, Shropshire, England, 12-13, 15
Latham, Robert, 37, 60, 119-123, 137, 155
Latham, Susanna Chilton Winslow, 37, 60, 119, 122-123, 137, 155
Latham, William, 119, 130, 197
Launder, Jane, 149
Launder, Richard, 211
Launder, Thomas, 46
Lawrence, Mercy, 87
Lawrence, Samuel, 87
laws in Plymouth
  based on biblical law, 26
  based on English law, 26
Leiden Separatist Congregation, 11, 132
Leiden, Netherlands, 11, 16-17, 26, 101, 126, 128, 130-133, 221, 250
Lennet, Hannah, 167
Leonard, James, 226
Leonard, Joseph, 199
Leonard, Phillip, 53
"Liberties of Women" in Massachusetts law, 80
light behavior, 78, 167, 173
Linceford, Anne, 179
Linceford, Francis, 179
Linley, Shropshire, England, 12

Linnett, David, 171, 217
Linnett, Penninnah, 217
Linnett, Robert, 217
Litchfield, Josiah, 113
Litchfield, Josias, 112-113
Litchfield, Judith Dennis, 112-113
Litchfield, Lawrence, 112
Litchfield, Sarah Baker, 113
Little James (ship), 131, 133
Little, Anna Warren, 235
Littlefield, Rebecca, 173
Littleworth Farm, Taunton, 141-142
Loe, Elizabeth, 53
Loe, John, 53
Lombard, Hannah Wing, 107
Lombard, Jedediah, 107
Lombard, Thomas, Sr., 107
London, England, 11-13, 51, 135, 153, 232
Longfellow, Henry Wadsworth, 135, 138-139
Lothrop, Barnabas, 62, 64, 239
Lothrop, Rev. John, 61
Lucas, Thomas, 32, 81
  death of, 82
Lumbard, Barnard, 209
Lumbard, Mary, 209
Lumberd, Bernard, 213
Lyme, Connecticut, 115

Maine, 58, 69, 209, 237
Makepeace, William, Sr., 209
Maker, James, 92
malnutrition, 22
Manomet, Native American settlement, 109
Marblehead, Massachusetts, 17, 212
Marchant, Abisha, 169
Marchant, John, 209
Markham, Gervase, 221
marriage, 215
  first in Plymouth Colony, 55   (white)
  gifts of land, 41
  husband's marriage duty, 61, 63
  husbands responsibilities, 54-55

laws, 54, 57
legal seperation, 21, 63
parental consent, 43
Quakers and, 56
standards and expectations, 55-56,
   80
vows, 12
Marshall, Richard, 82, 109
Marshfield, Plymouth Colony, 40,
   43-44, 46, 53, 106, 117, 119, 162-
   163, 191, 209, 228, 244-245
Martha's Vineyard, Cape Cod, 71,
   237
Mary II, Queen of England, 237
Massachusetts Bay Colony, 69, 80,
   140-141,212, 222, 237
   charter of, 237, 240
   laws of, 240
Massachusetts, Province of, 237-
   238, 240
Massasoit or Ousamequin, Native
   American Sachem, 94, 116-117,
   130, 133
Mather, Cotton, 19
Mather, Increase, 94-95, 117, 214
Mattashunnamo, Native American,
   36
Maverick, Moses, 17
May, Edward, 105
May, Henry, 17
Mayflower (ship), 11, 16-17, 20-22,
   36, 43, 54-55, 82, 102, 120, 123,
   125, 129-132, 136-137, 153, 170,
   197, 222, 232, 246
   children onboard, 14
   death onboard, 10, 180-181
   life onboard, 9
   returns to England, 14, 17, 25, 138
Mayflower Compact, 130, 153, 222
Mayflower Descendant (magazine),
   20
Mayne, Ezekiel, 49
Mayo, James, 169
Mayo, Samuel, 205
medical treatment, 197

with herbal remedies, 198
women as primary providers, 197
men, responsibilities as head of
   household, 155, 216
Mendame, Mary, 35, 178
Mendame, Robert, 178
Merritt, Elizabeth, 46
Merritt, John, 46
Metacom aka King Philip, 94-95,
   117
   death of, 94
   his unnamed son, 116-117
   his unnamed wife, 116
Michell, Jacob, 96
Michell, Richard, 203
Middleborough, Massachusetts, 102,
   105-106, 226
Mill River, 189
Miller, Joan, 83
Miller, John, 204
Miller, Obadiah, 83
Mills, Mary, 58-59
Minter, Desire, 130
   death of, 131
Mitchell, Edward, 206
Mitchell, John, 51-52
Moore, Elizabeth, 29
Moorecock, Bennett, 49
More, Catherine, 12-13, 16
   divorce of, 13
More, Christian Hunter, 14
   death of, 15
More, Elinor, 14
More, Ellen, 11-13, 55
More, Jane Crumpton, 15
More, Jasper, 11-14, 130
   death of, 14, 131
More, Mary 11-13
   death of, 14
More, Rachel, 13
More, Richard, 11-14, 16
   as servant to William Brewster, 14
   death of, 15
   excommunicated for adultry, 15
   marries, 14

marries (third time), 15
marries, bigamously, 15
sells shares of Plymouth property, 15
shareholder of Plymouth property, 14
More, Samuel, 11-13, 15
divorce, files for, 13
More, Thomas, 15
Morey, Hannah, 86
Morey, John, 86
Morey, Jonathan, 86
Morey, Mary Bartlet Foster, 86
death of, 87
Morison, Samuel Eliot, 22
Morris, Adonijah, 94
Morton, Ephraim, 50, 241
Morton, George, 50, 133
Morton, John, 248-249
family of, 182
Morton, Juliana Carpenter, 133
Morton, Lettice, 182
Morton, Lieu., 50
Morton, Lydia, 111
Morton, Nathaniel, 64, 111-112, 129, 131, 134-135, 181
Morton, Rose, 160
Muffee, Margaret, 229-230
Mullins, Joseph, 137
Mullins, William, 137
Musquash, Native American, 97
Myles Standish Burial Ground, 140

Nantucket, Massachusetts, 71, 237
Narragansett, Native American tribe, 195
Nash, Lieut., 78
Native Americans
assaults of women, 208-209
attacks by colonists, 94
attacks on colonist, 93
bounties on, 97
children as servants, 116
diseases, 185
execution of, 96

sold as slaves, 117
Nelson, John, 244
Nelson, William, Sr., 108
Nesfield, Sarah, 109
New Plymouth *See* Plymouth Colony,
Newcomen, John, 36, 102
New England's Memorial, N. Morton, 134
New England's Salamander Discovered, E. Winslow, 26
Newland, John, 150
Newland, Rose, 149
Newland, William, 85, 150, 156
Newport, Rhode Island, 73, 188
Nichols, Rebecca, 243
Nickerson, Joseph, 148
Nickerson, Nicholas, 190
Nickerson, Ruhamah, 148
Nickerson, W. Sears, 21, 203
Nickerson, William, 203
Nicolls, Sarah, 206
Nimrod, Negro servnant, 52
Norman, Hugh, 176-178, 202
Norman, Samuel, 205
Norman, Sarah White, 176-178, 202
North Carver, Massachusetts, 224
North Plymouth, Massachusetts *See* Playne Dealing
North River, Plymouth Colony, 200
Norton, Ephraim, 241
Nova Scotia, 237
Num, John, 96

Of Plymouth Plantation, W. Bradford, 19, 135
OKillia, David, 47, 252
OKillia, Sarah (daughter of DO), 47
Orchard, Dorset, England, 178
Ormsbey, Richard, 218-219
Ormsbey, Sarah, 218-219

Pakes, Thankful, 187
Pakes, William, 187
Palmer, John, Jr., 155, 163

Palmer, Rebecca, 205
Partridge, John, 246
Paule, Margery, 142
Paule, William, 35
Paybodie, William, 78
Peach, Arthur, 36, 174
Pecke, John, 207, 218
Peirse, Abigail, 157
Peirse, Michael, 157, 206
Penachason, Native American, 97
Perry, John, 79
Perry, Susanna, 201
Perry, William, 201
Peter, Native American (son of
    Awashunkes), 143, 193
Phillips, Annis (Agnes), 209
Phillips, Mary, 74
Phillips, Thomas, 209
Piant, Thomas, 97
Pierce, Alice, 77
Pierce, Capt., 109
Pierce, Elinor Child, 245
Pierce, Rebecca, 77
Pilgrim Congregational Church, 144
Pilgrim Hall Museum, 225
Pilgrim watchfulness, 26-27, 46
Pilgrim's *ideal* of womanhood, 253
Pincin, Ebenezer, 243
Pine Hills, Plymouth Colony, 233
Pittney, Sarah, 209
Pitts, Edith, 100
Plain Cemetery, Taunton, 144
Playne Dealing, 102, 105, 153-154
*Plymouth Adventure: A Chronical
    Novel of the Voyage of the
    Mayflower,* E. Gebler, 20
Plymouth Church, 69, 146, 148-149,
    222, 225, 240, 247
    punishments, 69, 149, 247-248
    women as members, 247
Plymouth Colony, 15, 18, 21, 23-24,
    36, 38, 40, 51, 56, 58, 69, 73, 88,
    97-98, 102, 107, 114 ,116, 123,
    125-126, 129-130, 133, 135, 137,
    139, 143, 159, 161, 164, 178, 181-

    184, 189-192, 194, 197, 199, 201,
    211, 214-216, 220-221, 234, 237-
    238, 240-241, 244
Plymouth Colony Courts, 67, 117,
    141, 209
    general sessions, 240
    town court, 240
Plymouth Colony merges into
    Massachusetts Bay Colony, (1691),
    237
Plymouth County, 237, 239, 241,
    244
Plymouth County Court of General
    Sessions and Common Pleas, 241
Plymouth Harbor, 131
Plymouth Rock, 137
Plymouth Town, 72, 108, 189, 231,
    244-245
Plymouth Colony's trading post, 88
Plymouth's Council of War, 116
Plympton, Massachusetts, 109, 112
Poole, Elizabeth, 140-144
    death of, 144
Poole, John, 142
Poole, Mary, 142
Poole, William, 140-143
Pope, John, 96
poverty, children placed in service
    because of, 101
Powell, Jane, 47, 252
Powell, Martha, 92
Pratt, Abigail, 85
Pratt, Jonathan, 85, 160, 245
pregnancy
    as evidence of fornication, 242
    death rate of women, causes, 183
    miscarriages, 73, 102, 181, 214
    stillbirths, 16, 181, 214
Prence, Elizabeth, 43-44
    marries Arthur Howland, Jr., 44
Prence, Thomas, 44, 84, 223, 234,
    237
Preston, Edward, 206
Prince, John Jr., 46
Prince, Rebecca, 223

Provincetown Harbor, Massachusetts, 55
Pryor, Daniel, 191
Pryor, Mary Hatch, 191
punishment at Plymouth, 29
  banishment, 34, 212
  branding, 94, 122, 178
  censure, 30, 31
  corporal, 25, 29, 42, 45, 57, 88, 118, 167
  beating, 30
  branding, 35
  public whipping, 15, 30, 32-36, 45-49, 52-53, 70, 72, 75, 77, 80-81, 83-84, 88-90, 93-94, 98-100, 104, 111, 113, 116, 146-150, 152-153, 158, 162, 167-168, 171, 173-174, 179, 192-193, 202, 206, 209, 211-212, 240, 242-243
  whipped at the cart's tail, 34, 52, 178
  financial, 29-34, 41-43, 45, 46-50, 53, 56-58, 61, 63-64, 74-75, 77-78, 81, 83, 85-86, 92-94, 98, 100, 104, 108, 113-115, 118-119, 124, 146-148, 150, 152-153, 156-159, 162-163, 167-171, 173, 192-193, 195, 201, 203-205, 207, 208-209, 218, 229, 242-243, 246-247
  hanging, 36-37, 39, 72, 102, 153, 175, 212
  humiliation, 30, 43, 47, 64
  letters/signs worn on clothing, 35, 178-179
  sit in stocks, 32, 35, 45, 57, 82-83, 85, 93, 104, 147, 152-153, 201-203
  imprisonment, 35, 47, 193, 246
  public apology, 156, 160, 162, 172
  verbal warning, 30
Purchasers, 114, 222, 232

Quakers, 44, 49, 51, 56, 84-85, 107, 146, 148-150, 171
Quanapawhan, Native American, 95, 96

Quebec, Canada, 251

Ramsden, Daniel, 82
Ramsden, Joseph, 37, 82
Ramsden, Nan, 244
Ramsden, Rachel Eaton, 30, 37, 82
Randall, Joseph, 167
Randall, William, 78
Ransom, Hannah (Susanna), 57, 58
Ransom, Robert, 57-58, 118
rape, 36, 87-88, 157, 207-208, 210-211
  as capital crime, 87, 210
  attempted, 92, 157, 206, 209
  difficulty in proving, 210
  of women, 157
  punishments for, 210
rattlesnakes, 194-195
Rehoboth, Massachusetts 94, 156, 187, 207, 211-212, 218, 225
Rhode Island, 78
Richard, Thomas, 178
Rickard, Giles, Sr., 31, 103, 151, 209, 244, 245
Rickard, Hannah Pontus, 244-245
Rickard, Hester, 151-152, 229
Rickard, John, 29, 151, 229, 245
Ring, Andrew, 223
Roanoke, Virginia, 71
Robinson, Bridget White, 130
Robinson, George, 156
Robinson, John, 25-28, 30, 67, 71, 101, 125, 129-130, 145, 171, 215, 221, 250
Robinson, Mary, 156
Rochester, Massachusetts, 177
Roes (Rose?), Joseph, 53
Rogers, Abigail Barker, 79
Rogers, Joseph, 77, 79, 182, 243
  family of, 182
Rogers, Joseph, Jr., 243
Rogers, Joseph, Sr., 243
Rogers, Thomas, 170
Rogers, William, 48, 160
Rose, Jabez, 243

Ross, Mary, 34
Russell, George, 31, 205
Russell, John, 209
Russell, Mary, 41
Ryder, Zachariah, 203

sabbath
    laws pertaining to, 148
    punishments for breaking laws,
    58, 148
Saconett (Sakonnet), Rhode Island,
    193
Saffin, John, 148
Saffin, Martha Willett, 148
Saints and Strangers, G. Willison,
    21
Sale, Edward, 211-212
Sale, Ephraim, 212
Sale, Margaret, 212
Sale, Rebecca, 211-212
Sale, Rebecca (daughter of ES), 212
Salem Witch Trials (1692), 161,
    164-165
Salem, Massachusetts, 15, 17, 163,
    222
Sam, Native American, 210
Sampson (alias Bump), Native
    American, 93-94
Samson, Henry, 167
Samuel and Bridget Fuller Society,
    225
Sanballett, Native American, 97
Sandwich, Kent, England, 136
Sandwich, Plymouth Colony, 28,
    47, 50-51, 57, 71-72, 84-85, 88,
    107, 149-150, 152, 169-171,
    177, 179, 182
Sassamon, John, Native American,
    36
Savory, Ann, 32
Savory, Benjamin, 110
Savory, Thomas, 110
schools in Plymouth Colony, 20,
    187, 224, 248-250
Scituate Military Company, 61

Scituate, Massachusetts, 31-32, 43,
    59-61, 65, 67, 99, 112-113, 115,
    158, 160-161, 163-164, 175, 190,
    201, 205-208, 229, 242, 243-244
Scottish Rebellion, 213
Scrooby Manor, Nottinghamshire,
    England, 126
Scrooby, Nottinghamshire, England,
    11, 17, 128
scurvy, 14, 22
Seabury, Samuel, 109
Separatism, 18, 126, 248
Separatists, 13, 17, 26, 67, 125-128,
    130-131, 146, 221
servants, 213
    abuse of, 99-100, 118-121, 123,
    207
    education of, 98
    indentured, 57, 98, 101, 116, 173-
    174, 203, 224
    sexual relations, 61, 72, 80, 166, 168,
    176
    in marriage, 61-62
    outside of marriage, 44
Sharp, Jane, 186
Shaw, Alice, 110
Shaw, James, 167
Shaw, John, 110, 167
Shaw, Jonathan, 110, 167
Shelly, Hannah, 171
Shelly, Robert, 93
Shirley, James, 231
Shrive, John, 168
Shrive, Martha, 115, 167-168
    marries Lewis Hues, 168
    marries Thomas Hazard, 168
Shrive, Thomas, 115, 167
Shute, Devonshire, England, 140
Silvester , Dinah, (*see also*
    Sylvester)161-163
Silvester, John, 163
Silvester, Joseph, 161
Silvester, Naomi, 163, 220
Silvester, Richard, 161, 163, 220
    death of, 163

Sippican, 249
Skiff, Elizabeth Cooper, 71
Skiff, James, 71
Skiff, Sarah Barnard, 71
slander and defamation, 61, 63, 79,
   145-146, 150-161, 171, 246
slavery in Plymouth Colony, 90
Slocome, John, 189
Slowly House, Plymouth Colony,
   233
Smalley, John, 189
Smelt River, 224
Smith, Bennett Moorecock, 110-111
Smith, Bradford, 22
Smith, Daniel, 241
Smith, Deborah, 150
Smith, Jaell, 209
Smith, Jeremiah, 110-111
Smith, John, 110-111, 160, 169, 209
Smith, Lydia, 160
Smith, Nehemiah, 224
Smith, Richard, 184
Smith, Sarah, 169
Smith, Thomas, 184
smoking tobacco, 203
Smyth, John, 49
Snow, Abigail Warren, 92, 233, 235
Snow, Anthony, 233
Snow, Jabez, 48
Snow, William, 167
sodomy, 36, 176, 202, 206
Soule, Elizabeth, 47
Soule, George, 48
Soule, Mary, 48
Southampton, England, 129, 139
Southworth, Alice Carpenter, 19, 21
   marries William Brewster, 23
Southworth, Constant, 64-65, 133-
   134, 200
Southworth, Edward, 132, 134
Southworth, Thomas, 133-134
Sparrow (ship), 132
Speedwell (ship), 140
Spooner, Hannah, 209
Spooner, William, 209

Sprague, John, 78
Spring, John, 59
Spring, Lydia, 59
Squanto (Tisquantum), Native
   American, 194
Standish, Alexander, 246
Standish, Desire Doty, 246
Standish, Myles, 38, 137-139, 141,
   234, 246
Standlake, Abigail, 243
Stanford, Rebecca, 246
Stanford, Robert, 246
Starr, Comfort, 198
Stevens, Elizabeth, 69-70
Stevens, Thomas, 70
Stinnings, Richard, 36
Stockbridge, Abigail, 157
Stockbridge, Charles, 157-158
Story of the 'Old Colony' of New
   Plymouth, S. Morison, 22
Strawberry Hill, 225
Streete, Mrs., 141
Studson, Cornett, 113
Studson, Robert, 65
Sturgis, Edward, 47, 203
Summers, Thomas, 62-65, 208
Sutliff, Abraham, 159
Sutliff, Sarah, 159-160
Sutton, John, 41, 159-160
Swansea, Massachusetts, 41, 102
Swift, Joan, 150
Swift, William, 47
Sylvester, Dinah, (see also
   Silvester)191
Sylvester, Naomi, 191
Sylvester, Richard, 191

Talmon, Peter, 78
Tatoson, Native American, 96-97
Taunton Iron Works Company, 141
Taunton River, 209
Taunton, Somerset, England, 178
Taunton, Massachusetts, 35, 73-74,
   102, 108, 119, 140-144, 184, 188,
   226, 231

taverns, alehouses, inns, ordinaries, 15, 114, 226-229
  homes used as, 226
  laws and licenses, 226-228, 230
taxation, 31, 223, 230, 233, 239, 249, 251
Taylor, Lydia, 205
Taylor, Richard, 43
Temple, Dorothy, 33, 173-174
Templer, Hester, 181
Thanksgiving holiday, 135
Thatcher, Anthony, 203
Thatcher, John, 241
Thayer, Abigail, 160
Thayer, Nathaniel, 160
thievery, 113-114, 201-203, 246
Thom, Native American, 65
Thomas, Goodwife "the Welsh Woman", 199-200
Thomas, Mary, 88
Thomas, Nathaniel, 241
Thomas, William, 38
Thornton, Robert, 142
Thorpe, Alice, 31-32, 45
Thorpe, John, 31-32, 45, 222
Thurston, Charles, 98-99
Tierney, Gene, 20
Tilden, Elizabeth, 158
Tilden, Joseph, 65, 158, 207
Tilden, Nathaniel, 207, 208
Tilley, John, 131
Tilson, Joan, 218
Tinsin, Native American, 178-179
Titicutt (Tecticutt/Tetticut), afterward called Taunton, 140
Titicutt Purchase, 143
Tobias, Native American, 36
Tompson, Lieut., 106
Torrey, Lieut., 113
Totman, Christian, 196
Totman, Dorothy, 196
Totman, Mary, 195-196
Totman, Stephen, Jr., 196
Totman, Stephen, Sr., 195-196
Totman, Thomas, 195

death of, 196
Tracy, Spencer, 20
Treaty with Native Americans (1621), 94
Trebey, Peter, 188
trial by touch or trial by ordeal, 91, 121
Trowbridge, John, 87
Trowbridge, Maria, 87
Tubbs, Benjamin, 79
Tubbs, Bethiah, 46, 77
Tubbs, Dorothy Jones, 78-79
Tubbs, Joseph, 79
Tubbs, Mercy, 252
Tubbs, Mercy Sprague, 77-79
Tubbs, Samuel, 77
Tubbs, William, 77-79, 200, 252
  death of, 79
  marries Dorothy Jones, 78
Tubbs, William, Jr., 77
Tupper, Anne, 179
Tupper, Thomas, 179
Turner, Abigail, 246
Turner, Goodwife, 149
Turner, John, 246
Turner, Joseph, Sr., 157-158
Turner, Nathaniel, 158
Turner, Ruhamah, 169-170
Turner, Susanna, 172-173
Turtall, Richard, 208
Two Mile Meadow, Taunton, 142

uncleanness, crime of, 35, 67, 72, 91, 174, 179, 206, 209
Upper Society See Plympton
Uttsooweest, Native American, 97

Vaughan, Elizabeth, 93
Vaughan, George, 93
Virginia Colony, 13, 186, 197
Virginia Company, 13

Wade, Elizabeth Hanford, 114
Wade, John, 114-115
Wade, Nicholas, 69, 114

Walker, Elizabeth, 187, 248-249
Walker, Francis, 48
Walker, James, 189, 199
Walker, John, 37, 119-123, 137
Walker, Michael, 187
Walker, Phillip, 187
Wallen, Thomas, 59
Walley, John, 241
Wampapaquan, Native American, 36
Wapanpowett, Native American, 97
Warner, Katherine, 58-59
Warren, Abigail, 232
Warren, Anna, 232
Warren, Elizabeth, 31, 232-236, 246
    death of, 235
Warren, Joseph, 232, 235
Warren, Mary, 232
Warren, Nathaniel, 182, 232, 234-235, 246
    family of, 182
Warren, Priscilla Faunce, 235
Warren, Richard, 232, 234
Warren, Sarah Walker, 232, 235
watchfulness *See* Pilgrim watchfulness
Waterman, Robert, 209
Watertown, Massachusetts, 59
Watson, George, 184, 190
Watson, Samuel, 184
Wattawamat, Native American, 138
Way, George, 59
Wellingsly (Hobs Hole), 32, 233
Weston, Thomas, 11, 13
Wetherell, Eunice, 242
Wetherell, Samuel, 242
Wetherell, William, 243
Weymouth, Wessagusset Colony, 161, 191
Whelding, Gabriel, 43
Whelding, Ruth, 43
Whitcomb, John, 118
Whitcomb, Robert, 49
White, Jonathan, 213
White, Nicholas, 209

White, Peregrine, 55, 241
White, Resolved, 14, 55
White, William, 55
Whitney, Thomas, 110-111
Whitney, Winnifred, 110-111
whoredom, crime of, 52-53, 89
widows, 23, 53, 55, 59, 66, 78, 102, 132, 142, 198-199, 204, 208, 215-220, 224-226, 229-230, 232-233, 235, 245
    as landowners, 232-235
    care of by family, 245
    debts of, 199
    laws of inheritance, 216, 218-219
    poverty of, 244-245
    probate, 216, 218-219, 223
    remarriage, 216, 218, 220
    widow's thirds, 217
Wilbore, Joseph, 188
Wilder, Roger, 130
    death of, 131
Will, Native American, 65
Willet, James, 41-42
Willet, Thomas, 234
Willett, Capt., 209
"William Bradford's Love Life", J.G. Austin, 19
William III, King of England, 237
Williams, Ann, 198
Williams, Elizabeth Lothrop, 61-66, 160, 238, 239, 252
Williams, Elizabeth Watson, 184
Williams, John, 60-61, 64, 99-100, 110, 160, 172, 173, 198, 208, 238, 252
Williams, John Jr., 61-66
    death of, 65
Williams, Joseph, 184
Williams, Roger, 223
Williams, Thomas, 31, 233
Williamson, Mary, 92, 228
Williamson, Timothy, 228
Willis, John, 123, 205
Willis, Richard, 50
Willison, George F., 21

Wills, Charles, 90
Wills, Rowland, 60
Windsor, Connecticut, 185
Wing, Daniel, 107
Wing, John, 189
Winslow, Edward, 13, 26, 55, 125, 220, 223, 231
  death of, 55
  marries Susanna White, 55
Winslow, Elizabeth Barker (wife of EW), 13
  death of, 55
Winslow, Faith, 92
Winslow, John, 37, 103-104, 123, 137, 223
  death of, 137
Winslow, Josias, 225
Winslow, Kenhelm, 122
Winslow, Major, 217
Winslow, Mary Chilton, 37, 135-137
  death of, 137
Winslow, Susanna White, 54-55, 220
Winter Harbor, Maine, 59
Winter, Christopher, 88-90
Winter, Jane, 35
Winter, Katherine, 205
Winthrop, John, 140-141, 143, 191, 212, 223
Wisewall, Ichabod, 238
witchcraft, 36, 161-165, 191
  in England, 164
  punishment for, 161
women
  abuse of, 205-206
  aging women -
    care of by community, 230-231
    care of by family, 230
  assaults on, 204-206, 208-209
    "crying out" required, 206-207
    two witnesses required, 206
  behavior in church, 145, 147
  behavior in court, 145
  emotional issues, 199-202
  in Plymouth Church, 247
  interdependence among, 247

  lesbianism, 176-177
  literacy of, 204
  menopause, 215
  mortality rate, 54
  poverty of, 198-199, 244
  professions of
    brewing ale, fermenting alcohol, 152, 229
    farm managers, 222, 224
    inn-keepers, 226, 245, 246
    land owners, 224
    midwives, 221, 225
    provider of medical care,198, 221, 252
  reputation, importance of, 155-157, 171, 252
  retirement, 215
  subservient to men, 125, 145, 247
  suicide of, 211-214
Woodcock, Deborah, 173
Woodcock, Israel, 173
Woodcock, Jane, 173
Woodcocke, John, 94-95, 218
Woodcocke, Native American, 96
Woods, Deacon, 245
Woodworth, Mehitable, 163-164
Woodworth, Walter, 163-164
Woolnough, Elizabeth, 15
Woonashenah, Native American, 97
Worden, Samuel, 92
Worksop, County Nottingham, England, 11
Wright, Brother, 223
Wright, George, 207
Wright, Martha, 243
Wright, Peter, 181
Wright, Priscilla Carpenter, 133, 223
Wright, William, 133, 223
Wyatt, James, 198-199
Wyatt, Mary, 198-199
  death of, 199

Yarmouth, Massachusetts, 47, 84, 176-177, 179, 181, 189, 198, 201-204, 209, 212

About the Author

DONNA WATKINS has published articles in magazines, journals, and newspapers, including the *Los Angeles Times*. She has an undergraduate degree in American Studies (CSULA), and she holds graduate degrees in Library and Information Management (USC) and American Studies (CSUF). She is also the author of *Diverse Gashes: Governor William Bradford, Alice Bishop, and the Murder of Martha Clarke, Plymouth Colony, 1648*. Donna's career included work as a librarian at the Pasadena Public Library. After years of helping patrons find books in public libraries, she has turned to writing her own. She resides in Fullerton, California, with her husband in a house full of quilts.

pp. 54-55 (White Family)